What people are saying about

Wisdom from the Christian Mystics

Every book David Torkington writes is about prayer, true deep prayer, but so simply expressed, so colloquial, clear as spring water and as refreshing. **We can so easily read about prayer, about love, about Christian service and in the emotional happiness of our reading come to think that we are actually doing what we are only feeling. Fortunately, no one is more aware of this danger than David Torkington. He is passionately committed to stripping from the reader those veils of illusion that allow what is said to be enjoyed in theory only.** His books should be mandatory reading.
Sr Wendy Beckett

Archbishop Ramsay used to say, 'There is a God-given space at the centre of each one of us which only he can fill.' This book, rich in its teaching and quotes from the Fathers, goes a long way towards helping us to fill that centre-space.
Bishop Thomas McMahon

The book is of course brilliant as only David Torkington can write it. The central point of the importance of giving quality time to personal prayer to be transformed by the Holy Spirit is truly bought out and is of course so utterly essential and truly misunderstood by so many. I don't think anyone is taught this these days; semi-Pelagianism is so rife. The current ethos is achieving everything on our own initiative. This encompasses every sphere of our lives. I think this is why there is so much breakdown because humanity is not meant to live without the all-encompassing love of the Father. David is a prophet who has truly been given his gifts to be a voice in the Church.
Sr Rosaleen Shaw OP, former prioress of St Joseph's Priory, Sway

This pioneering tour de force reintroduces the Christian mystical tradition that transformed the ancient pagan world. It should be read and re-read and used as a blue print for the radical restoration of Christian Spirituality.
Sr Bernadine, TSSF, Florence Province

David Torkington is a sincere and prayerful man whose writing is the fruit of a lifetime of prayer.
Anthony Lilles STD, Academic Dean, St John's Seminary, California

Torkington is a master of prayer. His engrossing style masks the depth of his practical advice and specifics about many forms of prayer from the traditional to the new.
Stanley M Grabowski, PhD in *Pastoral Life*

Mysticism is a frequently misunderstood word. It is sometimes presented as a modern phenomenon coming solely from the East and entering our Western world under the guise of the occult. In a beautiful, personalized portrait, the author depicts a real person delving into the depths of the human condition. It reveals a practice deeply imbedded in the original Wisdom of the Judeo/Christian tradition. This is a must read for both initiates to the subject and as a teaching method for those tasked to direct others.
Paul J Williams, Amazon reviewer

Wisdom from the Christian Mystics

How to Pray the Christian Way

Wisdom from the Christian Mystics

How to Pray the Christian Way

David Torkington

Circle Books

Winchester, UK
Washington, USA

First published by Circle Books, 2018
Circle Books is an imprint of John Hunt Publishing Ltd., No. 3 East St., Alresford,
Hampshire SO24 9EE, UK
office1@jhpbooks.net
www.johnhuntpublishing.com
www.circle-books.com

For distributor details and how to order please visit the 'Ordering' section on our website.

ISBN: 978 1 78535 774 9
978 1 78535 775 6 (ebook)
Library of Congress Control Number: 2017943734

A CIP catalogue record for this book is available from the British Library.

Design: Stuart Davies

Printed and bound by CPI Group (UK) Ltd, Croydon, CR0 4YY, UK

Contents

Other Books by David Torkington

Wisdom from the Western Isles - The Making of a Mystic

Wisdom from Franciscan Italy – The Primacy of Love

Inner Life – A Fellow Traveller's Guide to Prayer

A New Beginning – A Sideways Look at the Spiritual Life

Dear Susanna – It's Time for a Christian Renaissance

How to Pray – A Practical Guide

To Bobbie, without whom this book could never have been written, and to my brother Peter who inspired it. A very special thanks to Kevin Grant, former MD and editor-in-chief of the Catholic Universe and MD of the Catholic Herald, for his valuable advice and tireless work in editing the text.

Mystical Theology

It has always been believed that happiness depends on love more than on anything else. The greater the love, the greater the happiness. Yet for some unaccountable reason it does not always occur to people that, like everything else that is worth achieving, loving must be learnt. Far from being an exception to the rule, learning to love is more difficult than anything else, because human beings are insatiably selfish and learning to love means learning to be selfless. Mystical Theology is the study of how we learn to practise being so selfless that we are not only able to love others as never before, but also to yearn for, and to experience, the source of all love that resides in God. Take mystical theology out of Christian spirituality and you are left with laws, rules, regulations and rituals, and a moral teaching that is beyond reach. Take love out of the married or the celibate life, and people begin to seek substitutes that can be disastrous to themselves and to others.

Only love, not our love, but the love of God working through those who are taught how to receive it, can lead to the perfect loving that leads to happiness. If you wish to know the meaning of life then, you will find it in mystical theology. That is why Pope St John Paul II chose to study the teachings of the great Mystical Doctor of the Church St John of the Cross for his doctoral thesis. He was, like the author of this book, deeply influenced by the great Dominican theologian, Reginald Garrigou-Lagrange, perhaps the greatest spiritual theologian of the twentieth century, who taught him at the Angelicum University in Rome. His masterwork *The Three Ages of the Interior Life* synthesises the works of St John of the Cross with the teaching of St Thomas Aquinas. Following in that tradition Torkington was invited to lecture on mystical theology in the extra-mural department of the Angelicum in the late nineteen-seventies and early nineteen-eighties.

In this book Torkington uses his profound knowledge of what came to be called the New Biblical Theology to further the understanding of this synthesis, while at the same time emphasising what theologians of this movement have sadly neglected in the past. That is the daily mystical spirituality given by Christ himself to the early Church. This is of vital importance because it is upon this that the communal expression of life in Christ celebrated in the liturgy depends for its inner life and vitality. Bringing this spirituality back again for all is the focus of this book.

All quotations from the Bible are from *The Jerusalem Bible 1966*

Foreword

David Torkington has a unique gift of being able to express profound truths very simply. He has used it to good effect in his latest book on the Christian Mystics. He adopts an original approach that allows Peter, a hermit, to become the central character in the story. It is shot through with much autobiographical detail which not only helps the flow but adds greatly to the interest and communicates the heart-warming enthusiasm of the author. There is a particularly moving account of a night spent alone in the Basilica of the Holy Sepulchre which he describes as a 'life-changing' experience.

Like all David Torkington's books it is about prayer. He takes us right back to the mystical spirituality that Jesus practised with his disciples in their daily pattern of prayer. He then leads us to see how this was continued and brought to perfection after his glorification, giving prayer a new power in, with and through the Risen Lord. This would transform the lives of those early Christians by teaching them the daily prayer that leads to the prayer without ceasing.

He uses the word 'mystic' derived from the Greek word *Mysterion* to describe those first ordinary Christians who by daily living for God came to experience his hidden mystical love as a by-product of their selfless giving. They follow Jesus in what was known as "The Way" (Acts 9:2), journeying to the Father's home and the fullness of life and love. David Torkington leads us to see how this prayer is for all. Inspired by their example we endeavour to put prayer at the very centre of our lives as we seek to be caught up and transfigured in the Risen Lord.

This kind of prayer is very much a journey. We are encouraged to be strict in setting aside time and place; reading the Gospels; invoking the Holy Spirit. All of this helps to lead us to silent God-centred prayer. It will not always be easy and may well result in a dark night that purifies. In the end it is pure gift.

Lest this all sounds rather daunting, there is also a practical guide to prayer based on the Our Father and the acknowledgement that in the end each prays in the way that is best for them. Archbishop Ramsay used to say, "There is a God-given space at the centre of each one of us which only he can fill." This book, rich in its teaching and quotes from the Fathers, goes a long way towards helping us to fill that centre-space.

+Thomas McMahon
Bishop Emeritus of Brentwood

Prelude

I Remember, I Remember

"I remember, I remember the house where I was born, the little window where the sun came peeping in at dawn"
(Thomas Hood - 1826).

I remember the flying bomb that smashed that window to pieces and spread the glass all over the floor. I remember cutting my feet as I ran for the bedroom door. I remember grabbing my gas mask from the kitchen cupboard. I remember two buckets of sand for incendiary bombs guarding our grandfather clock. I remember dashing into the shelter built inside our dining room. I remember the sirens sounding as my mother bandaged my feet. I remember praying for the bombs to stop, for our family to be kept safe and for other families too, and for our relatives at the *front*. We prayed the same every night of the week before we went to bed, as we prayed at the Sunday Masses that were always crammed full. I remember how churches gradually emptied, as the forties gave way to the fifties, and peoples' pockets were filled with money once more. I remember how God gradually began to come second, as the *swinging sixties* put pleasure first.

I remember the Second Vatican Council, to help us turn back to God once more. I remember the re-birth of the ancient Liturgy in a language that we could all understand. But, as the seventies gave way to the eighties, I remember how it failed to do all that we had hoped to renew the Church that we loved. Priests and others left in droves and the churches began to empty more and more with each passing year. I remember the scandals that arose from those who remained behind. I remember the abuse, the cover-ups, and the injured innocents. If it's by their fruits that you are to know them, then there must have been something wrong with the soil that was right in the beginning. It was certainly not that the changes had gone too far, but rather that they had not gone far enough, I mean deep enough to reproduce the soil that once brought forth such exemplary fruit in the beginning. They had not gone deep enough to re-create the spirituality that Jesus had lived and bequeathed to his followers, to light them with the flame that set the ancient world on fire.

It was this that animated and energised the weekly liturgies that depended for their inspiration on the profound spirituality that Jesus had lived himself, and had handed on to his followers. Every day of his life he had prayed more than five times a day, as he had been taught to do at home, as had the disciples he chose to follow him. As he had prayed so also did they, as he loved and cared so also did they, as he served the poor and the needy, so also did they. As he learned to carry a daily cross and live and die for God, so also did they. When he was with them they did all these things with him, but after he was glorified they did them anew. Then they did them in, with and through him, to offer themselves to their common Father. They did it together at each Sunday Mass where they received the power to do it again and again in work, prayer and service to others throughout the following week. For the whole point and purpose of the Mass was and still is, in the words of Karl Rahner, "That our whole life becomes the Mass, the place where we continually offer ourselves in, with and through Christ to the Father."

There was only one Mass a week for more than a millennium that lasted for an hour or more like ours. But it received its power and vitality from every minute of the preceding week in which believers tried to observe the new commandments. Their daily sacrifices, offering, thanksgiving, praising, glorifying and adoring, were the means through which their love entered into God and his love entered into them. Their daily sympathy, empathy, caring, compassion and sharing were the means through which their love entered into him, in the neighbour in need, and his love into them. What would the final sacrifice of Jesus have meant, if it didn't embody all that he said and did each day for the Father who sent him, and for us for whom he was sent? What does our Sunday Mass mean or do for us, if we have done nothing to prepare for it in the previous week?

If there were to be another Council called to complement the last, then I would set our best scholars, theologians and liturgists to follow in the footsteps of Blessed John Henry Newman, and go back to the first Christian centuries once more, as they did before. No need to seek out the shape and form of the Liturgy, that has already been done, but this time to seek out and detail the profound mystical spirituality that Jesus practised each day with his disciples. Then see how it was continued and brought to perfection after his glorification, to transform the lives of all Christians by teaching them the daily prayer that leads to the prayer without ceasing. Let them, not only show how Christ became tangibly present in those who gave their lives for him in red martyrdom, but how the same happened in those who gave their lives for him in what came to be called white martyrdom. In those, in other words, who tried to convert every moment into the daily liturgy of selfless living and giving that enabled them to carry their daily cross for Christ. Let them explain for us the new means of Christian prayer called meditation, which taught how, from meditating on Christ as he once was, we can come to contemplate him as he is now, and through him to contemplate the Father. Let their scholarship and spiritual guidance help us to focus more attention on the weekly domestic and workplace liturgy that was so important to our early forebears. Once this is done, the same Sunday liturgy that we celebrate now will be transformed into what they called the Heavenly Liturgy, because that is what it will become, as our giving enables God to give to us in ever greater abundance, making something that we can so easily take for granted, into a foretaste of heaven on earth.

That all this be brought about we need to hear from priests, to be led by priests, to learn from priests. I don't just mean from those in the pulpit, but from those in their homes who are fathers and mothers, husbands and wives and from those in the workplace who are employers and employees, students and teachers, specialists and non-specialists, young and old, poor and sick. Their personal experience of selfless giving and receiving, suffering and dying in every nook and cranny of human existence is the example that we need to hear about, to help us joyfully exercise the priesthood that we are called to practise every day of our lives. They are already with us now, for I have been deeply moved, encouraged and inspired by their contributions, but we need to hear from more of them, not just as voices on the fringes but from the mainstream of the new spring that John Henry Newman promised but never lived to see.

For this new spring to dawn we need a deep spiritual and theological renewal, where scholarship is placed at the service of practical daily living, in and for Christ. When more and more theologians can be defined as the Desert Fathers once defined them – "Theologians are people of prayer and people of prayer are theologians" (Evagrius Ponticus). When liturgists give as much, and more time to detailing how we can transform the daily liturgy of work, prayer and play on which the Sunday liturgy depends. When more and more missives from above are directed to guiding us in our daily lives, into an ever deeper and ever more profound spiritual endeavour, until we can say as St Paul said before us, "It is no longer I who live, but it is Christ who lives in me" (Galatians 2:20). When this begins to happen, the touch-paper will be lit to set every sacrament, every sacramental, every structure and every institution in the Church alight with what, or rather with the one who originally set it on fire. Then more and more spirit filled, apostles will surge out, as before, to do for the modern world what was done for the ancient world, for nothing here on earth can resist the power of love, the love of God that can only be embodied in those who choose to receive it.

This book is the result of my personal journey back to the origins of Christian spirituality to rediscover and represent for today the spirituality that Jesus himself first lived before teaching it to his first followers. His hidden years, so often neglected because they do not seem to tell us anything of importance, are highlighted because they can tell us what is of the utmost importance - everything we need to know about his daily prayer life, through studying contemporary documents that detail the daily spiritual life of every orthodox Jew. This enables us to see and understand how what was shared with his fellow Jewish disciples before the Resurrection was transformed after the Resurrection. You do not find all this detailed in the scriptures, not because it is unimportant, but because it wasn't considered necessary to detail what everybody knew, what everyone practised every day of their lives, as Jesus had done before them.

When children go to secondary school their teachers assume that their pupils know how to read and write and have been taught the basic principles of mathematics. It is the same with the scriptures. They were written at a time when both the writers and readers shared a common daily spiritual life that did not need to be repeatedly restated, because it was lived day after day. It was therefore assumed, as the foundation for teaching other truths of the Christian faith. That is why it is both the scriptures and tradition together that convey the fullness of the spiritual legacy that Jesus left for us all.

I have not only been at pains to rediscover and represent this profound mystical spirituality that animated and inspired our early Christian forebears, but to re-emphasise both past and contemporary religious practices that still continue to embody them. I have tried to do this in such a way that the reader is not treated to a mass of historical scholarship, but rather to an introduction to daily Christian prayer in which the fruits of scholarship are learned without them realising it. To this end I have re-written this book six times, and then continually added many contemporary stories, analogies and metaphors to clarify what I am trying to say. The Christian message is not just for intellectuals, but for all. That is why I have adopted an unusual and hopefully engaging literary form, in the hope that I can reach a readership as wide as possible. I have done it to inspire as many readers as I can, to do what Jesus and his disciples did to make prayer the centre of their daily lives. It was in this way that they came to know and experience the hidden or mystical love of the Father transforming them from within, so that through them others might also be transformed and ultimately transfigured, both spiritually and physically as Jesus was after the Resurrection.

From all eternity, God's love conceived a plan to create beings of matter and form, of flesh and blood, made in his own image and likeness, so that they could return to the place where they had been conceived, as to their final destiny. St Paul called this plan the *Mysterion*. Jesus Christ was this plan, made flesh and blood, sent from eternity into space and time to bring it about by becoming the Way, the Truth, and the Life. He was the Truth because it was he who first began to reveal this plan and therefore the true reason for Creation. He was the Life because it was the inner life that animated him, that would draw others into him, so that he could become the Way in and through whom they could be led onward and into the love of the Father who first conceived them. That is why Christianity was first called "The Way" (Acts 9:2), a family of brothers and sisters set in a single direction, travelling together on the same journey home, in, with and through brother Jesus to the place where their Father was waiting to delight them with the fullness of life and loving for which they had originally been created.

The word mystic is derived from the Greek word *Mysterion* to describe those first ordinary Christians who radically consecrated their daily lives to entering into God's plan by entering into its perfect human embodiment, Jesus Christ, the *Mysterion* made man, the Way, the Truth, and the Life. This word was never intended to refer to spiritual self-seekers looking for extraordinary or esoteric experiences with which to divert or delight themselves, but to ordinary selfless Christians, who by daily living for the honour and glory of God, came to experience his hidden or mystical love received as a by-product of their selfless giving, as they journeyed on along the Way. Mystical theology then is merely the study of how human love can be sufficiently purified to be infused by the divine.

If you are married or wish to marry, mystical theology is a must, because it is simply the study of how human loving is brought to full maturity by practising to be a more selfless person. If you have chosen the celibate life, it means that you must learn from those who are living the married life, how to act selflessly, practising putting self second and someone else first, whether you feel like it or not. That is why the first great mystics wrote commentaries on the famous love poem, *The Song of Solomon* to explain the mystic way, by showing how the consummation of all human loving ends in a profound spiritual or mystical marriage.

This marriage is not just with another human being, but with the One in whom all love began, and in whom it finds its ultimate realisation. In early Christian spirituality no one doubted that this was for all, and that it was the beginning in this life of what would only reach its consummation in the next. Nor did anyone doubt that, like other marriages, this marriage involved a close and daily mutual interpenetration of loving that reached its most intimate moments in prayer. The sort of abstruse and intellectual arguments that made even some of the most respected theologians question whether the mystic way is for all, would have both mystified and horrified our forebears. It is just further proof that the prevailing spirituality that has reigned since the condemnation of Quietism is aeons away from the profound mystical spirituality bequeathed by Jesus himself to the early Church. It was both profound and mystical. It called all who would listen to him to a mystical marriage with him, destined to flower in a love that would completely possess and compenetrate the whole person, beginning in this life and reaching its climax in the next. If you feel the ultimate love for which you crave is beyond you, then this book is for you. Its formal object is to divulge a secret revealed to the first Christians that can raise human love to an infinitely more sublime level, making the impossible possible for those who take it seriously. How and through whom this is achieved, are the questions answered by the great Christian mystics. That is why their teaching is the subject of this book, helping those who wish to become genuine Christian mystics, totally committed to the Way, and to rescuing so many who have fallen a prey to counterfeit mysticism. The word 'mysticism' was never used by the Fathers of the Church. The many questionable forms of contemporary 'mysticism' that have become commonplace today will be dealt with at the end of the book. But first I have outlined the profound mystical spirituality that should be the basis for our daily prayer life, as it was in the beginning for Jesus and his disciples, both before and after the Resurrection. It is for all those who do not just want to gaze in awe at God's *Mysterion,* but who want to enter into it now, by entering into the *Mysterion* made man. This is the Mystic Way that is the subject of this book, or to put it more simply, *How to Pray the Christian Way.*

David Torkington Easter 2017

Chapter 1

The Mystic in a Barbour Sweater

He was kind, he was concerned and compassionate, but he was uncompromising too. My condition was incurable and I would be dead before the New Year was out. The doctor had never called me James before, it had always been Mr Robertson, but he called me James on that day as he took my hands in his and spoke to me like a father although he was half my age, and almost half my size. It was only supposed to be just another check-up, so neither my wife nor I had any reason to suspect what had come like a bolt from the blue. In fact, Ellena had gone out for the day fly fishing with a friend without the slightest suspicion that my doctor was going to give me anything other than yet another clear bill of health. I took the long way home through the New Forest to try to come to terms with the news that had turned my stomach into turmoil and my head into a hornet's nest. It was the autumn of 2014, the hottest year on record that had been crowned with the most beautiful autumn that I had ever seen, at least in England.

When I was a boy the family had a holiday home in New England that enabled us to escape the pandemonium that permanently prevailed in New York where I was born and grew up. This autumn in the New Forest almost rivalled the fall that never ceased to enchant me as a boy. I had a sudden desire to go back home once more to see the place where I grew up and to visit the magical forests where I fished with my father as a boy and played hide and seek with my brothers and sisters. But it was only a temporary whim. I married and made my home in Southern England and the New Forest became for me what New England had been before. I had in fact married twice. My first wife Jennifer, whom I met at university in the States came from Scotland, so we made our life together in Edinburgh where she died giving birth to our first child who died the next day. I met and fell in love with Ellena almost fifteen years later, on a visit to Franciscan Italy, and we had been married for over thirty years. Jennifer was a Presbyterian, Ellena was a Roman Catholic, but I was brought up an Episcopalian. Thanks to that retreat in Franciscan Italy, we both committed ourselves to living a serious Christian life and actively working to help others do likewise.

Ellena not only had a degree in English, but a theology degree too that enabled her to become the director of a retreat and conference centre called Walsingham House at Chingford, overlooking Epping Forest in North London. The incumbent director asked Ellena to take over his job as director when he was head-hunted to become the Dean of Studies at the National Catholic Radio and Television Centre in London. It was here that we were given the flat that became our first home. This enabled me to continue my academic career as a history lecturer at London University, while helping her at weekends. We so loved walking in Epping Forest that we bought, what was initially a holiday home in Brockenhurst in the New Forest, in Hampshire. It was a wise decision because the flat went with Ellena's job. We knew we would have to give it up sooner or later. It was wise, too, because house prices were still reasonable in the 1980s but they went sky high in the 1990s, especially in Brockenhurst that was in the heart of the New Forest with its fast train link to London. When, after about ten years, circumstances forced the Dominican Sisters who owned Walsingham House to sell up, we were not homeless or jobless either. I could still commute to London to continue my academic career, while Ellena accepted a job teaching at 'the Brock', as Brockenhurst College was affectionately called. I spent a good deal of time working voluntarily at the Catholic Chaplaincy in Gower Street, and Ellena did the same for a new retreat centre at Sway nearby. The Dominican Sisters who had to leave Walsingham House, eventually, and quite by accident, ended up in their new home only a few miles away from us.

We loved spending our holidays in Italy and usually ended them spending a few days at our favourite place, an enchanting little hermitage known locally as Lo Speco di Narni. St Francis used to go there for solitude and prayer and it was here that Ellena proposed to me and it wasn't leap year either! It was our special place. Having so much in common contributed to the happiest marriage that I could ever have hoped for. But what now, what, oh, what now? How was I going to break the terrible news, not just to my wife, but to my proven soulmate of the last thirty-five years?

She was so radiant when she came home, so excited, so full of life that I didn't know how to tell her of the death that was growing inside me. She had caught three trout, a four-pounder that she had taken to the smokery near Stockbridge, and two smaller fish, one for dinner, the other for our neighbour. How could I shatter her joy with the sorrow that welled up in me? But how could I hold it within me any longer for I must needs speak, and if I couldn't speak to my nearest and dearest, to whom could I speak? The fish ended up in the deep freezer and we did little else than weep and hug each other throughout a sleepless night. Poor Ellena was shattered, but she made me a cup of tea shortly after dawn before disappearing for the early Mass at Sway. When she returned she had changed. Oh, yes, there were many more hugs, kisses and sleepless nights, but she was never self-indulgent. In future all her care and attention was directed towards and for me, with no thought for herself. She had always been more practical than I and she immediately turned her attention to preparing for what was left of my future.

"I have been thinking," she said. "I think you should fly out to see Peter as soon as you can, and while you can." Peter, or Peter Calvay as he was known, was a hermit living in the Outer Hebrides who had helped me several times in the past. In fact, it was through him that I first met Ellena, and it was he who helped me when my first wife Jennifer died over forty years before. He helped direct my spiritual life, especially when I found myself in a black hole, not once, but many times over. Since that pilgrimage to Franciscan Italy, which he led over thirty years ago, my contact with him was mainly by post and then by email when we gave him a computer as a millennium present, to help him keep in touch with his many correspondents.

Peter's email was immediate. It was deeply moving and personal, too personal to share with anyone other than my beloved Ellena, but it was practical too. He was coming to the mainland in early March of 2015 on a very rare visit to join his brother and his wife to celebrate their twenty-fifth wedding anniversary and he would come earlier to visit us, if we could put him up. It might not be the silver lining that we were looking for, but it was none the less more than we could have hoped for in the circumstances. I was not only pleased for myself, but for Ellena too, who would need his shoulder to cry on more than any other when I had gone.

Just before the last Christmas post that I would ever receive, there came a large envelope from the parish priest of SS Anselm and Cecilia in London. It contained all the advertising material that he had prepared for the course I promised to give the following Lent. Understandably I had completely forgotten about it. What was I going to do? He spent a small fortune advertising in all the religious periodicals and newspapers as well as producing hundreds of leaflets. He hoped I was well, wished me a Happy Christmas, and hoped we could meet up early in the New Year to finalise all the arrangements. I was devastated and so was Ellena. What were we going to do? I couldn't possibly give the course now and who else could give such a specialised series of talks? Although I only lectured in English History I had made a private study of Church History specialising in the history of Christian Spirituality. My course was entitled Wisdom from the Christian Mystics and was to be given in the first week in Lent. "I simply don't know anyone else who could take my place," I said. "Oh, I do," said Ellena without a second thought. "Peter can. He is a brilliant speaker, as we both know, and who knows more about mystical theology than he does? And he said he is coming down in early March and your course is in the last week in February."

If it had not been for me feeling sorry for myself I would have been overjoyed when Peter accepted. His brother's wedding anniversary was on the 11th of March and, as he lived near Southampton everything should work out satisfactorily. Anyway, I told the parish priest of the revised plans and why. He was devastated for we were of a similar age, and we had known each other for a long time and he too had been an Anglican before he became a Catholic. I knew and liked him when he was a chaplain at London University. Of course he had heard of Peter Calvay and was delighted that he would take my place, although he said he still could not take in the news that shattered him.

In his life of St Antony, the great Father of monasticism, St Athanasius described him as he appeared to a group of would-be disciples after twenty years in solitude. They knocked down the door to his chosen retreat and begged him to make them his disciples. The man St Athanasius described, looked for all the world like the man who emerged from Brockenhurst Station on Friday 27 February 2015. Although I had kept in touch with Peter since I last saw him in Franciscan Italy thirty-four years before, I had not seen him since. His spiritual teaching never changed, but gradually deepened. But now I saw how all that I learned from him in the intervening years was embodied in him and in all he said and did. The familiar appearance of the man I knew and loved was still there, albeit thirty years older, but there was a quality of peace, joy and spiritual wellbeing that was more pronounced than ever before. When I shook his hand I felt as if I was shaking the hand of the man whom St Athanasius had described. The familiar shape and form was but the cast for the new-made man within, the man remade in the image and likeness of the man who had inspired him to go into solitude in the first place.

This Antony, however, was not dressed like an ancient hermit in a threadbare goatskin, but in a smart, brand new, green extra-large Barbour pullover with brown corduroy trousers, both of which Ellena had sent him. He reminded me of Joe Gargery dressed in his Sunday best as he arrived in London to meet Pip in *Great Expectations*. Goodness knows what Peter would have looked like if he did not humour Ellena by wearing the clothes she sent him for Christmas. One thing would nevertheless have remained the same, no matter what he was wearing, and that was his thick shock of hair, but now to our surprise it had turned completely white. We were delighted to see that unforgettable smile we knew of old. Although he would now be over eighty, he seemed to have lost none of his agility despite his handicap. Since the age of six when he was struck down with polio he had worn an iron calliper on his right leg and always carried a stick to support himself. This stick and the old brown leather holdall were the only two accessories by which I remembered him from our last meeting.

We spent most of our time on the train up to London reminiscing, so I had no time to ask Peter about his talks. My own talks on Wisdom from the Christian Mystics would have begun with St Augustine whom I used to summarise the teachings of the Fathers of the Church, before moving on to detail the mystical theology of Gregory the Great and St Bernard. I intended to spend a whole lecture on St Francis of Assisi and the Franciscan school with its emphasis on the primacy of love, before a full lecture on St Thomas Aquinas and the Dominican school, with particular emphasis on the Rhineland Mystics. The final talks would deal with the great Carmelites, St Teresa of Avila and St John of the Cross.

When I saw the people who turned up to hear the first talk I thanked God it was not me who was doing the talking. They had not come to hear a retired academic like me prattling on about something that had little to do with their daily lives, and for that matter with the spirituality for which they yearned. What they wanted was someone like Peter to set them alight with an exciting new and exhilarating mystical spirituality they could both understand and apply to their daily lives in a way that I could never have done. If what he said was a revelation to them, then it was a revelation to me too. All my communications with Peter were personal and to do with my own current spiritual problems, so I never saw the massive development in his theological thought in the last thirty years or more. But it was not just this profound new erudition that astounded me, but despite, or perhaps because of his solitude, it was how he was able to present it to ordinary people in a way they could understand, and in a way that could inspire them to live it in their daily lives. It made me realise that you need distance to see what closeness too often obscures.

Ellena had the foresight to record all his talks, so instead of listening to me trying to summarise them, they can be read in full. However, when I sent the text of the talks to Peter before going into print, he not only edited them, but added a lot more material to expand and clarify them. This involved adding many more stories, metaphors and anecdotes to make his points clearer. There is no doubt that they do help to enhance the book, but something of the brief spontaneity of the originals talks is inevitably lost. But unless you were actually there to hear him speak, without any notes and with such God-given enthusiasm, no written words however well-crafted, could capture the electric atmosphere that was generated by a man I can only describe as a living saint. Those people who heard him, heard something that they would never forget, and they received from him something more than just words, something or Someone who could help them change their lives permanently for the better.

Read the sermons of the Curé d'Ars and you'll see that they can read like an anthology of pious clichés. But when they were delivered with power, and love, they entranced his listeners, and ensured that by the end of his life forty thousand people a week were pouring into his parish to hear a living incarnation of the man in whose name he spoke. Listening to Peter must be like listening to a Curé d'Ars, but Peter's words never at any time sounded like pious clichés. The parish priest came up with a good idea to draw as many as possible into his talk in the church hall. Peter would take his place in the pulpit and preach in his place. It worked like a charm. On each of the following six days Peter would speak twice each evening except on the last when he only spoke once. He didn't seem to mind at all, nor did his listeners, nor, I believe, will you after you have read his first two talks. When Christ first appeared on the scene, John the Baptist insisted that in future, "He must grow greater, I must grow smaller" (John 3:30), so be it with me. My story now comes to an end, at least until the end of Chapter twelve. Henceforth it is to Peter that you must listen, not me, as he delivers his memorable lectures in the next eleven chapters. I will only make a few occasional remarks as the week unfolds.

Chapter 2

A Night in the Holy Sepulchre

(Peter's first talk)

When I was a young man, I received a phone call from Fr Kenneth Campbell, a Franciscan Priest whom I first met after a talk he gave on the Holy Land. He was born on the Island of Eriskay in the Outer Hebrides, but spent many years working in Palestine and Jordan. He had arranged a pilgrimage for Gaelic-speaking Catholics from the Outer Isles to visit Judea and Galilee, however, the Israeli government suddenly asked Fr Kenneth to escort the Canadian Foreign Minister and show him around the Holy Places, as he was a Catholic. Could I therefore act as a stand-in because he could not get back in time to meet the pilgrims at Luton airport? If I could, then after the formalities, I could board the 'plane with the pilgrims and so have a free holiday in the place I always dreamt of visiting, a dream I never had the time or the money to realise.

"If you want old ideas read new books, but if you want new ideas read old books." With these words my spiritual director gave me *Abandonment to Divine Providence* by the Jesuit French mystic, Jean Pierre de Caussade SJ. The book is perhaps better known under the title *The Sacrament of the Present Moment,* more usually used when the book is translated into English. I packed the book in my hand luggage and set off for the airport to act as a courier to Fr Kenneth's pilgrims.

On the first day I did the grand tour of all the major shrines in style with Fr Kenneth and the Canadian foreign minister. There are more Gaelic speakers in Canada than there are in Scotland and, as the foreign minister was one of them, he and Fr Kenneth spoke to each other in their common tongue knowing full well that the official car was bugged. When for my sake, he reverted to English whenever we left the car, I was amazed to hear the evidence for the authenticity of the Holy Places. After the Romans had destroyed Jerusalem in AD 70 they built their own pagan shrines over the place where Jesus had been crucified, and over the tomb from which he had risen from the dead to try and obliterate their memory. However, their action did exactly the opposite, guaranteeing their preservation until they were returned to Christianity when Constantine became the first Christian Emperor in AD 312. It was the church of the Holy Sepulchre that impressed me most, not its architecture, but because it was built over the place where Jesus died and over the tomb from which he rose from the dead. The whole atmosphere of the place touched me more deeply than I could have imagined.

Fr Kenneth, who had lived and worked in the Holy Land for most of his life, seemed to have a key to every place that you really should see, and even to places that you shouldn't! On the night before we left, his famous key opened a door that seemed closed to everyone else, and opened to me an experience that has affected me deeply to this day. Although the doors to the Holy Sepulchre are closed every night and cannot be opened until the next morning no matter what, I was given permission to remain inside for the whole night, with a room to myself in the Franciscan friary within. I spent little time in that room. Instead, I spent my time before the midnight office at Calvary, and the time after, alone in the empty tomb.

I was so overcome to realise that I was totally alone, the only person praying, within a matter of metres from the place where Jesus had died and from where St John and Our Lady had stood. There was a New Testament open before me at St John's account of Christ's death. The passage that told of the water pouring from the side of Jesus was underlined in red, for this was the key moment in his narrative. Once glorified he could immediately send the Holy Spirit whom he promised to send at the Last Supper. An outpouring of this mystical life and love had long since been likened to an unprecedented effusion of living water by both the prophets in the Old Testament and by Jesus himself.

Not long before his life came to its abrupt and agonising end, Jesus had taken his disciples with him to celebrate the Feast of Tabernacles in Jerusalem. On the final day, a priest filled a golden bowl full of water from the pool of Siloam outside the city gate and carried it into the Temple. There it was poured out before the altar in memory of the rock struck by Moses to give water to his people in the desert. While this was taking place a prophecy was read out. It promised a new and massive outpouring of the Holy Spirit when the Messiah would come. This was the moment when Jesus chose to cry out in a loud voice, "If any man is thirsty let him come to me. Let the man come and drink who believes in me." However, St John, who witnessed the whole event said, "He was speaking of the Spirit, which those who believed in him *were* to receive; for there was no Spirit yet, because Jesus had not yet been glorified" (John 7:37-39).

Little did St John know at the time that he would be there to see this outpouring with his own eyes, and the terrible circumstances that would precede it. Now Jesus himself would become the new rock, who when pierced at his death would pour forth the new living waters that the prophets had foretold. So that there could be no doubt about what was happening. St John emphasises this moment in the Passion narrative more than any other, as I read for myself on that unforgettable night. "When they came to Jesus they found that he was already dead, and so instead of breaking his legs one of the soldiers pierced his side with his lance and immediately there came out a flow of blood and water." The words, "a flow of blood and water," were underlined three times and so were the words that followed, making it clear beyond all doubt that what St John saw he saw at first hand. He was not just describing something that he heard from someone else, because what he saw was of such importance. "This is the evidence of one who saw it," he insists, "trustworthy evidence, and he knows that he speaks the truth, and he gives it so that you too may believe as well" (John 19:33-36).

For St John, the very moment of Christ's death was the moment when he was united with his Father - this homecoming was instantaneous. So too therefore was his glorification when he was filled by his Father's infinite love in such a way, that his whole person was filled to overflowing with the life of the Holy Spirit. The flowing of blood symbolised the final moment when he gave his all. The flowing of water symbolised the superabundant life and love of the Holy Spirit promised on that final day of the Feast of Tabernacles. However, what happened instantaneously in God's world and in God's time happened more slowly in man's world and in man's time, so that all would be made clear and there would be no misunderstanding for the Apostles.

They would first have to be convinced that Jesus rose from the dead before the consequences of his Resurrection could be spelt out in the weeks that would follow. In the so-called real time in which the Apostles lived, they had to wait until after the Ascension for the outpouring of the Holy Spirit in the Upper Room on the first Pentecost day. Jesus had made it clear that he came so that they might *see* and that *seeing* they would come to believe. That is why he wanted them to *see* him rising above them and passing through the clouds on his way home to be reunited with his Father in heaven.

Once again on that Pentecost day, St John was there for this epoch-making event, but this time with the other Apostles. They all saw and heard the signs, but now they experienced the love of Jesus, not as if he was standing close to them, but as he was entering into them through the Holy Spirit, as he had promised at the Last Supper. Now they could become true apostles because the word apostle means one who is sent, and they were immediately sent, propelled by that same Holy Spirit who possessed them, to share the Good News with others. As promised, this outpouring of the Holy Spirit was for all, for it was sent by

Christ, no longer just the King of the Jews alone, but the King of all creation and of all peoples to the end of time. On that day the promised Kingdom of God finally came. The Holy Spirit burst out, onto and into the world like an unstoppable supernatural sea of love. Like a spiritual tsunami, he would sweep out over and into all things, drawing all who would not resist him, back through Christ into the ocean of God's infinite loving. In the Risen Christ, in his glorified but human body, they would be drawn into the life and loving that flowed between the Father and the Son from all eternity. Since the first Pentecost day, the love of the Holy Spirit has been, and still is, endlessly flowing between the Father and the Son, drawing all who are in Christ into that loving. He is the means by which we are adopted into the family of God. By family, therefore, I mean that we have been taken up into Christ together with all those others, who like us, have been drawn up into the life of the Three in One.

I recently spent Christmas Day with my friend James, his wife, their family of four children and a foster child who used to spend some weekends and part of the holidays with them. After the four children were given their presents the foster child was given what appeared to be a boring pile of papers. But when he looked at them he dissolved into tears - they were his adoption papers. When he finally wiped away the tears he danced around the room in joy. Henceforth he would never have to go back to the orphanage. In future, he could call James his father, even his dad like the other children. This was the best news he had ever received, ever could receive. In the same way the new family into which we have been invited should be the best news that we have ever been given.

Some of you might have looked at that moving clip on U-tube when a convert from Islam told how, on reading the Gospels to see what the prophet Jesus had to say about Allah, he discovered something that changed his life. He discovered that Allah was not a distant God, but a tender loving father, his father, even his dad. Abba was the word Jesus used and told others to use when speaking to him. It was the word still used by young Arabs today to address their fathers. Those born Christians too often take for granted the world-shaking truth of why Jesus came, and the news he came to share with us. He is our brother and we have the same father, the dad who has given us new life and a temporary home with him in this life until we are ready for the home he has prepared for us in the next. This home that he came from and to which he would return will one day be our home too. It is here that we will share to eternity in the utter peace, joy and bliss of going out of ourselves through love into endless ecstasy. We will share this experience too, not just with Jesus, but with all those we have loved on earth, but purified of all the human weaknesses that once prevented us from loving them as we would have wished. This is what the first Christians called the Good News, the news that Jesus came to bring us. His message was that God is not just love but that he is loving us all the time and that he loves us not just as a father but as a dad.

In the Old Testament God is called Father only thirteen times and he tended to be a rather distant father, but Jesus taught that he is far more than that. He is a loving, tender father, a dad, because he not only loves us, but he wants to communicate his own inner life to us. In that life is the source and origin of every form of love that can be found on earth and every form of love that a person needs to become fully complete and mature, ripe and ready, not just for marriage with another human being, but with God. Jesus did not just tell people about this love, he showed them this love embodied in himself, and made tangible through all he said and did while he was on earth, through his tender loving human personality. When he was glorified he was still the same man as before, with all the human feelings and affections that he had on earth, but now they were brought to perfection.

But that is only half the story, for he has been raised above us, so that he can enter into us at every moment. If this is not good news, what is? God is not just Love, but Loving us at every moment. Three hundred years before the Resurrection the Greek philosopher Aristotle insisted that the supreme being, the first cause of all creation, must be pure act. In other words, he is what he does and he does what he is. This might seem a difficult concept to grasp, but it shouldn't be, if I could understand it when I was only six years old.

I was brought up on the radio. I used to ache for children's hour to begin and it would transport me into another world. One of my favourite other worlds was Toy Town and my favourite character was Larry the Lamb. He was always in trouble yet he was invariably well mannered and respectful. It was always, "Please, Mr Policeman, Sir," and "Please, Mr Mayor." I do not know who wrote the script but he knew a lot about children. He knew only too well that for a child, a person is what they do. If a man was always grumbling, then he was Mr Grouser. If he could perform tricks he was Mr Magician and if he made new things he was Mr Inventor.

We used to have a picture of the Sacred Heart at home and when my Mother explained who he was and what the flames around his heart meant, I remember pointing and saying, "It's Mr Loving." I could not have been more than five or six at the time, yet it was the first theological statement I ever made, and it was thanks to Toy Town and my good friend Larry the Lamb. I have to admit that when I began to study the new theology in Paris, even before the second Vatican Council, I became a spiritual snob and began to look down on the simple faith that I had been brought up on, and the devotions that had once sustained me. My artistic sensibilities were offended by those plaster statues of the Sacred Heart and the pictures of him that most Catholics, like us, used to hang with pride in our homes.

The Paschal mystery became the centre of the new spirituality that now sustained me. I began to understand the meaning and importance of the Resurrection as never before. It was not just a great historical event which happened two thousand years ago, it was much more than that. It was an event that is still happening now. Jesus is risen now. He is alive now, and the same power, the same love that raised him from the dead is accessible now to all who would receive it, to do in us what has already been done in him.

It took me many years to realise that, as T S Eliot once wrote, "The end of all our exploring will be to arrive where we started, and know the place for the first time." The wonderful truths that I learnt from my study of the new theology were not new at all. I was brought up on them, as were my parents and their parents before them. The plaster statues of Mr Loving might be a little old-fashioned by today's standards for some, but the truth behind the devotion to the Sacred Heart is the most important truth of our faith, and that truth is timeless. Who is the Sacred Heart but Jesus risen from the dead? He is not just represented as Love Incarnate but as Incarnate Loving. He is Mr Loving, transmitting the tender fatherly love of the God who created us so that he could become our spiritual dad.

During my student days in Paris I shared a room with a Russian student, Boris, who despite the regime that ruled in his homeland, kept the faith taught to him by his parents and his godparents. He was so religious that he decided that he would never return to his homeland, but instead would go to Mount Athos to become a Russian orthodox monk. On one occasion he persuaded me to go with him to visit his future home and it turned out to be one of the most defining spiritual experiences of my life. We arrived just in time to celebrate the feast day of the Transfiguration, and this was quite a revelation to me. In the Christian West, nothing much was made of this feast and to this day its meaning and significance has never been explained to me as it was during my sojourn on that holy mountain.

It was not only similar to the feast of the Sacred Heart, as it used to be celebrated when I was a boy, but much more. The transfigured and glorified Christ was central to the daily spirituality of the Orthodox faith, as devotion to the Sacred Heart was once in Western Catholicism. Just as pictures and statues of the Sacred Heart were to be seen everywhere in schools, convents and churches and in most Catholic homes, the same could be said of icons depicting the Transfiguration, in the homes of those who belong to the Orthodox Church. That is how it was then, is now and always has been. When I say that is how it always has been, I mean from the very beginning of Christianity long before the Orthodox Church was separated from the rest of the Christian Church. Even long before the art of painting icons ever began, the image of the glorified and transfigured Christ was indelibly burned into the minds, the imaginations and the hearts of every Christian, for as St Paul puts it in his great hymn, "He is the image (icon) of the unseen God" (Colossians 1:15).

This picture of the glorified and transfigured Christ was the same Christ who, in the words of the Creed, is seated at the right hand of God. Yet he is simultaneously at the centre and the heart of every Christian community and in every member of that community, closer to each one of us than we are to ourselves, as St Augustine put it. I brought a wonderful icon of the Transfiguration back home with me where, to this day it is the first thing I see when I wake in the morning and the last thing I see at night. It is the continual daily reminder that after he was reunited with his Father and the home from which he originally came, the glorified Jesus was, and is, the fulfilment of God's plan. Why? Because he is now, and always, pouring out the very life and love of the Holy Spirit, who can alone take us up into himself, and in, with and through him, into the life and loving of the Holy Trinity. He is the masterwork of his creation, its crowning glory, Christ the King. He is the supreme prophet too, because what God planned from the very beginning was not just promised by him, but fulfilled in him, and through him, when God's own inner life and love was transposed into human loving in Jesus, and then transmitted through him to other human beings.

The first time this profound truth was brought home to me was that night in the Holy Sepulchre. I returned to my room shortly before the midnight office to freshen up. I was desperate for a cup of tea but there were no facilities. So, without thinking I took out the small twelve-volt kettle that I used to make tea in my car to save me from the tepid dish-water that was served in motorway service stations and plugged it into the mains. There was a flash, a puff of smoke followed by the smell of burning and my poor kettle gave up the ghost. I had learnt my lesson – 240 volts into twelve volts will not go. It was then that the penny dropped - neither could the infinite love of God go into a finite human being. My poor kettle might have given up the ghost, but I had learnt a profound theological truth that I never realised before.

In the Old Testament, the infinite love of God simply could not enter into finite human beings. Nor for that matter could anyone see God and live, and the very thought of his infinite love entering our finite human being was totally inconceivable. Just as I would need a transformer to enable 240 volts to be converted into twelve, so God would need a transformer too, to convert infinite loving into human loving. That transformer was Jesus Christ. He was the perfect transformer because his human nature could convert the infinite love from his divine nature into human loving. Then he could communicate it to other human beings and transmit to them the love that he had received from his Father.

Now it was possible for God to do what had never been done before, something that I never understood before I plugged my kettle into the mains. Because the glorified Jesus had both a divine and a human nature he now became the perfect means of transforming the infinite love of God into human love and transmitting that love to other human beings who had not been able to receive it before.

Now, through Jesus, the whole of humanity could have access to the infinite love of God, to the end of time. It was this love that was destined to bring about a whole new world order that Jesus first called the Kingdom. It was a Kingdom of love. However, nowhere in the Gospels did Jesus say that the Kingdom had come, but only that it was coming. It finally came for all when, in the immediate aftermath of the Ascension, the infinite loving of the Father was sent out. This could never have happened before. Even the greatest of the patriarchs, prophets and priests in the Old Testament never received what was possible for the humblest of human beings, thanks to the transformed and transfigured human nature of Jesus. That is why Jesus said that, "Of all the children born of women, none has been greater than John the Baptist; yet even the least in the kingdom of God is greater than he is" (Matthew 11:11). If that is not good news, what is?

This unprecedented and definitive outpouring of love contains within it all that we can possibly hope for, all that we can possibly need. It contains within it all that is necessary for each one of us to grow, from being imperfect, into becoming ever more perfect and mature human beings. But first and foremost, it fills us with the truth. Whenever a person experiences the love of God, that love always imparts the truth too. It fills us with something of the truth about God for whom we now begin to yearn more than ever before. But it also fills us with something of the truth about ourselves too. These two characteristics of God's mystical touch, love and truth, can perhaps best be seen in someone else when he reaches out and touches them without any warning and with immediate effect.

This happened to a man called Saul as he was travelling from Jerusalem to Damascus. The dazzling light that he saw was nothing other than the love of God, but it was the love of God that reached out to him through Jesus the Son of God, the one his own people had crucified and with his approval. It was the man whose followers he was hunting down, throwing into jail, torturing, flogging and putting to death. Even now he was on the way to Damascus with letters empowering him to capture and imprison more of them. But suddenly, unexpectedly, he saw the truth about himself and about God. He saw that he was a merciless killer, an assassin, who had been putting Christ to death again in those whom he was persecuting. The words of Christ were quite clear, "Saul, Saul, why are you persecuting me?" "Who are you, Lord," he asked and the voice answered, "I am Jesus, and you are persecuting me" (Acts 9:1-9). Saul not only saw the terrible truth about himself, but the truth about his God who had been made flesh and blood in Jesus, who was no longer dead but alive once more, as he promised, and was living and loving in those who believed in him.

If Jesus was present in those whom he was persecuting, then the words of Jesus, spoken before his death, were true after all: "In so far as you did this to one of the least of these brothers of mine, you did it to me" (Matthew 25:40). Three days after this encounter with the Risen Christ, the blindness that followed the dazzling light, was cured and he was baptised. Now he could see clearly, not just with the eyes of his body, but with the eyes of faith. He saw that he was reborn into a family of believers who were his new brothers and sisters, who would support him on "The Way" beginning in this life and ending in eternity.

On that night as I prayed at Calvary I was not only bowled over by the profound theological insights that moved my mind, but by the terrible cost paid by Jesus that preceded the outpouring of divine love. It was what it cost him that moved me as never before. Like St Paul I would never be the same again; like St Paul I had to change my life and change it irrevocably. Simultaneously however, it aroused within me a deep and relentless yearning to come to know and experience something of the height and depth, the length and breadth, of the love of God that moved me to tears on that night, tears of sorrow and tears of joy. There was no time to lose. The book my spiritual director had given me had already made that clear to me. God was loving me here and now in what de Caussade called the sacrament of the present moment. I might not have sinned as Saul sinned, but I was no more than a nominal Christian. But now through all that I experienced that night, I knew I had to become a totally committed and radical Christian, and that meant now, in the sacrament of the present moment, without any further delay. So, without any delay I made my life over to God during the midnight office. Afterwards I approached the Guardian, as the superiors of Franciscan communities are called, and asked him to hear my confession so that I could begin again with a clean slate.

After confession, I told him what happened as I prayed at Calvary, and about the insight that I received when I blew up my little kettle. Although he laughed, he not only said that the insight I received was theologically correct, but that he would use the same example himself, if I didn't mind, as he had never been able to think of a better one. He emphasised that Jesus did not become a perfect transformer overnight - it took at least thirty years. When I asked him what he meant he asked me whether I had been to Bethlehem. He told me that I would have seen the exact spot where Jesus was believed to have been born and lay as a helpless baby. "That helpless baby might well have been what you called God's transformer, but it would take many years before he became a perfect transformer to channel his love to all humanity." Although in the years ahead, his divine nature would not and could not change, his human nature did, making Jesus an ever more perfect human being. Just as his physical muscles grew, so also did the spiritual muscles of his heart and mind. As St Luke put it, "And Jesus increased in wisdom, in stature, and in favour with God and men" (Luke 2:52). St Paul insisted that he was like us in all things but sin, so he would have had to grow as we do, to become a perfectly formed and mature human being. It would only be then that he would have the fullest possible inner human capacity to receive God's own life and love from his divine nature, assimilating and digesting it himself, before communicating it to other human beings.

To demonstrate this, the Guardian took out a large hour glass, once used to gauge the time given by the friars for personal prayer. He turned it upside-down to make his point. The sand in the top of the hour glass, he said, represented the divine nature of Jesus. The bottom part of the hour glass, that was empty, represented his human nature at the beginning. As St Paul put it, "he emptied himself, to assume the condition of a slave, and became as men are" (Philippians 2:7). Because there was, as St Paul insisted, no sin in Jesus to interrupt the steady inflow of divine love into his human nature, there was nothing to stop him being filled with that love at every moment of his life, as he was growing into a perfect mature human being. His human nature would not only be filled by the love of God, but that love could be handed on to other human beings who were open to receive it, both before and after his death. Before his death, it would be communicated physically to other human beings whom he met in the space and time world he then inhabited. But after his glorification when he was raised above that world of space and time, he could communicate what he received to all people of every time, entering them from the inside through his transformed human loving.

Henceforth he would become the perfect mystical transformer, able to convert and channel infinite loving into finite loving. He would do it in such a way that human beings everywhere and at every time could receive it. In this way, they could be drawn up into Christ and through him into the vortex of infinite loving that endlessly passes to and fro between the Father and the Son. Without Jesus possessing a divine and a human nature to facilitate this mystical transformation, God's plan to share his life and love with us could not have been brought about. That is why in the early Church they fought so long and so hard against anyone who tried to deny, on the one hand that Jesus was truly divine, or on the other hand that he was truly human. Without Jesus possessing both a divine and a human nature God's plan could not be implemented.

I realised I had to return to Calvary, there to make my vow in person at what must be the holiest place on earth. Yet at first I recoiled, not at making the vow that I had in fact already made, but at returning to the place where I had already learned and received so much. What did not frighten me before filled me with an understandable dread as I began to realize the dreadful things that happened there almost two thousand years before. I was no longer just a disinterested scholar whose mind was changed, but a penitent whose heart had been moved to make his life over to the one who gave his life for me.

I have read the works of many great saints, mystics and martyrs who have expressed, as one of their deepest desires, to have been there with St John and with Mary and other followers at the foot of the cross. Some have even prayed to share in some way in the terrible ordeal that Jesus had to undergo. I have never had such desires nor did I then! I felt physically fearful of returning to that infernal place where the forces of evil had been unleashed against the man I admired and loved more than any other. I did not want to look upon the torn, tortured, and tormented body of Jesus again at the very place where he had been crucified to death. Yet I felt I must, for it was a holy place where a titanic battle was fought and won, a place where the powers of evil were vanquished by the power of pure unadulterated goodness. They could not prevent or deter him from standing for truth, for goodness, for love, for what is right and decent. At the moment of his death he released an enduring shaft of love that contained within it the pure goodness that would empower hundreds of thousands, millions, billions of others, to stand up for all Jesus had stood for and to do so no matter what the cost.

When I knelt at Calvary again the dread that possessed me

disappeared. I felt as if I were bathed in the love that continually poured out of the man who was, in the words of St John, glorified at that very place. Now, filled with love, I slowly and solemnly made the vow to commit my whole life to the one who gave his all for me at this very spot. I then simply gazed at the cross and at the crucified figure of Christ and he appeared to me in a new light. For St Paul, the very dimensions of the cross spoke of the height and depth, the length and breadth of God's love that surpasses the understanding. Suddenly the terrible suffering that he had endured no longer filled me with dread but with love, for I saw, like Julian of Norwich before me, that I was looking at the flesh and blood embodiment of the love of the Three in One. It was a thought that had never struck me before. But after all, only a few hours before Jesus had been nailed to the cross he had insisted that the Father was in him and he was in the Father, and the bond that bound them together was the Holy Spirit. What had been revealed to Julian was therefore that the love that had constituted the Holy Trinity was manifested in human love on the cross more perfectly than at any other time or place on this earth.

I then returned to pray at the Holy Sepulchre where I was so overcome by the realisation that I was praying in the very place from which Jesus had risen from the dead, that I began to wish I could spend the rest of my life in that friary. This would enable me to return again and again, night after night, to what must be the holiest place on earth. Then suddenly, in a matter of moments I had a spiritual experience that changed everything. In one sense it was nothing spectacular, but in another sense, it irrevocably changed my whole attitude to the Resurrection that I had believed in since I was a child, but which had never really touched me in the way it touched me that night.

I do not claim that the words came directly from God; they most certainly came from my subconscious, but I'm sure God gave them a bit of a push. The words were these: "You are looking for Jesus of Nazareth who was crucified. See, here is the place where they laid him. He is risen now. He is not here. He has gone before you into Galilee." I changed instantly. I no longer wanted to live in that friary for the rest of my life. The empty tomb suddenly lost its importance, but not its significance. The meaning of the Resurrection struck me as never before. It was as if someone had said *ephphatha,* and my eyes were opened to a truth that I knew with my head, but which had never fully penetrated my heart. Although my spiritual understanding had not substantially changed, it was totally transformed in a way that I find difficult to put into words. It was as if I had spent years looking at the Resurrection from the outside, as framed in a stained-glass window, then suddenly seen it again, this time from the inside with the sun shining through it.

The Resurrection meant that Jesus had been swept up out of the world of space and time in which he had lived before, not to leave us alone, but to be closer to us than ever before, and, as he promised, "even to the end of time" (Matthew 28:20). Before the Resurrection Jesus was limited by the physical body into which he had freely chosen to enter. His choice meant that he could only be in one place at a time, so meeting him would have been as difficult as meeting any major celebrity in our time. But that has all changed now, because the same other-worldly love that raised him out of this world on the first Easter day enabled him to re-enter it on every day. So now he can enter into us as he promised, so that he can make his home in us and we can make our home in him, as he promised at the Last Supper. All this could be possible, not in some distant pipe-dream, but here and now. That is why de Caussade said that, "The present moment contains far more than we have the capacity to receive, for it is full of infinite treasures." Those infinite treasures are not only every form of love we need, contained within the love unleashed by our glorified Lord, but myriad virtues that love generates within us to return this love in kind, and to share what we have received with others. He calls the here and now the "sacrament of the present moment, because it is the only moment where time touches eternity, the only moment where the love of God can reach out to us and we can reach out to him, to begin and to continue the journey for which every human being yearns deep down within them. It is the journey to the ultimate mystical marriage where our love and the love of Christ become one, in the Three in One, and to all eternity."

The existentialist philosopher Martin Buber tells the story of the carpenter from Lublin in Poland who had a dream in which he saw a vast treasure reserved for him alone. After years travelling the world to find it, he returned home at the end of his life to find that the treasure was there all the time beneath the hearth where he warmed himself before the fire each evening. Like him we can spend a lifetime searching elsewhere for what is here, where we are now, wherever that might be, in this present moment. The love for which we were created and which Christ came to impart, can only be received here and now in the present moment, and at no other place than where we are now. Now is the moment to harness all the time and all the effort that could be wasted searching elsewhere to abandon ourselves, without reserve, to the One who first promised and then sent the love that can make all things new, beginning with ourselves.

The outpouring of God's love through Jesus did not just happen in the past, two thousand years ago, it is happening continually, but we can only receive and experience it here and now in the present moment. We can receive it now, because the baptism that once symbolised our personal reception of the Holy Spirit, is not just an event that once took place in the past, any more than the events that happened on the first Pentecost. They both symbolised that the very personal and infinite love of God is at this moment and at every moment being transmitted to us.

What happened at his Resurrection, was that the Jesus who was once limited by the space and time world in which he chose to enter, was limited no more. Now his glorified human being continually radiates like the sun that the early Christians used to symbolise his ever-loving presence. He radiates, not so much with light as with love, but unlike the sun that only shines in the day, his love radiates both day and night, for there is no time when his love cannot be received by those who believe in him. That is why the first Christians would rise at midnight when it was believed that Jesus rose from the dead, to meditate on his Resurrection, on what it meant for them then, and what it would mean for them in the forthcoming day. What the risen Christ and his love meant for them, the love of his Father meant for Jesus throughout his life on earth. That is why every moment of every day was the moment when he opened himself to receive God's love in his relentless daily prayer, and in the way in which he served those for whom his Father had sent him. There was no moment therefore in which he was not open to receive the love of his Father. It was therefore in imitation of him that the first Christians tried to do likewise. This enabled them to ensure that every moment of their day would be a moment to receive his love. Then this love would enable them to be drawn up into his continual and abiding presence, so that in, with and through him they would give glory to their Father in heaven, as he did. What they would then receive from God in return would enable them to experience something of that glory for themselves, and then show something of that glory to the world, as it infiltrated and shone through everything that they said and did, as pure unadulterated goodness.

Although it is true that this present moment, and every present moment, is the only time and place when we can open ourselves to receive the outpouring of the love that Jesus continues to send, love, most particularly God's love, is not magic. Not even God can force his love on us. Forced love is simply impossible as we should know from our own experience. We cannot force our love on anyone else, nor can anyone force their love on us. Forced love is simply impossible; it is physically impossible, spiritually impossible, theologically impossible, metaphysically impossible, impossible in every way. So, if we do not take the practical steps to turn and open ourselves to receive the divine love that is endlessly being poured out to transform and transfigure us as it transformed and transfigured Jesus, then we will remain the same. No, that is not quite true, because the spiritual life is rather like walking up a downward escalator; the moment you stand still is the moment when you start to go backwards. In other words, the moment you stop trying to open yourself to the only love that can change you, then you begin to go backwards, to deteriorate for, as Jesus said so clearly at the Last Supper, "Without me you have no power to do anything," but with him all things are possible, even the impossible, as the scriptures say repeatedly.

All these talks are dedicated to showing how to turn and open ourselves to receive the divine love that Jesus received fully at his glorification, by studying what Jesus did every day of his life to open himself to the love of our common Father. To be clear where we are going, let me state here briefly and simply what I first realised with such clarity as I continued to pray in the Holy Sepulchre. At every moment of his life Jesus was fully engaged in loving his Father with his whole heart and mind, with his whole body and soul, while at the same time loving others as he loved himself. This is the way he gave honour and glory to God.

These were the thoughts that were occupying my mind when, at six o'clock, the small Franciscan community came into the empty tomb where I was praying to do what Christians had been doing since Jesus rose from the dead. It was the most moving Mass in which I had ever taken part. When at the end of the great Eucharistic prayer the celebrant said, "Through him, with him, in him, in the unity of the Holy Spirit, all glory and honour is yours, almighty Father, for ever and ever," the 'Amen' resounded with such power that you could almost feel our offerings mingling with Christ's and rising to God the Father. At that moment I understood as never before how our offering becomes like a spiritual passageway that not only enables our love to rise through Christ to the Father, but enables the Father's love to descend into us through Christ. The profound mystical at-one-ment that then takes place is consummated in Holy Communion when we receive Christ and tangibly experience him entering into us. When Mass ended in the early church it always concluded with a clear directive as it still does today. That directive is, to take the Christ whom we have just received out into the world that he now wants to change through us.

Although I was born a Catholic I had never seen so clearly before the meaning of the faith into which I was baptised as a child. Nor had I seen so clearly the absolute importance of the personal daily prayer to which I now committed myself. It was here that I would try daily to open myself to receive the help and strength from God that I needed to love him in all I said and did each day, as Jesus himself did before me. Without doing this I would have nothing to offer when next I went to Mass, nor would I receive what I needed to make my whole life into the Mass.

A book my brother wrote some years ago won a prize at a book festival in Prague in 2002. He was in the middle of his acceptance speech when a parish priest interrupted him. "All this talk about personal prayer," he said, "What about the Mass, that's the prayer that really matters." My brother asked his translator to read out a quotation from Karl Rahner which my brother included at the beginning of his book. "The whole purpose of the Mass," he wrote, "is to so form us that the whole of our lives becomes the Mass, the place where we continually offer ourselves through Jesus Christ to the Father." This quotation sums up the essence of the spirituality that inspired the first Christians, a spirituality given to them by Jesus himself. It also sums up the ancient Christian spirituality that I want to share with you in my talks in this forthcoming week.

I stayed on in prayer after that Mass in the Holy Sepulchre, reflecting on the truths that I have just shared with you. They confirmed me in the vow that I made, although I did not know whether I would be doing this as a single or married man, as a priest, a religious or as a layman. However, I firmly believed that would be made known to me and it was, as you will hear.

* * *

Although Peter's talk had gone on far longer than the Parish Priest imagined, everyone seemed totally entranced. Nobody stirred at all, until the end of Mass when everyone moved *en bloc* downstairs to the hall for his next talk.

Chapter 3

The Secret Plan

(Peter's second talk)

After totally committing myself to God in the Holy Sepulchre I visited the great Carthusian monastery, St Hugh's Charterhouse, Parkminster in Sussex with the intention of living the enclosed eremitical life, two weeks after returning home. I was deeply impressed and I immediately came to the conclusion that it was here that I would like to spend the rest of my life. That is until I had a long talk with the monk who showed me around. It was obvious that he was deeply happy in his chosen vocation despite long periods of spiritual darkness when the light of God's love highlighted the sinfulness that kept him out. However, this did not deter me, for I had long since understood that before union with God could begin, it would have to be preceded by an inner purification, and I was eager for this purification to take place so that my heart's deepest desire could be fulfilled. What did eventually put me off was the monk's frank admission of what happened in, or rather after experiencing moments of ecstatic bliss when he experienced the presence of God penetrating him from within. His all but uncontrollable joy was only the half of it, for after moments of mystical at-one-ment he would be filled with wisdom too, with a spiritual understanding and insight into his faith that he had never experienced before. However, what had initially given him so much pleasure was counterbalanced by feelings of deep sadness. The problem was that he had no one with whom to share his joy, and the profound knowledge that he never understood before. What he wanted to do was to shout it from the roof tops, but all had to be contained within him for nothing could be shared with others, at least in the way he would have wished.

Despite everything else that attracted me to the Carthusian way of life then, it was this admission that decided me. I was a teacher by both inclination and profession and it was my greatest pleasure to communicate what I learnt to others. How could I remain silent for the rest of my life about the profound mystical insights which I received in the Holy Sepulchre, and most particularly about those other insights that inspired me before leaving the Holy Land? I was deeply impressed by Nazareth where the Holy Spirit first conceived Jesus in Mary's womb, Bethlehem where he was born, and the river Jordan where he was baptised with the power and strength to proclaim the coming of the Kingdom. When I went back to the Holy Sepulchre on the penultimate day it was full of tourists and, seeing that I wanted to pray, Fr Kenneth took me to what he thought would be the ideal place. He took me to the Garden of Gethsemane where Jesus prayed shortly before his final ordeal began. He prayed that he might be spared the terrible death and the appalling torture and indignity that would precede it. This was his prayer many times over. Fr Kenneth told me that the suffering that Jesus had to endure while making his prayer was exacerbated by his realisation that, although it would not be all in vain, so much of his spiritual legacy would be. So much of what he would leave behind him would be forgotten, misunderstood and misinterpreted by the perversity of so many men and women deformed and even depraved by human weakness, most particularly by selfishness, personal pleasure seeking, and the lust for self-aggrandisement. No wonder he sweated blood at the thought of it.

There is a great deal of uncontroversial evidence that more than 500 people saw Jesus after his Resurrection. However, is there any evidence that anyone saw him after his Ascension? Is there any evidence that he was seen in his new glorified life that was to become the means of transmitting the life of God to all men and women? Yes, there is. The three men were Peter, James and John, and the place where they saw him was on

Mount Tabor. It might have been before his death and Resurrection, but the Jesus they saw was a preview of the glorified Jesus who returned to this world after the Ascension. This was the new man who was transfigured before them. If the marks of the crucifixion had been seen on his body during his Transfiguration then his disciples would not have been so surprised and remonstrated with him when he spoke about his forthcoming death. The marks of his ignominious death were not to be seen on his transfigured body.

Immediately after the Resurrection Jesus still had the marks of his crucifixion on his body for all to see, so nobody could doubt who he was and what had just happened to him. It was a matter of identification to avoid any doubts, like that of Thomas. However, the Jesus whom the three apostles saw on Mount Tabor was the same Jesus, as he would have appeared after the Ascension, with all the marks with which the evil of man had disfigured him spirited away. And when they were looking at him in his transfigured glory they were, if they had only known it, looking at what would eventually happen to them too, and to those who would faithfully follow him. One day we will be transformed and transfigured too by the same Holy Spirit who glorified the Risen Lord, with the ravages of time and the deformities inherent in our human predicament spirited away.

This was how the glorified Jesus would have appeared on the first Pentecost Day, if he had been seen in the physical glory that enrobed him after his coronation in heaven, as Christ the king 'sitting at the right hand of God' to use the poetic metaphor used in the Creed. He was then fully radioactive, filled with the love of the Father. When human beings love, their love is both physical and spiritual, but as God has no physical body his love is entirely spiritual. As a mark of reverence therefore, his spiritual loving has traditionally been called the Holy Spirit. This is the loving that completely restored Jesus to the fullness of life, as man and God, after the Ascension. Furthermore, it was this loving that flowed out of him on the first Pentecost day, and for that matter on every subsequent day. It flows out of him like an infinite outpouring of loving, sweeping out to encompass the world, to surround and penetrate all who are open to receive it. Then, for this love is like a powerful magnetic force, it draws all who would not resist it, back into the glorified Christ and in, with and through him to give glory to God the Father, from whom they had all come in the first place.

When we reach this, our ultimate destiny, faith finally gives way to vision, a spiritual vision where we begin to experience what was only known by faith before. Saint Augustine says that in this, our final destination, we are taken out of ourselves to gaze upon the glory of God in a state of ecstatic bliss. However, Saint Gregory of Nyssa takes us even further, and in order to do so he has to manufacture a new word. He attaches two letters *ep* to the Greek word for ecstasy to form a new word *Epecstasy* to express the true nature of our ultimate destiny. It is not just to be taken out of ourselves into ecstatic bliss, but to be continually taken out of ourselves again and again and to all eternity. The more we give of ourselves to the Father, in Christ, then the more we receive what continually opens up within us, the capacity to receive more and more love. This ineffable process will go on and on, for there is no end to the journey into infinite loving. The reward of the traveller is to go on travelling, the solace of the searcher is to go on searching, for there is no end to this journey.

This is God's plan for us all, for the whole of humanity. It is what St Paul calls the 'Mysterion'. This plan is the source, the foundation and the ultimate completion of authentic Christian spirituality. For fear of failing to make myself understood about such an important matter let me explain it as simply as I can. God's purpose from the beginning was to create us to share in the ecstatic bliss that he experiences at every moment of his existence. To do this, he sent his son Jesus Christ with a human nature like ours, but with a divine nature like his. This enables his divine love to pass from his divine nature into his human nature. Here it is transformed into human loving in such a way that it can draw all who receive it back into him. Then in, with and through him we can come to know and experience the love of God to eternity. That is God's plan for us and that is our destiny. The word mystic derives from this word 'Mysterion', to denote a person who gives their whole life over to responding to God's plan. It has essentially nothing to do with searching for obscure, abstruse, or esoteric experiences. However, as a by-product of selflessly giving oneself to God's love, that love will at one time result in the pain of purification and at another time in the joy of being replenished and then transformed.

If you have never come across the word 'Mysterion' before it is because you have never read Saint Paul's letters in Greek; nor have I for that matter. The word itself means secret, or the secret. Whenever Saint Paul used it everyone knew precisely what he meant. Some words are so full of meaning that it would take pages of prose to explain them, yet we all know what they mean. Take the term 'the Budget' for instance; we all know what it means, yet it would take pages to explain its meaning in general, and its meaning for us in particular. In short it means that the government's plan is to take as much money from us as it possibly can. In a similar, but reverse way the Mysterion means that God's plan is to give us as much love as he possibly can to transform our lives in this world and then in the next. It summarises in a single word what he is prepared to do to enable us to share with him in the ecstatic bliss of loving and being loved that endlessly enthrals him from and to eternity. That is why he created us male and female, not just with minds and hearts that could receive it, but with bodies that could go on generating more human beings to be suffused by the divine. The plan is called secret because it was only revealed partially in the Old Testament, and was not revealed completely by Jesus in the New Testament. It was only after the Resurrection that, as promised at the Last Supper, all things would be revealed that were not fully revealed at the time. Saint Paul reveals this plan in its fullness at the beginning of his letters to the Ephesians and the Colossians (Ephesians 1:3-14, Colossians 1:15-20). But even then, the plan was still secret or mystical, because the inner life through which this plan was being brought about in each individual Christian could not be seen. But the way in which this inner life was manifested in unprecedented goodness, kindness, and charity to all could be seen, as we shall see. It was this remarkable Christlike behaviour that converted millions at the time and billions thereafter.

It was to draw people into this plan of God, and to continue to sustain and support them there, that Jesus left what the first Christians called the mysteries, a word derived from the word Mysterion. Later, when Latin supplanted Greek as the universal language of the Church, they were called the sacraments. That is why we also refer to the mysteries of the Rosary, because this prayer can enable us to meditate on the plan of God as it was being put into action, and as it was being brought to its completion. It has enabled countless generations of believers to follow the hidden or the mystic way into the Mysterion. They achieved this through reflecting, meditating and ruminating on God's plan step by step, as it was being implemented, and then finally contemplating God himself, in, with and through Jesus. Since my mother taught me to say the Rosary the fifteen mysteries have been extended to twenty to include what have come to be called the Luminous Mysteries, because they highlight the events in the life of Jesus between his hidden years and his death and resurrection. They are the Baptism in the Jordan, the Wedding at Cana, Proclamation of the Kingdom, the Transfiguration, and the Institution of the Eucharist. I find these mysteries a compelling addition to the Rosary that my mother taught me. On a personal note, I find meditating on the Sorrowful Mysteries immediately after the Luminous Mysteries deeply moving, if not heartbreaking. I find it almost unbearable to see the price paid by the utterly irreproachable to share his all with the utterly reproachable.

If you prepare for using the Rosary by re-reading the events in the scriptures highlighted by each particular mystery, then this becomes a powerful inspiration to the prayer that we can take with us anywhere, using our fingers if we do not have our beads to hand. It was for this reason that Pope Leo XIII said that the Rosary was "an incomparable prayer, the layperson's breviary that can lead a person onwards to the heights of sanctity." This is how so many of our parents and grandparents were taught to pray and were led on by the Holy Spirit into mystical contemplation without them ever realising it. Shortly before my mother died, she began to speak to me of her own spiritual life and of how, apart from the morning offering that she had taught me, and her night prayers, it was above all else the Rosary that was her spiritual mainstay. That is why she thought that she never grew up spiritually. In fact, she outgrew all forms of prayer that could not support her in the mystical contemplation into which she was led without ever realising it.

The only form of prayer that she knew had in fact guided her from the foothills to the heights of the spiritual life. That is why you rarely find arrogance or pride in someone whose spiritual ascent has been made thanks to the Rosary. My mother said she began by just saying each individual prayer slowly and prayerfully, trying to grasp their meaning and then making them her own. Then in time she learnt how to recite them in such a way that she could meditate on each mystery of the Incarnation in turn. Gradually, meditation turned into a profound loving contemplation. When this happened she no longer needed to count the beads as before, nor say the individual prayers, as a few heartfelt words rose up from within her to express her deepest feelings. Then, when words gave way to moments of joyous contemplative stillness, she no longer needed to do anything but savour in silence the fullness of love that she received and experienced more powerfully than ever before.

When this honeymoon period of prayer suddenly came to an end, as it always does, she suddenly found herself in what St John of the Cross called the dark night of the soul, although she never heard of him or his books. At this difficult moment in the spiritual journey many people give up prayer, because they simply do not know what to do. My mother did not stop, but she found that the only way to continue was to return to counting her beads as she did to begin with, and reciting the prayers, as she recited them before. It was the only way she could keep the distractions at bay that would otherwise have overwhelmed her, while enabling her to keep her heart fixed on the God who seemed to have abandoned her. In time, she no longer felt it helpful to recite each prayer in full, a sentence, a phrase or even a single word was all she needed to keep her on course. Then, she said, she would often resort to the short prayers or ejaculations as St Augustine called them, that she was taught as a young girl, such as, 'Sacred Heart of Jesus, I put my trust in you', or 'Jesus mercy, Mary help.'

When her spiritual desert became particularly testing, she turned to her spiritual director, Abbot Williams, for help. She had known him since they were in the same class at primary school. He told her that he could not have advised her better than she had advised herself, or perhaps as the Holy Spirit had guided her. He explained the meaning and purpose of what came to be called the Prayer of the Heart as used by the Desert Fathers. Virtually any short prayer is particularly effective when used *in extremis* in what later came to be known as the Cloud of Unknowing, when all other forms of prayer become all but impossible. The Abbot told my mother that when he was a young man he made a tour of the Franciscan hermitages in Italy as a papal visitator, where he found that the most popular form of personal prayer was the Rosary, precisely because it could be adapted to every phase and stage of the spiritual journey with such ease. He ended up at San Giovanni Rotondo where he visited the then famous Padre Pio who was virtually inseparable from the Rosary; it supported his mystical life more than any other form of personal prayer.

My mother needed no more encouragement to continue her prayer life as she had started, with the same beads that were in her hands when it ended. My father told me that in the years before she died she stopped using the Rosary, as had been her custom. But the beads were never out of her hands when she was confined to bed. The peace and contentment that radiated from her face was all the confirmation that he needed to convince him that she was already beginning to experience something of the peace and joy of the place for which she was preparing herself.

God's plan only became possible because of Jesus, the flesh and blood embodiment of God's love. As the Mysterion was first embodied in him, he was the first mystic. By that I mean, not only that he was the first person in whom God's love was embodied, but the first person to feel and experience the love of God as it reached out from his divine being into his human being. It is here, in him, and nowhere else that we come to know and experience the mystery of God's love, here and now, and to eternity. On a further personal note it was through meditating on the mysteries of the Rosary, taught to me by my mother, that I first began my journey, first to meditate on Christ, as he once was, and then to contemplate him as he is now, as I am to explain later.

I developed a new but personal way of saying the Rosary which I use from time to time in addition to the usual way. It has helped to remind me of God's plan, as it was being implemented in our world of space and time. This method of using the Rosary would not help someone in the depth of what St John of the Cross has called the dark night when one is being purified for perfection, but it can be very helpful both before and afterwards.

It need take no longer than the time to say the Rosary in the usual way – it may be shorter or longer, but it enables a person to take a brief overall glance at the whole mystery of God's plan as it is being worked out here on earth.

Begin by reverently taking hold of the crucifix to remind yourself that Jesus was glorified on the cross, filled with the supernatural and superabundant love that was fully unleashed upon the world on the first Pentecost day. Remind yourself that this love is being poured out upon you now and into you to the measure in which you are open to receive it. This is the beginning of a sublime mystical journey that will eventually lead you to *epecstasy*. Then begin counting the beads of the first of the joyful mysteries. You do not need to spend more than a second on each, for you are not using each bead to keep your attention on the recitation of the Hail Mary, but to help keep your heart and mind on the mystery of the Annunciation. Using your memory to remember this event, as you have read about it in the scriptures, and your imagination to visualise it, you will be reminded of its meaning and significance as part of God's plan. Then do the same with the other mysteries, all nineteen of them. By the time you have finished you will have seen in one swift sublime sweep how God's plan was implemented on earth. Then pray for the Holy Spirit who was at work in all these mysteries, to take you up, here and now in this present moment, into Jesus as he is now, so that in, with and through him you may give all praise, honour, glory and adoration to the Father. The speed with which you touch one bead after the other can help keep distractions at bay, as can the speed with which you glance at one mystery after another. However, the speed with which this method of saying the rosary is said is totally at the discretion of the one who uses it. I always use the large beads between each decade to remind me to say the Glory be to the Father – but all believers to their own. And remember, the moment you are inspired to stop, to pause, to contemplate more deeply what you are meditating upon, then do so. You do not have to get through or finish anything. The whole point of this form of meditation is to lead to contemplation and into Jesus and into his contemplation of our common Father.

To finish I would like to say something about all prayer and about the hidden inner dynamics within it. The baptism received by those who repented after St Peter had preached on the first Pentecost day did not just enable the Holy Spirit to enter into them during the baptismal rite itself. It would happen on every subsequent day and at every moment of every day for the rest of their lives, as long as they were continually repenting or turning and opening themselves to receive it.

There is a story of an old Chinese sage, who lived a thousand years before Christ and who was believed to be the wisest man who had ever lived. One day one of his disciples asked him an important question. "If you could do but one thing to change the world", he asked him, "what would it be?" Without hesitation, he answered "I would give back to words their original meaning." That is what I want to do to finish this talk this evening. Of course, there is not enough time to do this for every word, even if I could, but I would like to do it for one word. That word is repentance, for in practising repentance we are in fact practising loving, and, as we shall see, there is nothing more important. There is nothing more important, because it is only in the act of trying to love God that his love descends, to enter into our loving. Then it infuses our weak human loving with divine loving in such a way that we can return God's love in kind.

In Hebrew or Aramaic, the word repentance means to turn back to God and to turn back to him repeatedly. In these two languages, there is no such word for someone who has repented, but only for someone who is repenting and repenting continually. In the Old Testament, repentance was also used to mean turning back to one's father after a serious rift, a meaning embodied in the New Testament in the parable of the prodigal son. In the preaching and teaching of Jesus, every moment is the time and place to turn to the Father, so that, no matter what, he can gather us up into his arms and enfold us with his ever-ready, ever-forgiving, and everlasting loving.

If you were to search through the collected wisdom of humanity since the beginning to find what was considered the most worthwhile pursuit, you would find that the answer is happiness. If you were then to read all that has been written to discover how this happiness can best be attained, you would find that the answer is in loving and in being loved. It is for this that human beings crave more than anything else. Yet there is a strange, inexplicable quirk in human nature that makes people spend hours, weeks, months and years learning to do almost everything else, whilst forgetting to learn how to do what Jesus once called the one thing necessary. We believe that while every other human accomplishment has to be learnt, love just happens or it does not happen at all.

The Christian message teaches that when human loving is surcharged by the divine, it makes a person into an infinitely better lover, not just better able to love God, but to love other human beings too, most especially the one with whom you would wish to spend the rest of your life. But that is not all, it also makes them more loveable because, as they open themselves to God's love, his love fills them ever more fully with goodness, honesty, integrity, truth and with all the other virtues. It is this above all else that makes a person beautiful inside, and it is this that matters more than anything else. The way in which all these moral virtues and gifts are embodied and then exercised, in a man and in a woman, is different and yet complementary. This obvious difference led Plato to conclude that originally man and woman were as one being in God's ideal world, but in our world, they were created as two. They will therefore never be happy until they find their other half and become one again. Men and women are therefore complementary but, ideally, each embodies and manifests God's love in different ways that mirror what the Fathers of the Church called the anima and the animus in God - the masculine and the feminine. It should not be surprising then that God was called a mother as well as a father in the Old Testament; the truth is he is both.

So, quite apart from generating a deeper spiritual life by learning to love God, this very endeavour prepares a person to become more themselves. Then in becoming more themselves it makes them more masculine or more feminine and therefore more and more attractive to the other, whom they see as their other self and in whom they find their completion. That is why finding the right partner is often described as coming home, and their other half is called their soul-mate. It is tempting to believe in Plato's theory because in one sense he is right; the masculine and the feminine that we see as two on earth are indeed as one in heaven where they are to be found to perfection in God. One interesting conclusion to all this is that if the fullness of God's love is to be found in Jesus Christ then, despite his obvious maleness, both the masculine and the feminine, that are found to perfection in the Father, must also be found in the Son.

This perfect and balanced love can be seen by a careful reading of the Gospels. But it didn't end there because Jesus was the same human being after he was raised from the dead to be transformed, transfigured, and glorified. Yes, the same human being, but as his humanity was brought to peak perfection so also was the quality of his human loving in which the masculine and feminine love are as one. It was not only brought to perfection in him, but it was made available to others at the time and at every future time. Before, it was only available to the lucky few, but now it is available to all, for all the time to the end of time.

Love in any order, the human or the divine, can only be completed by returning it in kind. That is why we are told that the first of the new Commandments is to love God with our whole hearts and minds, with our whole bodies and souls. This love acts like a lightning conductor that directs the divine love that pours out of the glorified Christ into our human nature, and thence into our human being from where it infuses our human acting. I will return to this theme tomorrow, but now I want to turn to the question that I have already begun - how do we receive it?

Love, like anything else that is worth striving for, has to be learnt. We think nothing of spending years working to become a doctor, a lawyer, an accountant, a teacher, a nurse, an electrician, a plumber, a builder, but we seem to think no work is needed to learn how to love. Yet it is on this more than on anything else that our present and future happiness depends. We persist in believing and acting as if it is some sort of natural instinct that arises within us and either grows and develops or shrinks and dies with little reference to anything we do. The truth is, love can be learnt, love must be learnt, and we should give more time and energy to facilitating this learning than to any other, because our whole happiness as human beings depends on it and so does everything that we do. From the very beginning the word prayer was given to what we do to learn loving.

This practice of loving inside of prayer involves repenting not once but many times over. For no matter what means are used to raise the heart and mind to God, a hundred and one distractions from the world we have just left will pull them down to earth again, time and time again. If this happens fifty times in fifteen minutes it means that we have been practising selflessness by saying no to self and yes to God. We have been practising the repentance that St Peter said was essential if we are to be open to receive the love of God. That is why prayer is the place where we learn the selfless loving through repeated repentance that opens us to receive the love of God. That is why St Teresa of Avila said you cannot really pray without distractions. They teach you, in concentrated periods of time set aside for that purpose, to act selflessly until a habit of acting selflessly enables you to keep turning to God, directly in prayer, and indirectly outside of prayer as you turn to God in the neighbour in need. That is why St Teresa said quite bluntly that, "Prayer is the only way to perfection and anyone who points in another direction is deceiving you." That is why the whole of this book is dedicated to showing how we should use the example of Jesus himself and the pattern of daily prayer that he handed on to the first Christians to rebuild our own personal, daily prayer life.

The first three Christian centuries perfectly exemplify what happens when people are animated and inspired from the inside by the love of God. As we will see, although their prayer life is first developed at set times, it gradually overflows to encompass their whole lives. The love that they received drew them into the love of Christ and drew Christ's love into them. Nobody could see the inner life that transformed them because it was hidden from view. Nobody could see the Holy Spirit at work infusing his mystical love into them, but they could see the effect that it had. They could see that these Christians had something about them that they had never seen or experienced before. It was not so much an 'X' factor, but rather a 'G' factor because they saw in them something of the glory, the goodness, and the grace of God. It generated in them a quality of goodness and of loving, not just reserved for their own, but for all. It was this 'G' factor that enabled a small group of dissident Jews to grow into a vital and vibrant community of believers of all races, who transformed a pagan empire into a Christian empire in little more than three centuries.

The profound mystical spirituality that succeeded and triumphed in those early years did so because it generated a dynamic verve and vivacity that embraced every moment of every day. What was celebrated on Sundays was but the outward and communal expression of what came to be called 'the prayer without ceasing,' because it gradually overflowed from set times and places to infiltrate every aspect of the believers' lives and every action that they performed. No act of worship no matter how well it is presented, no matter how perfectly it exemplifies what once was, will succeed unless it expresses the daily mystical spirituality first given to the Church by Jesus himself. That is why we must embrace it once more. If we do not, then the consequences will be catastrophic. The terrifying truth is that God's plan can only be brought to completion by Jesus working now, through those who choose to receive him. If he is only treated as an outsider whom we keep on the fringes of our lives, or like the doctor to whom we only turn when we are in desperate need, then disaster is only a matter of time, and by all accounts time is running out. The moment to start again is here and now for we have all vacillated for too long.

That is why the French mystic, Jean Pierre de Caussade SJ (1675-1751), wrote *The Sacrament of the Present Moment,* because it is only in this moment that we can repent or keep turning to receive the Holy Spirit. It is for this reason that he said that the present moment is the only place on earth where time touches eternity. When we make an act of faith then, in our daily prayer, it does not mean that we are primarily affirming our faith in a body of truths, but in a body full of love, who rose from the dead on the first Easter Day. It means we believe in the glorified body of Jesus that pours out the love that he received from God his Father on the first Pentecost day, and on every day, on all who would receive it. This magnetic love is charged with a supernatural power that can draw us up into him, so that through him we can be continually drawn into the love of the Father, beginning now, and continuing to all eternity, so that the secret plan of God, the Mysterion, may finally be brought to completion.

* * *

Before leaving Peter distributed a little home-made booklet to everyone, so that they could have a look at it overnight before he explained it the next day. It contained a memory jog or a mnemonic that would remind the readers of the essential ingredients of the daily prayer that we should make each day.

When his disciples first asked him how to pray, Jesus gave them the Our Father. In his booklet, Peter used every letter of the two words 'Our Father' as a reminder of the essential ingredients of all authentic Christian prayer. In the next talk he would use the letters O-U-R as a reminder of the three essential features of Morning Prayer. The letter -O- would be a reminder to say the morning offering in one form or another. The letter -U- would be a reminder that as we make this prayer, we are uniting ourselves with Christ and with all who are in him. Then the letter -R- would be a reminder to review the coming day, resolving to do all and everything for the honour and glory of God. In the following talks, he would show how every letter of the word Father could be used too, as a reminder of how to pray during the day at a time set aside for that purpose. The letter -F- would be a reminder to make an act of faith, enabling us to express our belief as simply as possible and in our own words, in the God who is an ever-loving Father, in Jesus his ever-loved and ever-loving Son and in the Holy Spirit who draws all of us back through Jesus into God's kingdom of endless loving. Once we have briefly meditated on what God has done for us, and is continuing to do for us, it is time to make our response. To do this, Peter used the remaining letters of the words 'Our Father', accordingly. The letter -A- stands for the word abandonment, -T- for thanksgiving, -H- for Holy Communion, -E- for examination of conscience, and finally -R- for repentance. To help beginners, Peter included nine prayers of his own making, which I have included at the end of this book in an addendum. His little booklet ended with these words:

It is a good idea to begin daily prayer by trying to visualise our Risen Lord, as he is now, in the act of loving, in the act of sending out the inner mystical loving that revolves endlessly between the Father and the Son. The icon of the transfigured Christ helps me to do this now, as the picture of the Sacred Heart helped me before, but there are other similar images that can do the same. The Venerable Fulton Sheen once said, "In human loving all the powerful feelings come at the beginning, but in divine loving the powerful feelings come later," when we have been tried and tested. It is of vital importance therefore to persevere in praying whether we feel anything or whether we do not. Those who only pray when they have exhilarating spiritual feelings will get nowhere, because their behaviour makes it abundantly clear that they are only in it for themselves. Prayer, like all true love, must manifest a quality of selflessness that can alone lead a person on and into the love that surpasses the understanding, but in God's good time, not ours. At the end of his book *The Count of Monte Cristo,* Alexander Dumas, said that all the wisdom of the world is contained in but two words, waiting and hoping, and this sums up perfectly the teaching of St Luke's Gospel, sometimes called the Gospel of prayer. It is here that genuine patience is learnt, and remember, as St Catherine of Siena once put it, "Patience is not so much a virtue but the test of all virtue."

Chapter 4

Turning Straw into Gold

(Peter's third talk)

Fr Kenneth prepared a very special treat for his group on the final day of the pilgrimage. It was a treat few others had ever experienced. He was at the time the Fr Guardian of the Church of St Francis that had been in the possession of the Franciscans since 1335. This gave the Friars the privilege of looking after one of the most ancient and holy places in Christendom, one that very few pilgrims to the Holy Land have ever seen. It was the famous 'Upper Room' where Jesus shared his Last Supper with the Apostles. It was the place where he delivered the most profound and mystical discourse that has ever been given on earth. It was the place where ordinary bread and wine were transformed into Christ himself, and therefore the first place where those who ate and drank this sublime supernatural food received Christ within them. It was the place where Jesus told his disciples to repeat this sacred meal repeatedly until he came again. This would be a sign how, after his Resurrection, everyone who believed would be able to receive Christ within them, and so become one with everyone else who had Christ within them too. That is why Christ asked Saul on the Damascus road, "Why are you persecuting me?" With Christ in them and them in Christ, ordinary people who never dreamed such a thing possible before, would be able to reach out and up to God, would have access to God as never before. They would be able to pray to him and be heard, and would be able to thank him, praise him, adore him, give honour and glory to him, and with astonishing consequences. These consequences were that their prayer united with the prayer of Christ, opened a bridge over which human and divine love could pass to enter into one another, to mingle with each other and eventually to become as one, when human love had been purified of all that would prevent this ineffable union.

Then to our absolute amazement and joy, Fr Kenneth had arranged that we should have Mass in that very room where the first Mass was celebrated, but that was not all. The Mass would be said by a special friend of his. All previous Masses for the group had been said in Gaelic, but this Mass would be said in Aramaic, the language spoken by Jesus and used by him at the Last Supper, for his friend was Fr Joachim, who belonged to the Chaldean Church. He began by thanking Fr Kenneth for the privilege, because he knew that this holy place was only open, and then for very few, once or twice a year. He explained that this was not only the place where the first Mass was said, but it was the birthplace of the Church. It was here, where Jesus appeared to his disciples and confounded the doubting Thomas, where the Holy Spirit had descended on the Apostles on the first Pentecost. Fr Joachim did not preach as his English was not good enough, so Fr Kenneth spoke in his place, but his words were few and to the point because time was short - we had to catch the afternoon 'plane for home. What other subject could he speak about at the place where the first Mass had taken place? The essence of what he said was as follows:

"The whole of Christ's life was his Mass, the place where he continually offered himself to the Father, in and through all and everything that he did until his last breath on Calvary, when, as St John put it, he was glorified. It was then that he experienced the fullness of everlasting joy that he already experienced in part on earth. It was his lifelong giving and receiving that was made sacramentally present at the first liturgical Mass that took place, in this very place, at the Last Supper. It not only symbolised the lifelong giving and receiving that those who followed him had to imitate, but each Sunday it released the same love that Jesus received at his glorification. It was given to those who participated in these mysteries to the measure that their liturgical sacrifice represented the daily sacrifices made in all that they offered to God, for his honour and his glory, in all that they said and did each day, as Jesus did before them. In summary, the Mass is the Mysterion, God's plan made man, made bread, made wine, so that the mystical food and drink can draw all present into the priestly action of Jesus, not just during the sacred liturgy, but during the following week through all that is said and done for the greater honour and glory of God."

Many years ago my brother ran a retreat and conference centre in London. As he had to run the place on a shoe-string, he tried to do many of the odd jobs himself to save money. But he always had to call in a plumber when the drains were blocked. One day when the plumber was having his lunch my brother went to look inside his tool box to see if he could find the tool he used to save calling him again. It was then that he saw these words written in Latin inside the lid. "All for the honour and glory of God" (*Ad maiorem Dei gloriam*). This was the inner mystical meaning of all that he said and did each day, as it has been for all sincerely practising Christians from the very beginning, as it was for Jesus himself. St Paul simply put it this way, "Whatever you eat, whatever you drink, whatever you do at all, do it for the glory of God" (I Corinthians 10:31).

When in the first century the Martyr St Justin was writing about the celebration of the Mass, he said that, when, at the end of the Eucharistic prayer, the priest recited, "Through him, with him, in him, in the unity of the Holy Spirit, all glory and honour is yours, almighty Father, for ever and ever," the "Amen" of the faithful was so loud that it nearly raised the roof. Their "Amen" was so strong, so loud and so vibrant because the priest was not just summing up the offering that they were making at that Mass, but the offering that they were making with every fibre of their being at every moment of their lives, in and through all they said and did each day during the previous week. God's glory is nothing other than the mutual infinite loving that always was, is now, and always will be; what St John called eternal life. This glory of God was made flesh and blood in Jesus, but even in him it was only a shadow of the glory to which he was returning and which we are all called to experience one day, in, with and through him. Remember at the very moment when the first Martyr Stephen was dying, as he was being stoned to death, he cried out in joy that he could see the heavens opening and the glory of the Lord into which he was about to enter.

After offering all they had said and done for God and his glory the previous week, the first Christians knew they would receive God's love to the measure of their giving at Holy Communion, to prepare them to continue giving and loving in the forthcoming week. After Holy Communion, the whole community would join together in reciting or singing the Gloria. In the course of time this ancient hymn has been placed at the beginning of Mass, unlike the Anglicans who have kept it in its original place. When after communion they digested and spiritually assimilated something of the glory of God made bread and wine, they would proclaim this glorious and awe-inspiring hymn with all their hearts, for it summed up the very *raison d'etre* of their lives. With this song still ringing in their ears they would leave to transpose their words into action, their commitment to do all for the honour and glory of God.

St John insisted that the eternal life that constitutes the essence of God's glory is here now, at least in some measure in those who radically open themselves to receive it, as it was in Jesus before them. It was for this that Jesus prayed at the Last Supper. "I have given them the glory that you gave to me, that they may be one as we are one. With me in them and you in me, may they be so completely one that the world will realise that it was you who sent me" (John 17:22-23). It was in the act of doing this that God's honour and glory became embodied in them, enabling them to generate a quality of loving that the pagan world had never seen before, and a depth of inner spiritual peace and joy that they yearned to experience for themselves. This was not just evident in the way they lived, but in the way they died for the faith that we can so easily take for granted. Although the Gloria is not in its original place, the present liturgy of the Mass ends with the celebrant saying, "Go in peace glorifying the Lord with your life," so the original intention is nevertheless retained. The intention is that when we leave Mass we do not leave empty, but full of the goodness of God's glory, so that we bear witness to the love of God embodied in us and in all we say and do.

Those first Christians then, who bore witness to the glory of God most successfully, and so called others to turn to him and give their lives over to him, did so because they embodied within themselves the one in whom God's glory and God's goodness could be seen in something of its human grandeur. That is why St Irenaeus said, "The greatest glory to God on earth is man fully alive." The man to whom he was referring was the glorified and risen Christ and those who, like St Paul, in some way embodied him. When St Francis told his first friars how to spread the Gospel, he said that the first and most important way of doing this was by the way in which they would embody something of the goodness and glory of God in their lives, and then he said almost as an afterthought, that there is another way, and that is by preaching. However, no matter how great a teacher or preacher you may be, no matter how good you may be at explaining the faith to others, if you do not embody what or whom you are speaking about, you will fail. And, worse than that, you will positively give scandal as hypocrites always do.

Some years ago, a Catholic apologist, who was brilliant at defending the faith on radio and on the television, sadly denied the person in whose name she was speaking by an aggressive demeanour and by treating her opponents with disdain. Action had to be taken to make sure that this person no longer represented a faith that was contradicted by the way adversaries were browbeaten and bullied. The most impressive and effective Catholic communicators that I have seen on the media are people like Mother Teresa, Archbishop Fulton John Sheen, Archbishop Anthony Bloom and Saint John Paul II, because, as with Pope Francis in the present day, they clearly lived what they believed. The mere presence of such individuals does infinitely more good than all the clever arguments in the world.

The daily lives of the first Christians involved living out the Mass, in, with and through Jesus every day of the week, and at every moment of every day. It could be seen in the way they loved God their Father in prayer. However, it has to be said, important though this was, this inner prayer life could not be seen clearly by others, but something else could. This something else, that moved others so deeply, was how the love generated in their prayer overflowed onto others, not just onto their own brethren, but onto anyone in need. It was this quality of charity that they had never seen before that moved them so deeply that they wanted to join what was then called 'The Way' for themselves. It was then that they learnt as St Paul learnt before them that, "When you do this to one of the least of these brothers of mine, you do it to me" (Matthew 25:40).

If this prayer and this service of others was not practised in the previous week then the Mass at the end of the week would be meaningless, not in itself of course, or for others, but for those who would have nothing to offer. It is in giving that we receive, but if we have nothing to give then we have nothing to receive. If we have, however, then we will be filled with the goodness and glory of God that is our privilege and joy to communicate to others.

At the beginning of a school retreat that I attended many years ago, the retreat master began by asking us when we last felt really happy. One boy said when he was fishing with his dad, another when he was playing football, another when enjoying a film with his friends. A girl said it was when she was helping her mother with her shopping or spending time alone with her boy-friend, and so the examples multiplied. When we were asked what all these different experiences had in common, we all came to see that we were so lost in what we were doing that we forgot ourselves, at least for a time. The same thing happens when we learn how to live for God, at least for a time. That is why God teaches through Jesus how to live for him and for him alone, for his honour and glory, not our own. The truth of the matter is our puny efforts do not add one jot or iota to the happiness of God. He did not create us for his pleasure or satisfaction but for our own. The incredible mystery of God's love is that he does not actually need us to praise him and give him all honour and glory; he teaches us to do this because it is in doing this that we are taken out of ourselves to centre our attention on him, and to receive what he gives in return. This is the highest form of human action that eventually leads to moments of great happiness on earth and to eternal happiness in heaven.

From the very first centuries Christians would begin their day by offering all they would say and do throughout the day for God's honour and glory, so that their whole day would become the Mass. Later this offering came to be called the morning offering. A hermit whom I met in Italy many years ago called it the philosopher's stone, because it transformed ordinary commonplace things into gold. That is why we should always begin our day with the morning offering the moment we wake up. This can be done by repeating those last words of the great Eucharistic prayer, supplementing them with a few words of our own to help transform the day ahead into a daily Mass. "Through him, with him, in him, in the unity of the Holy Spirit, I offer all that I say and do today to give all glory and honour to you, almighty Father, for ever and ever. Amen." Notice that from the very beginning authentic Christian spirituality is theocentric, God-centred, not anthropocentric or man-centred. If it finally leads to coming to know and experience the love that surpasses the understanding, then like genuine human love this is always the result, the by-product of going out of oneself in pure other-considering loving into the other. When asked the meaning of love, the then Prime Minister Gordon Brown answered without hesitation, "Love is when someone else's happiness is more important than your own." It is when we forget ourselves in loving another that we surpass ourselves and find our true selves. When this other is God, then the love that he gives in return can completely transform and transfigure us beyond all our hopes and dreams.

Once the great Amen had assured the celebrant that the whole congregation had joined him in offering themselves in, with and through Christ to the Father, he would intone the Our Father. So now the whole assembly could pray to the Father, in, with and through Jesus, using the very words with which he had taught his disciples to address him. Although none of us understood Aramaic we all noticed one word when Fr Joachim began the Our Father – it was the word *Abba*. When we asked Fr Joachim about this after Mass, he insisted that when Jesus gave what has come to be known as the Lord's Prayer to his disciples it began, 'Our *Abba* who is in heaven,' or in English, 'Our Daddy who is in heaven'. Furthermore, he said that the whole teaching of Jesus could be summed up in this simple word, as from the very beginning God planned to become our Dad and to give us a loving home within him for ever. That is what he wants more than anything else because he loves us. These simple words spoken in broken English from an evidently holy man have remained with me to this day. From then onwards whenever I begin my Morning Prayer I begin with the Lord's Prayer and I use the word *Abba* as Jesus told us to do.

Let me explain what I do to encourage you to devise your own Morning Prayer for yourself. Once I have visualised the abiding presence of Jesus pouring out his love, I pray, "Lord Jesus, I know that you are here now, as you always will be, for you promised to be with us to the end of time. Help me to pray with you, in you and through you to God the Father who is always drawing us together in the love of the Holy Spirit, now, and forever." Then I try to say the Our Father as slowly and prayerfully as I can. I then call to mind all who are with me when I pray in Christ, asking for their prayers and praying for them; for family, friends and for all whom I have promised to pray. In this way, I can not only pray for them in words, but in all and through all that I say and do in the forthcoming day. Finally, I review all the things that I must do in the day ahead and resolve to do them as best and as kindly as I can.

Less than ten years before Constantine granted religious tolerance to all in the Roman Empire, one of the last of the Christian Martyrs, St Euplius, was tortured and scourged like Christ before him, and finally beheaded. All this took place in Catania in Sicily by the order of the prefect Calvisanus in the reign of Diocletian. In his interrogation St Euplius was asked why he would not offer sacrifices to the gods. He said he did, but his God was the Father of Jesus Christ. Nor did he need to go to a temple to offer sacrifices, for his whole life was a sacrifice to God, as it had been for Jesus Christ before him.

Two hundred years before Euplius, Christians used to insist that they had no temples, no altars nor for that matter did they have priests, as the pagans did. The same was true of their founder Jesus Christ. Although he was brought up and practised his faith in every other respect like a good orthodox Jew there is no evidence that he ever offered any physical sacrifices in the temple at Jerusalem. His mother and foster father did, like all his friends, relatives and disciples, but he never did. Why? Because the very essence of what he had come to do was contained in his total commitment to introduce a new form of worship that he had promised to the Samaritan woman. It was a form of worship that would come from the heart, and entail the complete and unreserved offering of oneself to God, in, with and through him, just as he had offered his all to his Father every moment of every day, to his death on the Cross. His followers were asked to do the same, and that means us too, and this is why the Morning Prayer that I am suggesting will help us do the same.

After Jesus' glorification St Peter taught that Jesus himself was the new temple, a spiritual temple and every Christian was built into him as spiritual bricks and mortar to offer themselves in, with him and through him to God the Father (1 Peter 2:5, 1 Corinthians 3:16, Ephesians 3:21). Furthermore, they were not only to do this on Sundays, but on every day too, and at every moment of that day, as Jesus had done throughout his life while he was on earth. The precise nature of the offering that God wanted was defined, so that there could be no misunderstanding. Before the Resurrection it was "to love the Lord your God with all your heart, with all your soul, with all your mind and with all your strength" (Mark 12:30). After the Resurrection the Old Testament commandment was given a new meaning and a new power that made what was impossible before, possible. Now the new offering was made possible, because it was offered in, with and through Jesus himself. He was not just the New Temple, but the new High Priest too. In the early days of the Church the word priest was only used for Christ and for every member of the Christian community who offered themselves daily to the Father through him. The first thing the early Christians would do each morning, therefore, was to renew the offering that they had made at the Sunday Liturgy. For over a thousand years daily Mass was hardly practised at all, it was certainly never the norm. For the early Christians, daily Mass was the daily offering they made to God through all they said and did each day. Although many practices of the early Church have been forgotten, this one has persisted in what we have known since childhood, as the morning offering.

On the day when Pope Benedict first used the Internet to tweet, he was asked by one of his respondents how married people living such busy lives could find time for prayer? He replied, "By offering everything that is said and done each day to God." First thoughts on waking each morning, he said, should be to offer the forthcoming day to him. It was my mother who first taught me to say the morning offering. She told me that by offering all that I said and did to God in the day ahead of me I would be able to transform ordinary little things into precious gifts for God, just as Rumpelstiltskin had turned straw into gold.

My mother owned a very old prayer book handed down to her from her recusant forebears. In the front it had listed the dates of many of my ancestors going back several generations. It also had their age when they died so I was able to find out where and when they were born. I did not need a genealogist to trace my forebears back to penal times and beyond, but that is another story. The story that I want to tell you concerns something I found in the middle of the book. It was the text of an ancient morning offering that they had all used for generations, my mother included. It was written on a well-thumbed card and in an archaic form of English. I have put it into a more modern version similar to the morning offering that my mother first taught me. It still gives me quite a thrill when I say my morning offering to realise that it was said by my ancestors going back for generations to penal times. Perhaps it was said by my ancestor, Sir Nicholas Tempest, who was hanged, drawn and quartered at Tyburn in 1539 with the Abbot of Fountain's Abbey, by Henry VIII for his part in the Pilgrimage of Grace (1536-37). This was a peaceful rising to protest against the ransacking and dissolution of the monasteries and the rejection of Henry making himself head of the Church in England. This is my modern rendering of this ancient prayer.

"Father, I offer you the prayers, works, joys and sufferings of this day, in union with the offering that Jesus made and continues to make in the Eucharist. I offer them with all who are alive in you, whether they are living or dead. May I draw strength from those who have already proved their faith and become the instrument of giving strength to those who have not."

My mother taught me to say my morning offering the moment I woke up in the morning. But above all she showed me how to put it into practice by her own example. It was not the little things that I noticed at first, but the big sacrifices that she made, that even I noticed. Like that terrible moment in her life when her own precious son, my brother, died in childbirth. It was with the help of her spiritual friend Abbott Williams that she gradually learnt to accept his death, as Mary had done as she stood at the foot of the Cross. Lessons learnt in such moments are never forgotten. They indelibly stain the memory and determine the way you think and act for the rest of your life, for better or for worse. In my mother's case it was for better not worse, as it had been for Mary. For both of them it meant that through their terrible ordeal, their motherhood had somehow been refined and deepened to the benefit of other children who looked to them for the motherly love that was always given without measure. I for one know this because I have experienced it for myself, and still do. My morning offering always reminds me of my mother for it was she who first taught me how to make it. It reminds me of the other mother too, who inspired her and who was given to us all by Jesus as he died on the Cross. So this is the time in my Morning Prayer when I say a Hail Mary to ask her to help me today, as I try to offer all I say and do to God the Father through her son, Jesus. I always try to remember my mother's terrible loss and to pray for her as well as for my brother.

It is as natural for sons to be absorbed with themselves as it is for mothers to be absorbed in them. There is usually selfishness on both sides, but with Jesus and Mary it was different. Neither of them was stained by the selfishness, the self-absorption that marks the rest of us. However, do not be deceived into thinking this made for a life of uninterrupted bliss. There could be and there were painful misunderstandings, separations and bereavements. If their close intimate and unselfish love for each other quadrupled their mutual happiness, then it did the same for their mutual sufferings too.

Anyone who has loved deeply knows that the greater the love, the greater the sensitivity, the higher the awareness and consequently they experience more keenly the heights of joy and the depths of pain, the agony and the ecstasy. If Mary experienced the heights at Bethlehem and Nazareth, then she experienced the depths at Calvary. The quality of her love meant that these *depths* had never been experienced by any other mother before or since. Nevertheless, the sufferings of the Son were even more. Added to the physical pain was a psychological pain of unimaginable proportions. It was the pain of seeing the most loving of all mothers in agony at the foot of the Cross, unable to do anything to help the most tender, loving and gentlest of sons. There were miracles before, there would be miracles again, but not for his own benefit or for his own family, even in their greatest need. Nevertheless, he gave her another son to take his place, the man he loved most in his life on earth. Despite the deep and all-enveloping spiritual darkness that was about to compound his physical agony, he turned to Mary and John and said, "Woman, this is your son. This is your mother" (John 19:26).

It did not take away the pain, but the mutual mourning of the new family he founded on his deathbed gave some measure of human comfort and support. It was the most he could do, the most human thing he could do. John himself understands this deeply moving moment in a profoundly personal way. From that time forward he takes the mother of Jesus to his own home to be his mother too. Not at the time, but later under the inspiration of the Holy Spirit, he came to see and understand another symbolic dimension to that fateful event. Mary was to become a mother once more to other children, conceived by the power of the same Spirit who conceived Jesus in her womb. These children would grow and grow and spread over country after country and down century after century. The motherhood that first embraced Jesus and then John would grow and expand to embrace other brothers and sisters united into a loving family that came to be called the Church. This describes a new spiritual brotherhood bonded together in the risen and glorified body of Jesus, by the same Holy Spirit who bonds the Father to the Son, from and to all eternity.

In Mary we find the most perfect expression on earth of the femininity of God. She perfectly embodies the feminine quality of perfect love, the motherliness that we all need in our spiritual as well as our physical lives. When Jesus said to his mother, "Woman, this is your son," he was not only giving her to John, but to all of us. Now in the same way that John took her as his own mother we must do the same, because we all need the soft gentle, warmth of God's motherly love made flesh and blood for us all in Mary.

When our family went to Mass each Sunday, they saw their mother totally absorbed in what they took all too easily for granted. Their selfishness meant that they had too little to offer, while she was offering a thousand and one acts of self-sacrifice made for them during the previous week. This meant that she received to the measure of her giving. Without any formal theological education, she discovered for herself that the Mass is not only a sacrifice, the place where we offer ourselves, in, with and through Christ to the Father, but something more. It is also a sacred sacrificial meal where we receive the love that he is endlessly pouring out, onto and into all who are open to receive it, through daily sacrificial giving. It was here that she received the help and strength she needed to go on selflessly giving in the forthcoming week, for the family that she loved so much. Each day she reminded herself of this, her sacred calling, by making her morning offering, as her ancestors had done for hundreds of years before her. If ever I forgot to say mine she used to say that the Curé d'Ars would say, "All that we do without offering it to

God, is wasted," and he was right.

It was my mother who first taught me something so profound that I could never forget. She said that even though I may make my morning offering alone by the side of my bed, I was not alone. Nor would I be alone even if I became a hermit and lived in the middle of some distant desert, or a prisoner locked up in solitary confinement at the other side of the world. My prayer would always be made in, with and through Jesus and so with all other living Christians wherever they are. She quoted the Our Father to press her point home. When we petition the Father, we do not petition him for ourselves alone as the prayer makes abundantly clear. It says, "Give *us* this day our daily bread and forgive *us* our trespasses as we forgive those who trespass against *us* and lead *us* not into temptation, but deliver *us* from evil. Amen." She taught me further that praying to the Father in Jesus also means praying with all those who have died and who are now alive again in him. That means with Mary and Joseph, with Saint Peter and Saint Paul, Saint Dominic and Saint Francis, with Saint Catherine of Siena, Saint Teresa of Avila and Saint Thérèse of Lisieux, and all the other great saints and mystics.

It also means praying for, with, and to, all my own relatives and friends both living and dead, who are alive again in him, and all who are dead, but not yet fully alive in Christ. She especially taught me to pray for the Holy Souls, those who have died but who are not yet fully prepared to be united with the Risen One for the sins and the fruits of their sins that keep them at bay until they are purified away. Unlike things cannot be united, so we must be cleansed from all that prevents us from having full union with Jesus, and we must be cleansed either in this life or in the next, before that which we desire more than anything else can take place.

Although it is perhaps understandable that Protestants find the idea of purgatory difficult to come to terms with for historical reasons, a change began to take place during the First World

War. It was when many hundreds of thousands were brought home in body bags, or were buried where they fell, that ordinary people of every Christian denomination flocked to church to pray for them to the dismay of the protestant clergy, who did not believe in purgatory. After all, if they were dead they were either in heaven or in hell, so what was the point of praying for them. However, one by one the Anglican Bishops in England, not only joined them, but led them in prayer for their loved ones. All, that is, but the Bishop of Liverpool, who belonged to the evangelical wing of the Church of England. He held out at least until he lost his son in action in 1917 and then he changed his mind. The doctrine of purgatory might not have been added to the Thirty-Nine Articles of Anglican faith, but it was tacitly admitted as they gave way to the overwhelming feelings and needs of their faithful. My mother not only taught me to pray for the Holy Souls but to them too. In fact, I always used to pray to them to wake me up if I needed to get up early in the morning, and they never let me down. Many years later when I was a student my parents came to visit me and I was proud to show them my extra-large bedroom and study. My mother was on her way out when she suddenly stopped and pointed to something on my bedside table. It was an alarm clock. "Whatever is that for?" she asked. She didn't wait for an answer, because she didn't want to embarrass me, but I can still see the expression on her face, and I know what she was thinking.

My mother also told me that this was the perfect opportunity to pray for others too, especially those who have asked me to pray for them. She said when you hear about people who are suffering all over the world, on the radio, the television or in the newspaper, you can reach out to them through prayer, because prayer is not limited by space and time as we are. One morning a lay brother, thinking that Padre Pio was out, burst into his room as he was lost in prayer. The saint dismissed his apologies with the words, "I was only praying for a happy death for my

Father." "But your Father died two years ago," the brother said, looking rather surprised. Padre Pio looked at him in disbelief. "I know he did." Prayer is not limited by the laws of space and time and that is why, although Saint Thérèse of Lisieux never left her Carmelite monastery, she was made patroness of the missions. Some years ago I went to see an opera at Covent Garden by John Tavener called *Thérèse*. Through sublime music and profound words, the composer showed how on her deathbed her prayer could reach forward to help soldiers who were to suffer in the first world war and backwards to those who had suffered in the past, as well as to a condemned murderer in the present that he might repent before he was executed, and this prayer was answered. The wonderful thing about praying for others at this time of the day is that they can be included in the prayer that is the rest of your day, as you try to offer up all you say and do for the honour and glory of God.

However, it must be emphasised that the morning offering is not a magic formula. It does not automatically transform the forthcoming day, and that is why something further is required. My mother told me that after she had made her morning offering she would spend a few minutes reviewing the day ahead, making a few resolutions that would enable her to try to consecrate every moment of the day to loving God. This would be done directly in prayer, and in all she said and did for him outside of prayer, and indirectly through loving the neighbour in need. It might be in pausing for brief moments of prayer during the day, but also in doing humdrum tasks that we keep putting off, like changing the sheets on the bed, putting air into the car tyres, defrosting the freezer or something that is more important. There is always that friend or relative who is sick or in need, whom we should telephone, or write to, or even visit for a few minutes. Alternatively, perhaps we should make a resolution to apologize to one of the family, a friend, or someone at work for the way we behaved towards them the previous day.

It is very difficult to stand up for someone who has been abused by authority at work, or elsewhere, or to speak the truth when no one wants to hear it, or to make a stand for what we know is right. But nevertheless, these are some of the more important things that could occupy our minds as part of Morning Prayer. Perhaps we could end with the most important resolution of all, to try and make the forthcoming day a day when we try as best we can to enable God's love to draw us up, not just into the life of Christ, but into his priestly action. It is only there that we will be able to love God as we should, by offering him all that we are and all that we do, but most of all by offering him the way we have tried to serve him in and through the neighbour in need. In this way, every day is a day in which we spend every single moment trying to observe the New Commandments, firstly by loving God, and then by loving him in the neighbour in need, just as Jesus did.

The spirituality of the Middle Ages was deeply influenced by a story that everybody knew from their childhood. It was the story of a Roman soldier and of his act of compassion for a fellow human being. The Roman soldier was later to become Saint Martin, Bishop of Tours, who was born at the beginning of the fourth century. He was still only a Catechumen when, on a cold winter's night, he cut his cloak in half to clothe a half-naked man who was starving to death outside the city gate. When the story was told that the poor man was in fact Christ, its impact was immense and lasting. It inspired everyone from the humblest of subjects to the kings who ruled over them. Clovis and the Frankish Kings who followed him carried the other half of that cloak with them wherever they went, even into battle. It helped keep the story of Saint Martin's act of charity alive, becoming the inspiration for countless works of charity in one of the cruellest and most barbarous periods in the history of Christendom. When Saint Francis of Assisi was moved to jump off his horse to help a poor leper, he kissed him on the mouth and gave him everything that he had. It was yet another example of the profound truth that kept charity alive through the Dark Ages. When the story was told that the leper was in fact Christ, it became yet another reminder of those unforgettable words from St Matthew's Gospel, "...in so far as you did this to one of the least of these brothers of mine, you did it to me" (Matthew 25:40).

Both Saint Martin and Saint Francis were deeply changed by their meeting with Christ in the neighbour in need. Pope Francis had a similar experience of the poor when he became Bishop. He learnt something deep and profound that he has since tried to convey to others. On the Vigil of Pentecost, he asked his audience a rhetorical question. "Do you give alms to the poor?" Receiving the expected answer, he said, "Very good, but when you give alms to the poor, do you look them in the eye, do you touch their hands?" Saint Francis had always given money to lepers before, but only through others or by tossing his purse to them from a safe distance, until that fateful day which, as he said in his final will and testament, was to change his life irrevocably. We are not changed just by giving, but by the way in which we give. This is the insight that Pope Francis discovered for himself. It is in the way in which we give to the poor that we can discover Christ in them, and through this experience be changed ourselves, as others have been changed before us.

One of the most important truths of the spiritual life that we neglect at our peril is that we will not ultimately be judged by the wonderful feelings that we have experienced in prayer. We will not be asked how many ecstasies we have had or even how many miracles we have worked, or people we have healed, but how we have served God in the neighbour in need. If we have done this, even if we have failed in so much else, we will be invited to share in his glory, because he will say to us, "For I was hungry and you gave me food, I was thirsty and you gave me drink, I was a stranger and you made me welcome, naked and you clothed me, sick and you visited me, in prison and you came to see me" (Matthew 25:35-37).

But if we fail to do this, then we will be condemned to hear these frightening words, "Go away from me... for I was hungry and you never gave me food; I was thirsty and you never gave me anything to drink; I was a stranger and you never made me welcome, naked and you never clothed me, sick and in prison and you never visited me. I tell you solemnly, insofar as you neglected to do this to one of the least of these, you neglected to do it to me" (Matthew 25:41-46).

The morning offering and its implementation then, is not just a nice, pious practice for those who have the time to do it, but something on which our ultimate destination depends. It is the place where the whole of the forthcoming day is dedicated to loving God through a continual process of prayer, self-sacrifice and the service of others. In this way all that is said, done and suffered, all that is enjoyed and celebrated, is offered in, through and with Jesus to our common Father. This is the new worship "in spirit and in truth" (John 4:24), that Jesus promised to the Samaritan woman and is put into practice. We are called to take part in the priestly action of Jesus every moment of every day of our lives. We can be encouraged by the words of one of the Desert Fathers who insisted that we will ultimately be judged, not so much on what we have achieved, but on how best we have tried. In the words of the French philosopher Simone Weil, "A person is no more than the quality of their endeavour." That is how God will judge us even if nobody else does.

I never spoke to my father about his or my spiritual life for that matter, but I know that after reading Thomas Merton's autobiography, *Elected Silence, or Seven Storey Mountain* as it was first called in the United States, he became very interested in the Desert Fathers. It must have been the way they offered their day and everything in it to God that affected him most, because after his death I found a quotation from John Cassian on the final page of his missal which helped him to keep his morning offering on course throughout the day. It was a short prayer recorded in the works of John Cassian. It seems my Father used it throughout his day whenever he was in need. The prayer was simply, "O God, come to my aid, O Lord, make haste to help me." John Cassian said that the prayer was taught to his disciples by Abbot Isaac and later used by St Benedict with which to begin the divine office throughout the day. Under this little prayer my Father copied out the following words from Abbot Isaac, written for the benefit of his followers:

"You must continually use this prayer in your heart, whatever you are doing or whatever office you are holding, or journey you are undertaking; in adversity that you may be delivered, and in prosperity that you may be preserved. You should be so moulded by the constant use of it that when sleep comes you are still considering it so that you become accustomed to repeating it even when you sleep. When you awake let it become the first thing that comes into your mind, let it anticipate all your waking thoughts. When you rise from your bed let it send you down on your knees, and thence send you forth to your work, and let it follow you all through the day."

Abbot Macarius used to tell his disciples to say simply, "Lord, to the rescue," or call upon him by name by using the holy name Jesus whenever they were in danger of losing their way or forgetting what they were about. Abbot Macarius was believed to be the originator of the Jesus Prayer. Later it developed into the prayer, as we know it today, which was originally composed by Saint John Climacus, "Jesus, son of God, have mercy on me a sinner." These short prayers, were not only used by the Desert Fathers, but have been used continually throughout subsequent centuries. They have always been used to help Christians keep their attention fixed on their calling throughout the day and to help them when distractions or temptations threaten to engulf them. One of my mother's favourite little prayers that helped her throughout her day was, "Jesus mercy, Mary help." My primary school teacher, Miss Holt, taught us all to say, "Sacred Heart of Jesus, I put my trust in you."

Morning Prayer wasn't the beginning and end of daily prayer, for it was the custom of the early Christians to pray at least five times a day, as Jesus had done. It is still possible for us to do this, as I believe my father did. I remember asking him why he put little stickers on his wrist watch. One was pointing to nine o'clock, another to twelve o'clock, and the third to three o'clock. He merely said it was a little device to help him remember something. In earlier times when Christian Europe was predominantly rural, the Angelus bell that pealed three times a day, called everyone to prayer wherever they were and whatever they were doing. This was a world that neither my father nor his forebears had known, for unlike my mother, they were all Protestant. His parents were converts and like them he was always reticent to speak about his faith. When it came to the spiritual life he was an intensely private man who found it difficult to speak about his own journey. However, one thing I know for certain was that he always tried to find some time each day, in addition to all else, to enter into what my mother called his inner garden shed for his daily prayer. In future talks I want to speak about this prayer that should be part of every serious Christian's day.

Chapter 5

Mystical Marriage

(Peter's fourth talk)

On my arrival back in England after my unforgettable pilgrimage I was sitting in Waterloo station watching the commuters, the tourists, the retail therapists and other miscellaneous men and women rushing past me. They were of all ages, all colours and all different shapes and sizes, but they all seemed to have one thing in common. They all seemed to be busy, in a rush, totally preoccupied. I felt as if I was caught up in a *Lowry* painting, watching all the people passing to and fro, but these people were not burdened or bent with manual labour, their souls had not been sedated into submission in the *dark satanic mills.* They were upright and busy about their own business, they all seemed to be moving with purpose and intent, but what would they make of the pilgrimage that I had just finished, of my faith that had just been reinforced? What on earth would it mean to them; how could it enrich their lives even if they stopped long enough to listen. I felt like an outsider, an interloper who had just landed on Platform 1 from planet Zog. Then, suddenly, a young man of no more than eighteen or nineteen years started to walk towards me smiling. I began to get worried when he quickened his step and opened his arms as he approached. Before I had time to take evasive action, the girl sitting next to me jumped up to be enfolded in his arms. Like a flash of lightning I saw the light; everything made sense that had made no sense before.

The more I thought about it, the more I realised that we had everything in common. They were not soulless zombies after all. What did each one of them really want, what did they all have in common? Deep, deep down beneath the surface they all wanted to love and to be loved. They all wanted to have a home, a family, or at least to be part of a loving family where they could feel safe and secure. They all wanted to have a place they could call home, where all the personal selfishness, the petty jealousies, the small-mindedness and the pernicious prejudices in themselves and in others could be spirited away, so that nothing would come in the way of the perfect love, the perfect family, the perfect home for which they had always yearned. And, if all their dreams could come true, they would not only want to live in this perfect new world forever, but, ideally, they would want it to become ever more perfect, ever more enjoyable, ever happier and for this happiness to go on for ever. If this could be offered to them, would they not listen, would this not be good news, the best news they ever heard?

What they all wanted deep down within them, is the love to bring all this about. Now this is the essential teaching of our faith. We believe that all our deepest hopes and dreams that are exactly the same as theirs can, no, will come true. They will come true only if we have sufficient faith to believe in and turn to the love that is continually pouring out, at this moment and at every moment, from the God who is the fullness and source of all love. This is what St John meant when he said that "God is Love" (1 John 4:8). This was the truth that I came to understand in a unique way as I prayed at Calvary in the Holy Sepulchre only a few days before.

Some years ago, I had dinner with friends in London. When I was leaving their home, I was introduced to their father, who was busy digging in the garden. Taken by surprise and not knowing what to say I asked a rather stupid question. "And what are you doing?" I said. "I do be digging the garden," he replied, glancing at his son as if to say, "Who's your fatuous friend?" Intrigued by his answer I asked a nun who taught Irish in Dublin what was meant by the expression, "I do be digging the garden." She said that it is the English rendering of what is called in Irish, the present continuing tense. It means, "I have been digging the garden,

I am digging the garden and when you stop asking the obvious, I will continue to dig the garden."

There is no such tense in English, but it perfectly expresses the meaning of the Aramaic idiom, as spoken by Jesus, and in this case by St John, when he said, "God is Love". He was not trying to give a definition of what love is in itself as a Greek philosopher would do, but he was describing in his own language that God is Loving; that is what he is, and that is what he does, and does continually. This is what St John was taught in the synagogue as he was growing up. It was here that he learnt how God loved his people in the past and how he was still loving his people in the present, and how his love had prepared a glorious future for them. Then, when he became a young man, he tangibly experienced this love in a deeply personal way through the love of Jesus, the man sent to bring the dream of a glorious future into reality. After the Resurrection, he continued to experience the love of God, still reaching out to him from Jesus through the Holy Spirit. The message of St John that you find on every page of his Gospel, is that God has been loving us, that he is loving us now, and that he will continue to love us from here to eternity. This is the God in whom we believe when we use the letter -F-, in the blueprint for daily prayer. It helps to remind us to make an act of faith in the love of God that first filled Jesus, raised him from the dead and now pours out of him onto and into all who would receive him. It is this love, the Holy Spirit, who becomes for us like a beam of light that enables us to look up, as it were, to see the world of infinity from our limited world of space and time. We can only see it in brief and incomplete glimpses, or as St Paul puts it, "Now we are seeing a dim reflection in a mirror; but then we shall be seeing face to face" (I Corinthians 13:12).

That is who God is, from our point of view, 'looking up', into what he has done and is still doing through Christ. But looking inward from God's point of view, he not only is what he does, but he experiences who he is. His existence is one lifelong, uninterrupted and eternal experience of loving and being loved in a place that has traditionally been called heaven, from where we have all been conceived and called to join him. To try and appreciate what this means, use your memory for a moment to remember the most treasured moments of loving and being loved that you have ever experienced in your life. When you have done this then multiply this by infinity; imagine that these moments never began and never ended but simply went on and on for ever. Imagine further that these experiences of loving and being loved are tangibly felt by someone infinitely more sensitive than yourself. Only then, in some infinitesimally minute way might you be able to glimpse from afar what it must mean to be God and what it must be like to live in this other world that we call heaven.

Then, while making your act of faith, realise the truth, the most exciting, exhilarating, invigorating, and intoxicating truth that has ever been proclaimed. This truth is that Jesus has come to fill our inmost being with a love that can transport us to this other world where all our hopes and longings, all our deepest desires and yearnings will be fulfilled. St John insists that this other world is already with us. It is not so much over there, but all around us, if we only knew it.

When Fr Kenneth took us to the place from where it was believed that Jesus ascended into heaven he gave us a fascinating little talk. He said that the ancient Jews believed the world was rather like a gigantic, transparent baking bowl turned upside down. God's heavenly throne was placed above it, from where he surveyed all that was going on in his world, which oddly enough doubled as his footstool. The bowl was upheld by what the Old Testament called 'the eternal hills' and it had open windows through which God could send his messengers or angels, because, as we have seen, no one could see God and live. He also used these windows to send wind, rain, and snow whenever he thought fitting. Between the 'eternal hills' the world was as flat as a pancake with the different landmasses separated by the primeval waters, and held up by pillars that rose from the depths, where the sea monsters Rahab and Leviathan dwelt guarding *Sheol*. This was the place where the dead dwelt to await the coming of the Messiah to free them, as Jesus was to do when he descended into hell.

Jesus had little enough time to teach his disciples all he wanted them to know before his death, so, as there was no time to teach them a new cosmology he concentrated on theology. He concentrated on teaching his disciples all that God did, was doing and would finally do for them and for those who would follow them. In doing this he used their existing knowledge, to lead them on to the profound, new spiritual truths that he had come to impart. That is why he rose heavenward and passed through the clouds to make them understand that he was going back to where they believed God lived, high up above the firmament. He did indeed go back to the Father to be united with him, but as God is omnipotent - all powerful, so also is he omnipresent - present everywhere. So, to be reunited with his Father, Christ did not need to rise or ascend heavenward. He only did this so that his disciples would know his destination. But his destination was not so much 'up there' as 'in here' into a different dimension, because God is everywhere. As God is everywhere so also is the love, or rather the loving that St John said is his very essence and existence; it is what he is and what he does all rolled into one.

In the ballet 'Cinderella', when the lights change and the thin gossamer curtain suddenly becomes transparent, the drab and dreary kitchen disappears to reveal all the grandeur and splendour of the royal court. Like heaven itself it had been there all the time, not out there, or up there or in some other place, let alone in some distant world beyond the universe, but where we are now. Only the light of faith can reveal this world to us in this life. However, I believe that the moment we die will be the moment when we will be astounded, dumfounded to realise that this other divine and heavenly world is in no other place than where we are now. For it has been there all the time in another dimension, for in the dimension of supernatural love and loving, its centre is everywhere and its boundaries are nowhere.

The purpose of these talks is that this loving that surrounds us will go no further unless we freely choose to turn and open ourselves to receive it, as Jesus did at every moment of every day whilst he was on earth. He was the first mystic, the first to receive continually the hidden or mystical love of God. When we follow him, and continually try to do likewise, we too are mystics, learning as he learnt, to practise 'the prayer without ceasing' – a way of life in which we strive at all times to receive the only love that can transform us into him.

There are two fundamental and undeniable truths, one that God exists and two that we exist. How then can we come from anywhere other than him? Further, how can we come from him, except through his loving? That is what God is, and that is what he does, no more, no less. Now loving is not a reason for creation - not because it is irrational for such a superior being to want to create lesser beings, as the Greek philosophers believed, but for something further. Love is supra-rational, if I may paraphrase Pascal; "Love has reasons that the reason knows nothing about." St Augustine said that the pure goodness generated by the mutual loving that is spiritually embodied in the Three in One must needs overflow, it cannot be permanently contained within itself. God's pure Loving Goodness overflowed to express itself into another physical dimension, in a world of matter and form, of flesh and blood, all created by, and in, his Loving Goodness. Then this Loving Goodness, called The Word, because it was the perfect expression of God, was made flesh in a human being, Jesus, who although he was born a helpless baby would grow into Christ the King, the masterpiece and crown of God's glorious creation. Then he would overflow with the love that he received so that we could receive that love too and the pure unadulterated goodness that love generates. This in its turn would give birth to all the fruits of goodness and therefore to all the virtues that are born of goodness. All this takes place not in a vague void or vacuum, but within us because, as the Gospels make clear, the Kingdom of God is within us. So, when you make your act of faith in the love of God, realise why his love is being poured out, and how it is re-making and moulding you from the inside into the image and likeness of the sender. Realise too how this process will continue as long as you continue to remain open and receptive each day to receiving it though the selflessness learnt in practising daily prayer and good works.

To help remind me of these profound truths I try to visualise in my imagination, the picture of the transformed and transfigured Christ that hangs on my bedroom wall. Other depictions can be equally helpful, like one of the great Renaissance paintings of the risen Christ, or of the Sacred Heart, or a more modern depiction of Christ radiating the life and love that can alone transform us into the person whom God has created us to become. But this act of faith must be immediately followed by the heartfelt prayer that asks for this love to permeate us to the very foundation of our being. This is so that we can be filled with all the love that we need to nourish us to grow spiritually and physically. For it is only in this way that we can first become more mature and more secure human beings as the prelude to becoming transformed and transfigured into the glorified Christ.

When Helen, said to be the most beautiful woman in Greek antiquity, fled with her lover to Troy, she did not receive the welcome she expected. Although her lover was Paris, the son of the King, he and his courtiers were reluctant to admit her. One look at her face rightly confirmed that her husband, the King of Sparta, would indeed launch a thousand ships to retrieve her. She was therefore understandably interrogated about her motives for deserting him. The King was on the point of rejecting her when she cried out in her defence, "Do we not all know that the gods have made us to love and to be loved, and so achieve our destiny? I can only achieve that destiny here in Troy and with your son, Paris, whom I love with all my heart."

One thousand years later Jesus came to tell us that our God has also created us to love and to be loved, as part of the preparation for the infinite loving that is our ultimate destiny. Learning to love, here in this world, prepares us for the ultimate love for which we all yearn in the next. That is why marriage is a sacrament and that is why, first and foremost and before all else, Jesus went to Cana in Galilee, not just to give his blessing to human marriage, but to show how human loving can be transformed when, as it is being learnt, it is suffused with and supercharged by the divine.

This was for St John, who tells the story in his own unique way, the meaning of the miracle of the changing of the water into wine. He does not call it a miracle, but a sign, because what the miracle signifies is more important than the miracle itself. This sign has long since been interpreted as symbolising how, just as Jesus can change water into wine, he can change the old order into the new; the Old Covenant into the New Covenant. However, the context in which he performs this action gives it a more specific meaning. Now, and in future, thanks to the incarnation, human love will be suffused with the divine.

Water can indeed quench our thirst, but when water is permeated through and through with the fruit of the vine and allowed to ferment, it is filled with properties and powers that far surpass water alone. This is what happens when human love is permeated by divine love. At Cana in Galilee Christ's first miracle demonstrated this, as a sign, by transforming water into wine. The sign announced loud and clear, at least to people who knew the meaning of signs and symbols in a way that was lost to later generations, that in future marital love would be transformed by being suffused by divine love. That is why this sacrament is so special. It is the only sacrament of the seven in which those receiving it, the husband and wife, and not the priest or the bishop, are the normal ministers. In other words, it is they who transmit the love of God to one another through each other's love for one another, through the selfless sacrifices that they make for each other every day and every moment of every day for the rest of their lives. This love is then literally handed on to their children, even before it is received directly and independently from God.

I first experienced God's love through my parents' love as an infant, even before I was baptised. In my case my baptism confirmed what had already happened, was happening and would continue to happen through my parents' love for each other that overflowed onto me. Long before my mother taught me how to pray, how to turn to receive God's love independently, and long afterwards for that matter, her love continued to sustain me. I well remember when I was ill as a very small child, how my mother swept me up into her arms and placed me in my parents' bed between her and my father where I felt safe, secure and loved. When I was later handicapped with polio, her love was lavished on me, eventually giving me the security to live my life independently and even to seek out the contemplative life. Without her love for me that would not have been possible, nor would it have been possible for me to journey on through the dark nights of spiritual purification where the fire of the Holy Spirit would begin to purify me. I would never have persevered, nor ever have come to experience, albeit in brief glimpses, the love that surpasses the understanding. That is why St Bonaventure said that contemplation is first learnt at the mother's breast. For myself I know this to be true.

It is for all these reasons that I have placed a picture of my mother next to the icon of the transfigured and glorified Christ. My brother has placed a similar picture of our Mother on his wall too, but he has placed a picture of his wife there as well, and for the same reason. St John was adamant that where there is love, there is God. My brother knows as well as I do that God's love reaches out to him indirectly through his mother and his wife as well. And for those who have not been as fortunate as I have been, for those who have not had such special love from their mothers, their fathers, their husbands or their wives or from other relatives or friends, then Christ, the source of all and every form of love, is needed and needed desperately. He can and will give all that is necessary for those who turn to him in their need, for he is the origin and source of all love. He always gives to those who turn to him; in the measure that they give, will they receive – in ever fuller and in ever deeper measure.

Whenever and however God reaches out to touch us, we always receive both love and truth simultaneously. His truth enables us to see with ever greater clarity the truth about God and the love that he continually showers on us, leading us on to the destiny he has prepared for us. But he also gives us the grace to help ourselves and others too, to come to know him, and to join us as we travel along 'The Way'. Then in the same way and at the same time he shows us the truth about ourselves, how far we are from him in the selfish way that we have been pursuing our lives, and what needs to be done to purify us of all that keeps his love out. The more we respond to his continuous love, the more his love inspires us to reach out to him with ever greater endeavour. It does this by suffusing and supercharging our human endeavour with the divine, as water was changed into wine at Cana. In this way, all the virtues that we need to become fully secure and mature human beings in Christ, are infused in us as we try to exercise them.

However, nobody, as the Stoics themselves finally discovered, can generate by their own unaided human endeavour, the necessary virtues to become perfect or even near perfect human beings, never mind into becoming other Christs like so many of the saints. That is why this book is called *Wisdom from the Christian Mystics*, because all authentic Christian mystics know for themselves and teach that it is only through the hidden, the secret, the invisible or the mystical life that endlessly pours out of Christ that we can be purified of all that separates us from his love. Then at the same time this love helps to generate within us all the virtues that we see embodied in Jesus, the first and greatest mystic, that were made visible in all that he said and did. Put simply you cannot have, or live a perfect moral life without the mystical life that Jesus offers to us, suffusing and supporting our weak human life from within.

The more we open ourselves to receive this mystical life, which is nothing other than the Holy Spirit, we see that we will eventually have to submit ourselves to the second baptism to which John the Baptist first referred before Jesus himself confirmed it (Matthew 3:11; Mark 10:38; I Peter 1:2-4 and I Peter 4:12). The first baptism is of water, the second is of fire where mystical purification is brought to completion (James 1:2-4). I will return to this theme later for upon it everything that I must say is based. No purification, no change, and without change we do not just stop going forward, but we start to go backwards, and continue to go backwards until we allow the fire of the Holy Spirit to transform us.

The more we are open to the love of God then the more his love can make up for the deficiencies that would otherwise prevent full human maturity and the capacity of giving ourselves in pure selfless loving to another human being and ultimately to God. The more a human being is open to receive the love of God as they grow to human maturity, the more able they are to make the long and lasting personal relationships upon which every successful marriage depends, and to achieve the happiness to which they aspire. That is why the early Christians committed themselves to a spiritual marriage with Christ during the mysteries of baptism. In this marriage, they would learn the selflessness that would open them in ever fuller measure to the love that would enhance all other human relationships, most particularly in sacramental marriage to their future husband or wife.

All the great mystical writers, from the beginning, used the analogy of human love to show how ultimately our love of Christ takes us up and into the love of God. That is why they repeatedly used the most beautiful love poem in the Old Testament, the Song of Songs or the Song of Solomon to describe and detail the mystical journey through Christ into God. It was originally sung as part of every Jewish marriage ceremony. It would have been sung by Jesus himself with all the other guests as they escorted the bride from her old home to the new home that she would henceforth be sharing with her husband. In the early church, it was Jesus himself who was the first bridegroom for the believers. It should not therefore be surprising that for centuries to come, the mystical marriage with him was seen as the high point of the spiritual life for religious and lay people alike. Later however, although many spiritual writers rightly used the mystical marriage to denote the high point of the mystic way, they wrongly believed that it is only for a chosen few, usually only for those dedicated to God in religious life. This is not the case and never was in the profound mystical spirituality taught to the first Christians by the Fathers of the Church. They received this teaching from Jesus himself, long before religious life, as we know it, ever existed. It is for all.

The first Christians were told of the spiritual marriage to which they were all called before they were married in the usual way. This was the marriage to Christ that took place during the rites of Christian initiation. They were taught that the preparation and the spiritual purification that they had to undergo for this marriage would help them develop a habit of selflessness and empathy for others. Without this, marriage to another human being would never last, or develop beyond the purely superficial when first passions fizzled out. There are therefore two marriages for a Christian, the sacrament of marriage and the spiritual marriage to which we have all been called in baptism.

When the new Christians emerged from the baptismal pool as one with Christ, they were led in procession into the Christian community where their marriage was consummated for the first time in Holy Communion. This marriage however was not the end of, but the beginning of love, a love that would be demonstrated time and time again every day and in every moment of every day, for the rest of their lives through all that they said and did.

The five times a day that they prayed, as Jesus did with his disciples, was not a daily drudgery but a daily delight. It enabled the married mystics to touch and be touched repeatedly by the One to whom they had committed themselves in a mystical marriage that begins in this life, but which is only completed in the next. Every Sunday this mystical marriage was consummated in Holy Communion, reinforcing their love and supercharging it with the power to continue expressing their love for God. When both marriages, the human and the divine are lived to the full, they simultaneously enhance each other. For the loving, selfless sacrifices made in each enable the participants to join Christ, the new high priest, at every moment of their day, offering with him and through him the new worship "in spirit and truth" that Jesus promised to the Samaritan woman (John 4:23). That is why, when the early Christians came to offer themselves to God in an act of communal worship at the end of the great Eucharistic prayer, St Justin said, as I have mentioned before, that the sound of the great 'Amen' was proclaimed with such power and gusto that it all but took the roof off. Why? Because that 'Amen' represented all that they had done, all that they had given, and all the sacrifices that they had been making to God, in both their spiritual and their human marriages that complement each other.

When we marry, we marry into our lover's family too, to experience the family that made him or her what they are. This is sadly not always a pleasant experience, but in the mystical marriage into which Christians enter through baptism, they come to know and experience something of the ultimate mystical family where all their hopes and desires will find perfect completion. This is the life of the Three in One whence Jesus came and to where he will return with everyone else when love has prepared and transformed them. This is our ultimate destiny, the home where we were first conceived and to which we are to return, to bathe in the endless loving in which God resides, from and to all eternity.

When we pray each day then, the letter -F- is to remind us of the ever-continuing outpouring of God's love that comes to us in the sacrament of every present moment. It may come to us directly in prayer or indirectly though the love of our husband or wife or of our children or brothers and sisters, relatives and friends Either way he is loving us now through Jesus, so that his infinite loving can be transposed into human loving in such a way that we can experience it here and now. Furthermore, we can experience it in such a way that it can fill us with whatever sort of love that we are lacking, whatever form of love we need to grow, as Jesus grew, into a perfect human being. Then in him, with him and through him, to be raised up, as if by some powerful magnetic force, to be enfolded by the love of our common Father and to remain there in our true home to eternity. This is what we believe in when we make our daily act of faith, in God our Father and in Jesus Christ his son, sent so that we can become sons and daughters of the unutterably Other who dwells in light inaccessible, made accessible to us, because that light is love.

If the passers-by at Waterloo station could only be convinced of this then they would be overjoyed, because what we call the Christian message is not just for the few but for all, and it fulfills all our deepest desires and longings. That the message has still not reached them is our fault and the fault of our predecessors, who have failed to make them see, because what we would like them to see has not been practised as it should have been in our lives. So, it is time to put this right.

When we have made our act of faith slowly and prayerfully, mulling over what it means, reflecting and ruminating on all that has been said, to penetrate its meaning with all that human and divine understanding can do to enlighten us, it is time to pause in contemplative stillness. Gradually, a sublime realisation will begin to stir in the utmost depth of our being. For once this act of faith has been reflected on and understood, we will inevitably be inspired to make another act. This time, it is an act of total abandonment to God through Jesus. What other response could we possibly make? If this is asking too much, then sadly it means that we have become wedded to a purely nominal faith doing the bare minimum. It means that we have become completely oblivious to God's ongoing plan, to sweep us up here and now into the man Dom Eugene Boylan called 'This Tremendous Lover'. For it is here, even in this life, that he wants us to experience something of the ecstatic bliss that will be ours to eternity in the next.

* * *

On the journey home, we asked Peter questions that kept us talking all the way. Despite this he was up early in the morning and after breakfast he walked to the local church where he remained until lunch time, as he had done the previous day. Then, after his siesta, we set out once more for London. On the Monday the church had been less than half full, so everyone could easily move into the parish hall to listen to Peter. However, news of his talks had spread, so we needed to remain in the church to fit everyone in.

Chapter 6

Abandonment – *Shema*

(Peter's fifth talk)

On returning from my pilgrimage to the Holy Land I sent a long letter to my brother telling him of the profound events that I had experienced inside the Holy Sepulchre. I also sent him a copy of The *Sacrament of the Present Moment* which impressed him deeply. He was at the time a Franciscan student studying theology in preparation for his ordination to the priesthood. He had just completed reading the book when his year were beginning to study what they then called "Sacred Eloquence". In plain English that means, how to preach. Each student had to prepare and deliver a sermon to his fellow students as if they were a typical Sunday morning congregation. My brother, brimming over with enthusiasm after reading de Cassaude, told the congregation that they should abandon their whole lives to God in every present moment, which is the sacrament of his all-abiding presence.

The reaction of his listeners, and that included several well-seasoned preachers as well as his fellow-students, was unanimous. It was decidedly underwhelming. You simply cannot expect to place a burden on the laity that even religious find difficult. They have families to provide for, mortgages to be paid for which they must work around the clock, and they have a hundred and one things to do that religious do not have to think about. I know that my brother in his enthusiasm might have asked too much too soon because his intended listeners had for many years been living in a secular world. It was the world of the swinging sixties, of rock 'n roll, pop, tamla motown, and heavy metal. It was the Age of Aquarius, of skimpy fashions, of drug addiction and of a promiscuity unparalleled in recent years. You really could not ask Generation X to abandon themselves totally to God. The best you could do was to inspire them to go to weekly Mass and return to the confessional, along with a little encouragement, my brother was told. It might have been different for the older generation at least twenty years before, when sirens were summonsing them to air raid shelters, when the sound of bombs dropping, and the drone of doodlebugs overhead made them reach for their rosary beads. However, after twenty years of the good times when they were told they had never had it so good the edge of their piety had been blunted.

Before the swinging sixties, before Buddy Holly and Elvis Presley, and even before Bill Haley and the Comets had set these Isles throbbing with the sound of Rock 'n Roll, I fell in love for the first time. I was only sixteen, but it was the real thing. My Juliet who was so beautiful, so pure, so perfect in every way seemed utterly beyond me. How could she possibly feel even so much as a spark to match the flame that set me alight with love for her? I simply could not believe it possible. How could such a beautiful creature even want to look at a gauche beanpole like me who had not even grown out of pimples and into poetry? Yet, despite my incredulity some of my friends assured me that she did. I still could not believe it, even when some of her friends told me the same. If, after a barn dance at the local church hall she had not told me herself, I would never have believed it. But she did and I floated around for weeks on cloud nine. Now I was prepared to do everything to be with her, to experience her love reaching out to me. I was prepared to do everything and anything for her, leave home, give up the comfortable life to which I had become accustomed, and endure any other sacrifices asked of me. Abandoning myself to her love would not have been the last, but the first thing that I would have wanted to do.

The problem my brother faced when his sermon was ripped to pieces by his peers, was that neither they nor the imaginary congregation really believed in the love of God deeply and personally except as an article of faith they had never personally experienced, a least at any depth. If they had, and did, then abandoning their lives to him would have seemed the obvious and natural thing to do, as obvious and as natural as it would have been to abandon themselves to the lover who first enthralled them. However, there is a problem with the love of God that I have already referred to when I quoted the Venerable Fulton Sheen saying, "In human loving all the powerful feelings come at the beginning, but in divine loving the powerful feelings come later." This means that we must do what I had to do when I was first told that I was loved, I had to take it on faith. In faith we have to search for God's love and continue for a long time before we begin to experience it. In order to seek the love of God, daily quality space and time for prayer must be found, because it is only here that we will come to know and experience the love of God that alone can change our lives, giving us the same strength and support that Jesus himself sought. He needed the love of God as we do too, so the best way to seek it is by following his example, the example of the daily prayer that continually opened him to receive the love of God his Father. That is why prayer has always been paramount in the Christian tradition. That is why the great mystic St Teresa of Avila used to say, "There is only one way to abandon oneself to God and that is to pray; anyone who points in another direction is deceiving you." Making an act of abandonment to God is one thing, then finding the daily quality space and time to do this in prayer is quite another, but the very act of doing this is a clear sign of the good intentions that God will never ignore.

Forty years ago I was challenged by a canoness. I had just finished a weekend course on personal prayer at a retreat centre in north London when she took me aside to share her misgivings with me. Her dedication to liturgical prayer had made her somewhat dismissive of personal prayer which she felt was all well and good for the laity, but not for semi-contemplative nuns like her, whose spiritual meat and drink was primarily and almost exclusively the Prayer of the Church, the corporate expression of the faith of the community. "I have read the New Testament from back to front and many times over," she said, "but I can find no evidence there for the personal daily prayer that you have been advocating in your talks. Admittedly", she conceded, "there is mention of Jesus praying at the beginning of his public ministry, and at the end in Gethsemane, but there is nothing to justify the sort of daily private prayer that you have been talking about this weekend, apart from a couple of occasions when Jesus went alone into the mountains for prayer."

Let me explain what I tried and failed to explain to her, because our spiritual life and well-being depends on it. The canoness was right in this, that after reading the Gospels she could find no evidence for the sort of daily prayer I was speaking about, but she failed to understand the reason why. I for my part had failed to convince her because at that time I failed to understand why the Gospel did not explain in detail the inner daily prayer of Jesus. Now, and this is so important, they did not detail the daily prayer life of Jesus, because they all knew it, and so did everyone else for whom they were writing at the time. They all knew it, because they all learnt this pattern of daily prayer from Jesus himself and they were all practising it every day of their lives – so why stress the obvious?

If you love good food you will undoubtedly be a devotee of Delia Smith, Mary Berry, Nigella Lawson, Gary Rhodes, Rick Stein or some other master chef. No matter whether you read their books, listen to them on the radio or watch them on television, they all make an understandable assumption about their students. They not only assume they have ovens, but that they know how to use them, and they use them often, many times a day. They assume they know how to cook. It was the same with all the writers of the New Testament. They assumed, or putting it more strongly, they knew that their readers all prayed regularly every day, as they did themselves. They did not therefore detail when they should pray, because everybody knew. Nor did they detail how everyone should pray, or the prayers that they should use, because they all knew that too. It would be stating the obvious. Nor did they have to describe endlessly how the love they received in prayer would enable them to love others as Jesus had done before them. Nor, for that matter, did they have to keep underlining how these, their daily efforts would become the offering they made with their brothers and sisters at the weekly Mass. This is why for Catholics it is not just the scriptures, but the scriptures and tradition that convey the full teaching of Christ to successive generations.

You do not have to tell fish how to swim, it is what they do. You did not have to explain how to pray to the first Christians, it was what they did. It was the living environment in which they lived and moved and had their very being. Read the New Testament with what I have just said in the forefront of your minds and you will be able to understand them in a new way, a far more profound way than ever before. However, if you re-read the New Testament while practising a daily prayer life similar to that of the first Christians, you will not only understand them in a new way, but much more. For the Holy Spirit who inspired the scriptures in the first place will be inspiring you too. This will enable him to lead you on, and into the One whose life, death and Resurrection the Scriptures have been written to glorify. The first Christians learnt how to pray each day and throughout the day from the Apostles, who in their turn learnt it from Jesus himself. He for his part had learnt how to pray and when to pray from his earliest years from his parents, like any other Jewish boy. That is how we know when and how he prayed and even the content of his prayer. The Gospels therefore do not spend any time telling their readers how he prayed during what were called the hidden years because it was assumed, because everybody would have known, because that is how they prayed themselves each day.

In the immediate aftermath of the conversions that took place on the first Pentecost Day, the essential features of early Christian spirituality were described by St Luke. "These remained faithful to the teaching of the apostles, to the brotherhood, to the breaking of the bread and to the prayers" (Acts 2:42). These prayers were the prayers that Jesus had said throughout his life, and with his disciples at the end of his life. Some were said at home, some at meal times and some each day in the synagogue or in the Temple, if they happened to be in Jerusalem. Even after the Resurrection they continued to go to the synagogues to pray, or to the Temple, as they had done with Jesus. The practice is often referred to in the *Acts of the Apostles*. A few telling quotations will have to suffice to make my point. When Christ appeared to St Paul in the Temple where he had gone to pray, he was told to leave Jerusalem. In answer, Paul told Christ that he knew that the Jews were after him, and he knew the reason why. "It is because they know that I used to go from synagogue to synagogue, imprisoning and flogging those who believed in you" (Acts 22: 19-20). In other words, after the Resurrection the first Christians still went to the synagogue to say their daily prayers, including the *Shema*, and that is why Paul knew where and at what time he would find them. They prayed at the same set times that they prayed when Jesus was still with them, in the synagogue as well as the Temple if they were in Jerusalem. In the very first line of Chapter 3 of the Acts, St Luke writes, "Once, when Peter and John were going up to the temple for the prayers at the ninth hour" (Acts 3:1). On another occasion when St Peter was on his way to Jaffa St Luke writes, "Peter went to the housetop at about the sixth hour to pray" (Acts 10:9). There are other brief glimpses of their daily prayer life such as, "One day as we were going to prayer…" (Acts 16:16). These texts were not trying to teach their readers that they prayed daily, as they had always done, everyone knew this because that is what they all did. The fact that they were going to pray was not in itself surprising or remarkable. It was just the writer's way of putting into time and context for his readers something that immediately followed. As we will see later, their prayers, whenever and wherever they were said, had a new context and a new power after the Resurrection, because they were now offered in, with and through their Risen Lord. When the Jews finally excommunicated Christians from their places of worship they had to find their own in what came to be the prototypes of the first Christian churches.

But with the passage of time later generations forgot what was commonplace for the first Christians. It was so forgotten that I had to spend hours failing to convince a contemplative nun that personal prayer was a daily imperative for Jesus, his disciples and the first Christians. I failed to convince her because it was only many years later that I started to study early Christian spirituality for myself and came to discover what might be called for early Christian writers the elephant in the room. Or to be more precise, the elephant beneath the texts, the great assumption that was once understood by all, but which must now be stated explicitly to people who think you are making up something that never was, like my friend the 'contemplative nun'. The daily personal prayer that was commonplace and understood by all Christians must now be stated explicitly. If it is not we will never understand and therefore be incapable of reproducing the profound mystical spirituality that once set the Christian world ablaze and the pagan world alight with what finally drew them out of darkness and into the light.

Although we do not know a hundred and one things that Jesus did in the hidden years, we do know the most important things that he did. We know when he prayed, where he prayed and how he prayed, continually abandoning himself to his Father. We know that he prayed first thing in the morning to consecrate his day to God, we even know some of the prayers and some of the psalms that he would have used for that purpose.

We know that he would have prayed last thing at night too, and some of the prayers and psalms to which he would have turned. Further to this he would have gone to the synagogue each day, to say a prayer called the *Shema.* For the Jews, and therefore for Jesus too, this prayer embodied within it a total abandonment to God by promising to love him with their "whole heart, with their whole soul and with all their strength," as they had been commanded to do, as the first and greatest of all the commandments (Deuteronomy 6:5). This prayer was said three times each day in the synagogue at the third, the sixth, and the ninth hour. If for whatever reason a good Jew was prevented from doing this then at those same times he would stop his work, or his journey or rise from his sick bed to say the prayer that was meant to dedicate every moment of every day to God. All this was in addition to Tuesdays and Thursdays when a more formal service was celebrated with prayers and readings from the Old Testament when the *Shema* would be recited together. This service was later to form the basis for the first part of the Mass as we know it today. They also said another prayer whenever they came together for meals, to thank God not just for the food on the table, but for land that was given them to provide for it. They thanked him too for all he did for them in the past, was doing for them now, and had promised to do for them in the future. This prayer was called the *Berakah.*

The times set aside for the recitation of the daily *Shema* were not arbitrary, for it was at these times that the sacrifices were being made in the Temple at Jerusalem, and so if they were in Jerusalem, Jews and even the first Christians, would go there to pray at these set times. The offering of themselves to God at these times each day was a reminder that they were making their offering with the whole of the Jewish community with whom they shared their common faith in the same God, to whom they were travelling, as to their ultimate destiny. When they were blessed with the opportunity of going to the Temple in Jerusalem their prayers were made tangible in the material offerings that they made on the altar, offered for them by one of the priests.

Although we know for certain that Jesus prayed the *Shema* while he was growing up, there is no evidence that he personally offered sacrifices in the temple, (*Karbanot*) for one important reason. The sacrifice that he had come to make was not of lambs, or sheep, or oxen or of anything else for that matter. He had come to offer himself. He embodied within himself the new temple, the new form of priesthood and the new form of sacrifice that he would bequeath to his disciples. While he was with them they prayed with him, but after the sending of the Holy Spirit they prayed not only with him but in him too, and through him in such a way that they could pray as none of their greatest forefathers had been able to pray before. Now they were able to understand for the first time the meaning of the new "in spirit and truth" (John 4:24), that Jesus had promised to the Samaritan woman. Like Jesus they no longer needed to go to the Temple to offer material sacrifices, because the sacrifice that God wanted now was nothing other than themselves, and, as nobody else could do this for them, they were, each one of them, priests. Now they were able to make the only offering that God wanted, and make it in such a way that he could receive it, because it was made in, with and through his Son Jesus, the one and only true High Priest.

The essence of the ancient Jewish prayers was still used by the first Christians after the Resurrection, but they were transformed. The prayers that were once said with Jesus before the sending of the Holy Spirit were now prayed in, with and through Jesus, into whose mystical body they now lived and moved and had their very being. The inner dynamic power and vitality on which the early liturgy depended was the quality of the daily prayer and service of others during the previous week that was offered at Mass, in, with and through Jesus, to their common Father. However, what is supposed to be a liturgical climax can turn out to be an anticlimax if those who come to Mass bring nothing to be offered, because their previous week was barren and bereft of trying to practise the two new Commandments that Jesus gave us. Our daily endeavour to implement them *is* the offering that we bring with us to offer, through Jesus at the weekly Mass. If we come with nothing, then we receive nothing, and the Mass becomes meaningless, not in itself, or for others, but for those who bring nothing to offer when they enter the church.

After Our Lady appeared to three girls in Northern Spain the eldest asked her if she would take them back to heaven with her. She replied, "Whatever for, for your hands are empty." What would she say if we arrived for Sunday Mass with our hands empty? Any great enterprise of any moment whether it is a wedding, an anniversary, or even an important game or match, or any crucial event for that matter, will only be as successful as the time given preparing for it. The Mass is no different, except that it is the most important event in our lives, on which our lives depend. Regular failure to prepare for it will lead at best to spiritual stagnation, and at worst to spiritual suicide.

Renewal in the Church does not primarily depend on a perfectly designed liturgy, but on the quality of the spiritual lives of those who participate in it. Let us suppose that I had a magic wand and I could wave it to give everyone the liturgy of their choice each time they went to Mass. It might be the new liturgy as introduced by the Second Vatican Council, with a perfect translation of the text and with all the rites and rituals perfectly designed to satisfy everyone. On the other hand, it might be the old Tridentine Mass in Latin that so many of us were brought up on, or a grand sung high Mass with music by Perosi, Palestrina or Purcell, or the mediaeval Mass that was so loved by some of the greatest saints that have ever lived, or the ancient Mass known to the Fathers of the Church which was said in Greek long before the introduction of Latin. Or what about Mass according to the Chaldean rite said in Aramaic, the language that Jesus himself would have used at the Last Supper. The introduction of any or all of these rites in themselves would do nothing to change us personally and permanently, or the Church to which we belong, unless they were animated and inspired by the same profound daily liturgy of spiritual endeavour as practised by the first Christians in imitation of how Jesus prayed and served the neighbour in need throughout his life on earth.

It is not the outside of the cup that matters, but the inside of the cup, the intrinsic quality of the personal spiritual life of those who participate in the liturgy. Get the first right without the second, and you have a recipe for the disaster that St Paul predicts in his letter to the Corinthians, "If I have all the eloquence of men or of angels, but speak without love, I am simply a gong booming or a cymbal clashing" (1 Corinthians 13:1-13). Love's endeavour is the offering that makes the Mass what Jesus wants it to become. If you take that away the gongs may boom and the cymbals might clash, but nothing else will rise from us to give glory to God in heaven or on the earth that he created. It is our spirit-filled endeavour, demonstrated in the personal prayer that we have made, and in the good works that we have performed, and all that we have suffered, thanks to the grace we have received in prayer, that we offer through Jesus to the Father when we take part in the Mass. Many years ago I failed to convince a canoness about the absolute importance of personal daily prayer as practised by Jesus and his first disciples. I do hope that I have managed to convince you, because without it we cannot practise the first commandment properly, nor therefore receive the grace to practise the second.

It took me a long time to decide whether or not to use such an uncompromising word as abandonment in today's secular climate, to encourage people to abandon their lives to God for fear of asking too much as my brother had done. But frankly I have no choice. If we really believe in God and what he has planned to do for us, has already done for us, and is doing for us now to unite our destiny with his, then there is only one way to respond. He has chosen to give us his all; how can we do less than give our all for him? The trouble is we have grown up in a Christian world where nominal, or part-time Christians abound and the truth is we are probably numbered amongst them. All too many people who claim to be Christians do so because, in a vague general sort of way, they subscribe to a high-bred Christian ethic that owes as much to Socrates of Athens, and Seneca of Rome, as to Jesus of Nazareth. This is thanks to the moral spirituality of the Renaissance that so many of my generation unwittingly imbibe with their classical education at school. No wonder my theology teacher said that ninety percent or more of us are Pelagians, who, of course, believed they could reach God and even observe all the moral teachings of the Gospels by their own unaided endeavours.

The early Christians had no problem abandoning themselves to God totally, as the man to whom they committed themselves had done throughout his life on earth. They knew what was being asked of them from the beginning and they gave it because they were Christian and that is what Christians did. The vast majority of the first Christians were baptised as adults. This meant they would have had to spend a minimum of two years in preparation, during which time they would pray more than five times a day, as well as fasting on certain days and participating in the first part of the Mass, then called the *synaxis* that had taken its shape from the twice weekly synagogue services that Jesus first attended with his disciples. In addition to this they would have to give up going to games in the amphitheatres, taking part in a seedy *soirée*, accepting jobs that entailed making oaths to the pagan gods or that compromised their religion, and so many other things, that were part and parcel of everyday life in the Roman Empire, particularly if you were seeking preferment. While they were under instruction several times a week, and praying five times a day, they were seeing the Christians whom they were being prepared to join giving their lives for their belief in Jesus. Indeed, you would not become a Christian unless you had counted the cost, and that cost might mean losing all your property, all your wealth and your health too, in terrible prison conditions. Here torture was to be expected, followed by the most hideous forms of death imaginable at the end of it. In short, no one became a Christian without deciding to abandon their life to God totally, no matter what the cost.

If there were any doubts about what they were about, the baptismal ceremony itself would dispel them. Just before the Easter Mass they would have to abandon their old clothes as a sign that they were abandoning their old lives. When they were plunged into the baptismal pool three times, it was to make it clear once and for all that they were dead to their old way of life to take up a new life in Christ the Risen One. That is why when they came out of the water it was like coming out of the tomb into which Jesus was placed, not just to show that they had died with him, but that they had risen to a new form of life as he had done. When they came out of the water they were dressed in a shining white garment similar to the one Jesus was wearing when he rose from the tomb.

To make it clear that becoming a Christian meant becoming another Christ, they were anointed with chrism like prophets, priests, and kings before them. As the vast majority of the first new Christians all underwent this ceremony as adults they were totally conscious of what becoming a Christian meant. However, the vast majority of newly baptised today are children, who cannot possibly remember their baptism never mind the symbolism, so growing up to become a half-hearted or nominal Christian is so much easier. Their total and daily abandonment to God was the reason why the early Christians were able to achieve what seemed to be the impossible, transforming a pagan into a Christian empire in such a short time. In comparison we achieve so little, yet there are so many more of us.

I can still remember how faith deepened during the Second World War, and oh, how we prayed in the Churches and at home. However, it faltered the moment it was over and the wheels of industry began to turn once more, and people had more money in their pockets to spend on luxuries that they had never had before, as the fifties turned into the swinging sixties. Do we really need our lives to be devastated by wars, disasters or the threat of impending Armageddon before we are brought to our senses? If the love of God is going to be the guiding principle in our lives, and not just fear, then now is the time to begin anew, inspired by our Christian forebears who consecrated every moment of every day to God, in and through everything they said and did. Now then, is the time in our daily prayer to make an act of total abandonment to God in Christ in whom we have been reborn, and in whom we live and move and have our very being. If we find this too demanding, then it is a reality check. It means that there is something seriously wrong with our faith and it is time to do something about it, like programming more quality time in our daily life, to turn to the only One who can revive it. There are many ways that we can do this. Where there is a will there is a way. My father put little markers on his wrist watch at nine, twelve, and three o'clock to remind him to follow the example of when and how Jesus and his disciples had prayed before him. If we really believe what God has done and still is doing for us then we will find a way to follow in the footsteps of our early forebears come what may.

When the first Jewish Christians were excluded from the synagogues, they still said the *Shema*. Furthermore, if they were excluded from family meals that they once enjoyed, they said the *Berakah* in their new Christian families when they met in each others' houses. However, in future they always ended these prayers with the words, "In, with and through Jesus Christ," who was, as he had promised, with them always. "For where two or three meet in my name, I shall be there with them" (Mathew 18:20). The measure in which the first Christians gave to God each Sunday determined the measure of the grace he was able to give them in return. Then this grace suffused their prayers and their good works making every moment of every day the Mass, the place where they continually offered themselves to God, through Jesus in whom they lived and moved and had their very being.

Chapter 7

Thanksgiving – *Berakah*

(Peter's sixth talk)

I saw my grandfather forty years after he died. I loved him with all my heart, not because he gave me toys, bought me ice cream or took me to the funfair, but because he loved me so much. I was only eight years old when he died of a heart attack and I cried myself to sleep. The next day my mother told me that he loved me very specially, so much so that he made special plans for me and so I should always pray for him each day when I said my Morning Prayers. That is why I felt so guilty when I saw him again forty years later. The truth of the matter is I had forgotten to pray for him as often as my mother wanted me to. It was Christmas Eve when I saw him. I usually shaved in the morning, but as I was going to midnight Mass I thought I better make myself a little more presentable. I had removed all the shaving cream from my face apart from a white moustache under my nose, about the same size as the white moustache my grandfather always wore, that tickled when he kissed me. I never thought I looked like him, but there he was looking at me from the bathroom mirror. Oh, yes, it was him all right, but he did not look as kind or as loving as the man I remembered.

When my mother died thirty or more years after he did, I was devastated. I not only missed her more than I could say, but I particularly missed her help and encouragement when I was going through the most difficult period in my life. I not only felt spiritually bereft, but I was physically bereft too, without a home to call my own. It was then that my grandfather came to the rescue. When my mother said that he loved me very specially I knew what she told me was true because I had felt his love, but what she said about his plans for me meant nothing at all, at least until a letter arrived. It came from the family solicitors with news about which I knew nothing. He had left all his money directly to me. My mother only held the capital for her lifetime so she could live off the interest, which in those fairy tale days was considerable. Now everything came to me. At last I was safe and secure, at last I could have a home to call my own, but what was even more important, I felt loved, even though those who loved me were dead. Their love lived on and I could now live on to begin a new life. Thanks to them, to their tangible love for me, all went well, better than I could ever have hoped, so well in fact that self-absorption and self-satisfaction had made me forget those who loved me most, and what they did for me. That is why the face that looked back at me from the mirror that Christmas Eve might have looked like my grandfather, but it was covered with a guilt that I had never seen on his face.

When I went to midnight Mass it was to realize that I had forgotten someone else too. Just as my grandfather had given me all he could to show his love for me, God had done the same. He had not shown how much he cared for me by the money he left me, but by the love he left me – his own personal love made flesh and blood for me in Jesus who was born on the first Christmas day. This enabled God to do through Jesus what he was never able to do before. God's infinite love which was in the past too powerful to enter into finite human beings could do so in the future, thanks to the birth of Jesus. Once his human being was filled to overflowing with God's infinite loving, it was transposed into human loving, enabling all human beings to receive God's infinite loving through him. That is why Christmas is such a sublime and inspiring feast, because in the baby in the crib we see the beginnings of God's plan for us that was brought to completion on the first Pentecost Day. It was then that for the first time on earth his human nature became radio-active with the infinite loving mercy of his Father, so that on that day and on every day, he can pour that loving mercy out, onto and into all who are open to receive it. For the first time in my life I began to realise, not just with my head, but with my heart just how much God has done for me and I resolved to make sure that I gave due thanks to God in future in my daily prayer.

However, it was the following Christmas that I came to see and understand a deeper reason for giving thanks to God. Making a formal act of thanksgiving to him each day had made me realise that we are all quick enough to storm the gates of heaven when we are in trouble or when we need something, but we are not so quick when it comes to saying thank you. It is in saying thank you as we should, that we are led into the sort of prayer that can change our lives permanently for the better. It is not enough just to thank God for what he has done for us, and continually does for us, but we need to thank him for something further, as I discovered for myself. Instead of Christmas crackers the parish priest bought Christian crackers for the parish party. So instead of wearing paper hats everyone wore paper haloes instead and received miniature plastic saints, and instead of side-splitting jokes they had to meditate on mind-bending religious epigrams. Mine not only bent my mind, it tied it in knots for weeks trying to work out what on earth it meant. It was ascribed to a certain H Smith (circa 1630) and went something like this, "He is not thankful before God who only thanks him for his benefits."

I do not think I would ever have fully unravelled its meaning had I not been to a retreat given by Archbishop Anthony Bloom three weeks later. At the end of the retreat the sister in charge said, "I not only want to thank you for what you have given us, but to thank you for being you." It was a popular religious cliché at the time that usually made me squirm, especially when the said sister, not only thanked me for unblocking the convent drains the day before, but added the, "Thank you for being you" bit at the end of it. However, when applied to Archbishop Anthony Bloom it certainly made sense, and gave sense to the religious epigram that had been tying my mind in knots ever since the parish party. The Archbishop had given us a lot to think about in his talks, but he gave us far more by just being who he was, a remarkable embodiment of the man in whose name he preached. It was silly to thank me for being me, just because I unblocked the convent drains, but it was not silly to thank him for being who he was. Who he was, was far more important than what he said, though what he said moved me more than any other preacher before or since. Now I could see what Mr H or Ms H Smith meant. If we only thank God for what we manage to get out of him or for what he has done for us, then we have hardly begun to thank him as we should. He should be thanked for being God, for being goodness, justice, truth and beauty, for displaying his inner glory in the glory of creation that surrounds us, and for the masterpiece of creation in and through whom we are drawn up to share in his own inner life and love.

When I first began to thank God for being God, it was as if I was raised beyond myself and into God's world, if only for a brief moment where my prayer life reached higher peaks than ever before. If you don't know what I mean, try this little experiment. When you've thanked God for what he has done for you, start thanking him for what he is and what he does for everyone, just by being what he is. Take your favourite prayer or hymn of thanksgiving or praise, like the Gloria from the liturgy for instance. Then recite it slowly and prayerfully and you will find you are taken out of yourself, out of your world and into God's world where you praise him, thank him and give him glory with all those who have learned to thank God just for being God. You will find that the further you enter into his world, the more you will forget yourself and the world where you only thanked him for what you get out of him. Then you will come alive, more alive than ever before, if only for a time in the world where you want to be for all time. Thanking God for being God leads into the heights of prayer where thanksgiving leads to praise, and praise to glorifying God. Glorifying God leads to adoration, when we just want to gaze upon him with a profound reverence and awe that takes us out of ourselves if only for a time into brief moments of rapturous bliss. In these moments we come to know by experience what Teilhard de Chardin meant when he said, "To adore means to lose oneself in the unfathomable, to plunge into the inexhaustible, to find peace in the incorruptible, to be absorbed into the immeasurable, and to give one's deepest to the One whose depth has no end." Without us realising fully what has been happening, our thanksgiving, praising, glorifying and adoring have paved the way for our love to enter into God and his love to enter into us. And our daily sympathy, empathy, caring and sharing have paved the way for our love to enter into God in the neighbour in need, and his love into us.

I remember taking a small group of young women to a Franciscan hermitage in Umbria. The women who lived there were semi-hermits. When I asked the superior to explain to my group why they were there and what their life was all about she led them into the little church and everyone knelt with her to pray. Every quarter of an hour or so she prayed aloud and it was always the same prayer and in Latin: *"non nobis, Domine, sed nomini tuo da gloriam."* – "not to us, Lord, but to your name give glory." Eventually after well over an hour she stood up and led the group out. "Now," she said, "You see what our life is all about." Nor were the girls put off, because, as she spoke her face blossomed into the most other-worldly and sublime smile that they had ever seen. It was as if we were speaking to a modern Moses whose face shone with the reflection of the God with whom he had been communing.

Saying thank you was terribly important to Jesus - remember how disappointed he was when only one of the ten lepers came back to thank him. However, he did not just tell others that they should remember to say thank you, but he practised what he preached many times each day. The Jewish religion is at source a domestic religion that, like charity, begins at home. It was here that in addition to prayers before going to bed and on rising in the morning, Jesus first heard and participated in the famous *Berakah* at every meal time. It is very difficult to translate the meaning of this prayer, because it is so pithy and pregnant with meaning that no other single word can do it justice. *Berakah* means thanks, praise, blessing and giving glory to God and much more, all embodied in a single prayer. I suppose it was the Jewish equivalent of the ancient Christian hymn the "Te Deum" only of course much shorter so that it could be said before every meal. It was not only addressed to God for the food and drink that was on the table, but for the land from which the food and drink had been harvested. It was this land that was given to them through Moses after their miraculous escape from Egypt. The shorter form of this prayer would be said daily by the father of the family or the one who took his place when a child grew up and attached himself to a Rabbi who would preside in his stead. On major feasts like the feast of the Passover, this prayer would be far more solemn and include so much that could not be included in the daily *Berakah* said at ordinary meals.

Jesus may have said his *Berakah* three times a day, but his thanks to his Father did not stop there, it was transposed into all he said and did. If you really want to thank someone for what they have given you, try to find out what they want more than anything else. Jesus knew what his Father wanted more than anything else; he wanted him to spend his life on earth telling the world that they had a loving Father and showing them how to receive his love, and then having received it, how to share it with others. That is why he prayed more than five time a day to receive the help and strength to do it. That is why, as well as saying his *Berakah* at every meal, he went into the synagogue too, three times a day to pray, saying the ancient prayer, *Shema,* to consecrate his whole life to loving God with his whole heart and mind and with his whole body and soul, and to loving his neighbour as himself. When Jesus was young the *Berakah* would be prayed by the father of the family. Later, it would be said by Jesus when his disciples gathered around him for meals. This prayer would take on a special significance when used on the great feast days like the Passover.

The best known, best loved, and most often quoted words from all the writings of St Augustine are, "You have made us for yourself, O Lord, and our hearts are restless until they find rest in you." They are the best loved because they sum up our deepest desires and longings implanted in us by God himself. We want to love and be loved here on earth, but we want that love to go on deepening and becoming ever more complete, not just now, but forever. This desire can only be ultimately fulfilled by being permanently plunged into the fullness of love that resides in God. Throughout the Old Testament this all-consuming desire ran like an unquenchable undercurrent. But it continually rose to the surface to express itself in poems and prayers, in canticles, psalms and prophesies. It was always there, expressing itself in the sacred dramas endlessly re-enacted on the great feast days. It was here they celebrated God's promise to give them the love they longed for in the past, that was available to them in the present and which would ultimately captivate, enrapture and enthral them to all eternity in the future.

The last Passover that Jesus celebrated with his disciples was not just a case in point, but it was the point of everything that God had planned to do and bring to perfection from the beginning. The disciples Jesus charged with the task of preparing for the feast would have purchased a lamb to be sacrificed to God in the Temple. Before the sacrifice it had been their lamb, but after the sacrifice it became God's lamb or the Lamb of God. Now, believing that it was impregnated with the presence of God, it was eaten by all at the Passover meal. Its communal consumption signified and symbolised the desire for the communion with God that they all desired, as well as union with one another, symbolised by sharing the same sacred food. I use the word symbolised, because despite the profound meaning expressed in this sacred rite, it did not, could not, fulfil their deepest desire for union with God. The prophets had been adamant that this union would only come about when the Messiah came. But on that holy and hallowed night, the Messiah was there with them, and about to fulfil all that had been promised, all for which his people had longed and desired, and for that matter all for which human beings had, and would always long for and desire.

When the old rite that only symbolised union was over, for the first time Jesus enacted the new rite that would bring union about. There was now no need for a new lamb, no need to go back to the Temple, no need for the priest to offer it to God for them as before. Jesus himself was the Lamb of God, as John the Baptist already proclaimed him. He was the Lamb of God because at every moment of his life he was offering himself to God his Father. As he was doing this, his Father's love was possessing him ever more fully. That is why he said to Philip on that very night, "Do you not believe that I am in the Father and the Father is in me" (John 14:10)? The offering that Jesus was making throughout his life was the offering that he put into words three times a day when he said the *Shema,* and put into practice through all he said and did throughout the rest of that day. That is why he was the first of a new brand of priests. They would no longer need to go to the Temple to offer themselves to God by offering something to represent them, for now the new offering would be themselves. This would be the new sacrifice "in spirit and truth" (John 4:24) that Jesus promised to the Samaritan woman. In future then, they would offer themselves as Jesus had done, and so became priests themselves, as they offered all they said and did each day to the Father through him, the new and only High Priest. They would receive all that he received, to lead them on and into an ever-deepening union with God.

The sign and the sacrament of this new priesthood and what

it would bring about, took place at the Last Supper when the old rite was concluded. The old Temple and all it stood for would soon be destroyed, levelled to the ground by the Romans, as Jesus foretold only a few days before. This would make no difference to the new priesthood into which all his followers would be incorporated. They could and would offer themselves to God wherever they were and through whatever they were doing. They would no longer need lambs or livestock of any sort to do what God now wanted them to do for themselves. The sacred rite, the sacred mysteries in which this new worship would be celebrated by his future priests was now to be enacted by Jesus. Space was made at table for the bread that was soon to become the "bread of life" (John 6:35) that Jesus had already promised to his disciples. Their friendship was then in its infancy, and some of them nearly left him with so many others, because he not only told them that he was "the bread of life", but that they must eat this bread if they were to have life in them now, and eternal life hereafter (John 6:50-51).

Now the time had come for Jesus to fulfil what he promised. He took the bread and the wine, two readily acquired commodities, and transformed them into his body and blood. In eating and drinking this sacred food, then and in future, they would be taken up into union with him, and in, with and through him, with God the Father. Then, and forthwith, all the deepest hopes and longings of the whole of humankind were fulfilled. This was the mystery in which the Mysterion of God was made tangible. But it did even more than that. Each time they were taken up into Jesus, the Lamb of God, they received the same life and love that replenished him throughout his life, so that in the same way it could replenish them too. This spiritual power and energy would enable them, not only to exercise their priesthood whenever they came to Mass, but throughout the rest of their lives, and in all they said and did to give glory to God, as Jesus had done. Then, these daily offerings and sacrifices, made increasingly more powerful and effective by the inner spiritual energy with which they were infused at Mass, would be offered again to God the next time they went to Mass, but this time with the rest of the Christian community. In this endless mystical cycle of giving and receiving, in and outside of community prayer, believers would be fitted ever more fully into Christ and in, with and through him, into union with God the Father. This is why, when at the end of the great Eucharist prayer the celebrant said, "Through him, with him, in him, in the unity of the Holy Spirit, all glory and honour is yours almighty Father, forever and ever," the "Amen" of those present nearly raised the roof. For those words represented what they were doing and what they would continue to do in every moment of their daily lives.

Once those words were said it became the custom to recite the Our Father as we still do today, for now in Christ, he was their Father, the God of love for whom the whole of humanity had yearned and would continue to yearn to the end of time. For more than a millennium, Mass would only take place once a week for the majority. That is why, in the Our Father, the faithful would pray, "Give us this day our daily bread" (Matthew 6:11). This daily bread was nothing other than the life and love of Jesus himself, "the bread of life" who continues to give himself to all who turn to love him, through all they say and do each day.

After the Lord's Prayer was said, Jesus himself is addressed twice, the faithful begging him for mercy and for forgiveness in preparation for the holy communion which is about to take place. "Lamb of God, you take away the sins of the world, have mercy on us." When the first Passover lambs were slain before the Exodus from Egypt, the Israelites were told to paint their doors with its blood, so that even though they were sinners, they would be saved from the punishment that would be meted out to the Egyptians. This is the mercy that we all need, most especially at this point in the Mass when we are about to receive the Lamb of God, in whom and through whom we are united with the Father. When in the autumn of his days the redoubtable Hans Kung was asked what he would say when, after his death he would come face to face with God, he said he would cry out, "God have mercy on me, a sinner." When G K Chesterton was asked why he became a Catholic, he answered only half audibly to spare his own embarrassment, "To have my sins forgiven." Mercy and forgiveness is what we all need, and need most especially at this moment in the Mass when we are about to receive the Holy Communion for which we will never be worthy, but which God nevertheless continually gives us.

Once the first Christians had relished what they had received in their weekly Holy Communion, they were full of rapturous joy, because of the union they experienced with God through the Lamb of God made bread, but also with each other, in him. That is why they all joined together in singing or reciting the Gloria, which was then in its original place after the reception of Holy Communion. No one could see their love of God, but what could be seen was its effects, as that love overflowed onto each other, and onto others outside the confines of the Christian community. It was this love, a quality of love that non-believers had never seen before, that moved them so deeply that more and more of them came knocking on the door, and more and more places were set at table. After due preparation they would be able to participate in the sacred mysteries and in the Holy Communion that set the early Christians alive with love they had first seen and experienced in their new-found brothers and sisters.

Whether they were Jews or non-Jews they would all come to know and love the *Berakah.* It was the prayer of thanksgiving offered to God for what he had done in the past, was doing in the present and would be doing for his people in the future. This prayer continued to be said by the followers of Jesus after the Resurrection, but most especially when they came together as a family on Sundays. This prayer became the context in which the mysteries first enacted by Jesus at the Last Supper would be presided over by one of his chosen representatives thereafter. To begin with the event for which they gathered was actually called the *Berakah*. But as the common language in the Roman Empire was Greek, the Greek word for thanksgiving, *Eucharist* was eventually used to replace the Hebrew word. We know the word well enough, because we still call the Mass the Eucharist today.

Quite apart from going into the Synagogue to pray three times a day, as Jesus did, the early Christians also went there on Tuesdays and Thursdays for a more formal synagogue service, as had been their custom with Jesus. But when the Jews refused to admit them any longer, and when persecution made it dangerous to meet too often, they began to have their twice weekly synagogue service just the once for the sake of safety, and that would be immediately before the *Berakah* or the *Eucharist* on Sundays when they celebrated the Resurrection of their Lord. The ancient synagogue service was gradually Christianised with readings from the New as well as the Old Testament, showing how the old was fulfilled in the new. When it was over and all the preparations were made, the celebrant would begin the Christian *Berakah*.

The prayer would begin, as it always had done, with the person presiding in place of Jesus using words similar to those still used today, that had their origin in the ancient Jewish *Berakah*:

Priest: Lift up your hearts. People: We lift them up to the Lord. Priest: Let us give thanks to the Lord our God. People: It is right and just.

What we call the Eucharistic prayer or the Canon of the Mass, originated in the *Berakah,* that ancient prayer of thanksgiving used by Jesus throughout his life and most particularly at the Last Supper. If we are going to let the Mass form our daily prayer then the letter -T- in the Our Father is a reminder to thank God for all he has given us, is giving us, and will continue to give us personally and communally, and most of all for his sublime plan for us, his Mysterion, and his Mysterion made man in Jesus, to bring that plan to fruition.

The extraordinary and the sublime generosity of God is such, that as we do this, he gives us here and now in the present, a hundredfold in return, and continues to do so the more we thank, praise, worship, love and adore him. As we continue to do this in the liturgical Mass and in the Mass which is commensurate with our lives, our journey into God continues, leading us ever more deeply into the mystery of love. The journey stretches from here to eternity, where the searcher finally enters into a profound and ongoing Holy Communion with the One who dwells in the mystical maelstrom of mutual loving that constitutes God's very being. Faith in what is to come is fortified by hope that is derived from the tangible experience of the love enjoyed in the profound and intimate Holy Communion that has already begun here and now. At Mass this is the time to reflect upon and to relish what we have received and on the one who is making his home deep down within us. For a thousand years and more when Mass was only celebrated on Sundays, a time was set aside each day as part of daily prayer for what came to be called a spiritual Communion. It should be part of our daily prayer too, and the letter -H- for Holy Communion is a reminder to do this each day.

At the Last Supper, Jesus revealed himself in a unique way as the Lamb of God in whom God's presence dwelt. His disciples had already been to the temple where, as usual at Passover, they offered a lamb to God. For the Jews, it was a common belief that having accepted the offering of a lamb during the sacrificial rite, God came down to penetrate it with his presence. This food therefore, was sacred. So too were those who ate that lamb, because in eating it they believed they would enter into a mystical communion with God. This mystical communion united those who shared this sacred food, bonding them ever more deeply together as a family. Their upbringing as orthodox Jews therefore, had prepared the first apostles for what came next, when Jesus said that he himself was the Lamb of God in whom God's presence dwelt. He had spent his whole life offering himself to God in sacrifice in such a way that God had penetrated him with his presence. That is why when John the Baptist pointed Jesus out to his followers he called him the Lamb of God. And that is why Jesus explained at the Last Supper that his Father was in him, and he was in the Father (John 14:10). In future then, he would be the Lamb of God, and eating this new sacred food would enable them to enter into him. At the same time, what, or rather whom, they received would bond them together ever more closely into a new family with no one excluded. This new family would later come to be called the Body of Christ, and later still the Mystical Body.

Although the Jewish rites and rituals would be unknown to newcomers, they nevertheless yearned, as did the Jews, for the fullness of love that resided in their maker. This inborn longing was rooted deep down in all, rich and poor alike, so it was indeed 'Good News' to hear that the love they desired could be received in the sacred meal that Jesus had left for his followers to perpetuate. The meat eaten by the Jews was changed to bread by Jesus at the Last Supper, but what or rather whom was received when eating this sacred food remained the same. Now, as promised, Jesus became the Bread of Life. Bread was the staple diet of most people and far less expensive than meat, so Christ's presence could become available to all, and regularly, regardless of their station in life. It is important to remember, however, that the Jews in those days were brought up in a world of signs and symbols that are new to us and therefore too often misunderstood or taken too literally. When for instance, Jesus said that, "If you do not eat the flesh of the Son of Man and drink his blood, you will not have life in you" (John 6:53), he was not referring to the sort of meat you see in a butcher shop nor to the blood that it contains, but to his whole person - body, blood, soul, and divinity, as the Church made clear later.

When Jesus foretold that he would become the Bread of Life, he was not only referring to his presence in the Eucharist, but much more. He was referring to his daily, moment by moment and ongoing presence, as the Bread of Life in the lives of his followers. In short, he would become the staple diet of their daily spiritual lives too. In modern times, it might be possible to interpret the words in the Lord's Prayer, "Give us this day our daily bread," as referring to daily Mass, but in ancient times when daily Mass was unknown and would remain virtually unknown for over a thousand years or more, it referred to the daily Bread of Life that was Christ himself, who is prepared and poised at every moment to nourish us with the spiritual food which is nothing other than his own life and love (see John Chapter 6).

During the Second World War, I used to come home bearing gifts given to me by American GI's waiting for D-Day. They had obviously been moved by the iron calliper on my leg. We called the gifts that endeared me to the rest of the family, manna from America, because it reminded us of the manna from heaven with which God fed his people in the desert as they were fleeing from Egypt. They were oblong pieces of candy, the like of which we had never tasted before. I called them paradise bars. They were made from all the exotic fruits I had heard about, but never tasted thanks to German submarines. These dried fruits were blended together in such a way that they melted slowly in the mouth, tantalising the taste buds with indescribable delight. Although everybody in the family loved them, no one seemed able to describe the taste, although each of us was convinced we had never tasted anything that so completely satisfied our deepest desires before. Furthermore, they were crammed with vitamins to keep every soldier ready and alert to do their duty each day. That is why we called the bars manna from America. The Bread of Life that Jesus first promised and then gave to his followers was perfectly adapted to cater for their daily desires too and to the needs of whoever received it, like the manna from heaven that foreshowed it in the Old Testament.

The paramount importance of daily personal prayer for the first Christians was continually emphasised by their spiritual mentors. It was there that they performed in an intimate and personal way what was performed in an open and communal way at the Sunday Mass. There they would pause to digest and assimilate the love they received, so it could seep into their spiritual metabolism to saturate them with supernatural life and love. This is the God-given power and energy that can reinvigorate our whole inner being, so that our outer being can begin to proclaim the glory of God to the world, which is in such need of what only he can give it.

The letter -H- in the mnemonic is a reminder then to pause in our daily prayer in silent contemplation for a time to reflect on the Holy Communion that is taking place within us, disseminating the mystical food without which we would languish and die. It is a time to ruminate on and relish the profound mysteries that are at work deep down within us, and to digest and assimilate their sublime meaning and importance for us now and for our future. It is time too, to allow these truths to percolate through, to penetrate our hearts and minds, and then gaze for as long as possible at the indescribable mysteries that Jesus came to share with us and in us. That the heaven that we are bound for is within us, is a fact that Jesus affirms repeatedly in his profound mystical discourse at the Last Supper. This is the time for us to speak with him and to share with him our most secret thoughts and desires. At the Last Supper when Jesus spoke about these sublime truths he repeatedly insisted that this would be the time to ask whatever we wanted and to be assured that our prayers made in his name would be answered. What happens in these brief moments of daily spiritual communion makes a person desire more space and time to penetrate and contemplate these sublime truths at greater length and in ever greater depth. Inevitably a person feels the deep inner pull that is at times clearly tangible, to seek out more space and time, to do what we have been created for. And so we experience, in some small measure, what we will one day experience without measure, in our true and everlasting home from home. I will speak later about how this prayer begins and develops in these sacred moments.

* * *

I had to go to the hospital on the Wednesday for further tests, so my wife went up to London with Peter. As she recorded the talks, I could hear them later. Apparently, the church was absolutely packed as more and more people wanted to hear him, including many priests and religious who were not at his first talks.

Chapter 8

Loving Mercy – *Hesed*

(Peter's seventh talk)

The Mass to herald the Year of Divine Mercy in 2016 was prepared by the parishioners with the help of the curate and a group of the Sisters of Mercy. The readings, the psalms and the prayers had all been chosen to echo the overall theme of asking God to give his loving mercy to all those present and to the whole world that would be lost without it. The visiting preacher came straight to the point. "Why waste your time praying for God's loving mercy?" he said. "Whether you pray for it or not, his loving mercy has been sent out, is being sent out, and will continue to be sent out whether you pray for it or not. Why not save your breath to cool your porridge, or rather save your breath to pray that we will be given the strength to take the steps to receive it, by finding time to do so in our daily lives."

In the Old Testament the word *hesed* was used to describe the loving mercy of God. It has been translated by the Latin word *gratia* in the New Testament that gave birth to the English word grace. Fortunately, nothing is lost in translation, in fact everything is gained. Now that the Holy Spirit has been sent, and is continually being sent, his love is no longer referred to as *hesed* but *gratia*, or grace. It is the same love of God that revolved between the Father and the Son from and to eternity, but now, thanks to the glorified Christ, it is sent out with the power to do something that was never needed to be done before. For now, its power to forgive sins is seen, as this love is directed to sinful human beings to dispel the sinfulness that would otherwise keep God out. That is why all the sacraments give grace, God's loving mercy that first forgives the sins that would otherwise prevent him making his home within us, as he promised at the Last Supper. There is only one thing that can prevent God making his home within us and that is the sickness of sin and selfishness that does to the mystical body of Christ what high cholesterol does to the physical body. It must ultimately be controlled, if not totally rooted out. This is a long process and can never be fully achieved without God's help and the acceptance of the suffering that this will mean. All this is part of the deep mystical purification inaugurated, sustained and completed by the Holy Spirit in mystical prayer beyond the first emotional beginnings. To avoid confusion, let me make it clear that just as Jesus is God's 'love made flesh', so also is the food given to his Apostles at the Last Supper his 'love made bread'. So also, therefore, is the less tangible but nonetheless equally real God-given bread with which he chooses to nourish us each day. This daily bread for which we are told to pray in the Lord's Prayer then, is simply the love of Jesus made mystical bread, with which to nourish us with all our daily spiritual needs. If you do not eat ordinary food you will progressively become weaker and weaker and finally die. In the same way, if you do not eat God's mystical food you will in the same way become progressively weaker and weaker and die spiritually.

A series of talks I gave to Cistercian monks in Cameroon, enabled me to spend many hours with the holiest man I have ever met. He was in his 'eighties and I learned far more from him than his fellow monks learnt from me. He told me how, for many years he had been in spiritual darkness where many times over he questioned the faith that led him to the monastery where he was called upon to guide others. Then, one day he became ill and was admitted to the monastery hospital where he received Holy Communion each day. On three distinct occasions, just as he was about to receive communion, he heard these words, "Only you have been keeping me out." He insisted that he did not hear them in his head, or through some sort of inner revelation, but, "Out loud, and as loud and as clearly as you have been speaking to us during your talks." Simultaneously he found himself immersed in the love of God in such a way that he became continually caught up in what he could only describe as a weak ecstasy. In other words, he did not lose consciousness, but the profound experience of Presence remained with him, continually restoring and surcharging the faith that had all but deserted him before.

In one way or another we all must be purified of the selfishness that prevents the pure love of God from possessing us. The spiritual life is a journey from selfishness to selflessness, because only a selfless person can become one with the utterly Selfless One, who is all pure, undiluted loving. This is a lengthy business that will be commensurate with the whole of our lives. Unless a person makes a genuine attempt to rid themselves of the selfishness that keeps God out, then they will make no spiritual progress. Unless we try to change our self-centred lives outside of prayer, our prayer itself will never develop beyond the most rudimentary stages. Even from a psychological point of view, if we have behaved badly all day, then prayer will be quite impossible at the end of that day. In fact, one of the reasons why people run away from prayer is that they know it will mean coming to terms with themselves, and doing something about their shoddy lifestyles.

Even though we may make the morning offering as sincerely as possible, and genuinely try to implement it in the forthcoming day, we will ultimately fail unless something is done to cure the scourge of selfishness that can destroy even our best of intentions and our sincerest efforts. God wants us to do all that is within our power to strip away all and everything in our lives that prevents us from being totally united with him at all times. Only then will he be able to possess us as fully as he has planned. If we do not see the sin and the selfishness that prevents our growth in the spiritual life, it is not because we are sinless, it is simply because we are blind and we need to cry out with Bartimaeus, "Lord, that I may see" (Mark 10:46-52).

In one of the most memorable retreats I have ever attended, Archbishop Anthony Bloom began by telling the story of a retired headmistress who offered her services to him as a chauffeur. As they were returning home one Monday afternoon she stopped the car in Kensington to pick up her new glasses from the opticians and proceeded to try them out for the remainder of the journey. It was less than a mile, but it turned out to be the most terrifying journey either of them ever made; her driving was atrocious. She climbed out of the car shaking all over, opened her handbag, took out her driving licence and ceremoniously ripped it into little pieces. "I'll never drive again," she said. "Why ever not?" asked the Archbishop. "Because," she replied, "there is just so much traffic on the road."

So, if we don't see it is because we are spiritually blind and need to do something about it. That is why the letter -E- in the Our Father is to remind us to examine our conscience each day, to pause for a few moments to review our lives since we last prayed. It is time to ask God to show us everything we have done or failed to do that has kept him out. For it is this selfishness that prevents him from making his home within us, as he would wish and as Jesus promised on the night before he died. After this has been done, it is time to make an Act of Contrition for how we have failed in the past. A formal act of contrition could be used, or perhaps the recitation of what came to be called The Jesus Prayer said several times over, slowly and prayerfully. "Jesus, son of God, have mercy on me a sinner," but a sincere expression of personal sorrow, in our own words would be better still. Then we could make a firm purpose of amendment, in other words, a genuine decision to try and behave better in future.

Some years ago I shared a flat with a man called Carruthers. If morals make the man, and manners make the gentleman, then Carruthers was the finest gentleman I ever met, or so I thought for the first few weeks. However, as the weeks went by, I began to see that his manners were no more than a thin coat of veneer that hid the chipboard man within. Casual visitors were as impressed with him as I was to begin with. He was always so terribly sorry for everything. He was so terribly sorry for beating me to the bathroom, so terribly sorry for keeping me waiting for half an hour, so terribly sorry for failing to clean the bath. He was so terribly sorry too for emptying the fridge when his friend came around, for leaving the washing-up for me the following morning, and for leaving my car with an empty tank when he borrowed it without asking. The trouble was, he was not sorry at all and he kept on behaving in the same old way day in, day out. It is one thing to say you are sorry, it is quite another to mean it. If you mean it, you do something about it. No act of sorrow, no promise to do better next time however heartfelt it might sound, will do us any good, if we do not resolve and seriously endeavour to do better next time around.

Finally, as we become a little more aware of the moral stumbling blocks that usually trip us up, it is time to try and forestall them. If there is a lazy streak in us, or if we have a hot temper, or are prone to making smart alec remarks at the expense of others, it is the time to take the necessary steps to avoid falling into these same faults in the forthcoming day. St Paul was the first to realise with such clarity that it is in fact our very weaknesses, and that even includes our sins, that can become stepping stones to sanctity, if they only convince us of our utter need for God. For, "My grace is enough for you: my power is at its best in weakness" (2 Corinthians 12:9). This is good news, because the truth is, in this life we will never stop falling. "When you stop falling you will be in heaven, but when you stop getting up, you will be in hell" (Peter Calvay).

At the feast of Pentecost, the Jews celebrated the day on which God gave the Law to Moses. However, the first Pentecost after the Resurrection was the day on which God gave his new law, the law of love. This law was not primarily a list of commandments like the laws given to Moses, but the same personal love that became embodied in Jesus. It was this love that enabled Jesus to practise to perfection the New Commandments that he taught his disciples, namely, to love God with their whole heart and mind, and with their whole being, as he did; then to love others as he did too, and still does. This love was given to Jesus throughout his life on earth, and was given in full measure after his Resurrection, and in such a way that he would be able to give it to others to inaugurate a new era, the Kingdom of Love. After the Resurrection, the unique and transcendental love that Jesus received from God enabled him to love not just one person, or even a group of persons as he had done before, but every person alive at that time and in time to come. So when the crowds who gathered on the first Pentecost, demanded to know how they could receive the love of the Holy Spirit, St Peter told them that they should repent.

When he told them to do this, he was telling them in language that they understood, how to turn to receive this love that had already begun to change St Peter and the other Apostles. In other words, they had to turn away from the adolescent world in which they had been living, where self-seeking, self-indulgence and self-absorption was the norm, to turn to be filled with the love of Jesus, his Holy Spirit. This love would take them out of themselves and into the new world order that Jesus had come to inaugurate. In this world, love would transform them, by enabling them to enter into the Risen Christ. The fruits of this love, justice and peace, goodness and truth, peace and joy and all the other virtues, would be seen embodied in his followers, as they were embodied in his life on earth. That is why he said, "It will be by their fruits that you will know them." (Matthew 7:16).

The love that was unleashed by the Risen Christ will never stop pouring out now and for always, but it will only be received by those who choose to turn to receive it, or in the words of St

Peter, who choose to repent. Every Jew knew what it meant to repent, it meant turning back to God, for that is what the word repentance meant throughout the whole of the Old Testament. However, for Jesus, this traditional word took on a new meaning. For the first time Jesus, had taught his followers that God was none other than their ever-loving Dad (*Abba*), and repentance therefore meant turning back to him. It meant turning back to the true home where we were all originally conceived, and to where we will all one day return. The word *Shub* in Hebrew actually means to return. The prophet Isaiah uses this word as Jesus was to use it later, namely of the return of errant sons back to their Father. Jesus came from the home where we were all conceived, to take us back with him to live with him in a family bonded together by the love that endlessly surges out of his Father, to enjoy utter, ongoing and ever-increasing joy to all eternity. Many of those who listened to St Peter had an immediate conversion experience. The love that touched the Apostles touched them, and they wanted to change their lives immediately. A conversion experience is one thing, but repentance is quite another. Repentance means turning to receive the love that is forever pouring out of Jesus, not once, but time and time again. How? By relentlessly turning away from all and everything that would impede it, even though this might mean a complete and radical change of life and utter abandonment to God.

God the Father lives outside of space and time, in eternity. In him there are no yesterdays, nor tomorrows, there are no befores nor afters. He simply is, now in the present moment. Here he is utterly engrossed in, and enjoying the life of uninterrupted loving. When Jesus rose from the dead to be united with God his Father, it meant that he too was taken outside of space and time. Here his utter delight and joy is not just to love and experience his Father's love, but to become the means through which that love is channelled to those he left behind, as he promised at the Last Supper. God is only alive and loving now, in this present moment, so it is only now that believers can turn to receive his loving by continually repenting. Yesterday is gone, tomorrow is to come, so it is only now that a person can turn to God to receive the love that is relentlessly pouring out of him, and into us through Jesus. That is why Jean Pierre de Caussade called the present moment a sacrament, because it is only now that we can abandon ourselves to the love of God. The only way to do this, is not by making a grand gesture, as people often do after a conversion experience, as I did when I nearly joined the Carthusian order, but by freely choosing to repent here and now, today and repeatedly every day.

In the Christian tradition, there can be no such thing as a mystical life without an ascetical life. If we do not make the continuing effort to receive the love of God each day, then not only is the continual outpouring of his love pointless, but the Incarnation will have been pointless too. If everyone behaved like this the affront that this would mean to God would be so enormous that you could not blame him if he simply destroyed what was created with the best of intentions, but which proved to be a complete waste of time. If recent apparitions of Our Lady are to be believed, this is a distinct possibility. She makes clear that if we do not radically change our lives and repent, then a calamity avoided in the past by those who did repent, will be visited on those who do not, and in the immediate future. Even if it could be proved that these apparitions did not happen, the fact remains that, if the very *raison d'etre* for God creating the world was being continually ignored, and nothing was being done about it, what would be the point of keeping it in existence? God is not in the business of continually doing something that is pointless. The call to repentance, and all that we have to do to keep turning to God, is of paramount importance, and it would seem more urgent today than ever before.

A contemporary mystic assures us that only Christ is holding back the hand of God. Quite naturally many God-fearing people tend to take such language literally, and we are led to imagine Christ actually holding back the vengeful hand of God to prevent him annihilating what has long since seemed to have been weighed in the balance and found wanting. What this means in theological language is that Christ is still just about sufficiently present and active in enough good people to prevent God annihilating the rest of humanity. The story of Noah illustrates my point. God promised him that if he could only find sufficient people who were good, decent and God fearing, as he and his family were, then the impending disaster might be prevented. We all know what happened next. It would seem that we are in a similar position today, although to date there must still be just about sufficient good and decent people to offer humanity hope of a temporary reprieve.

However, that number is dwindling rapidly, and if more do not choose to take their place, and in sufficient numbers to bring about radical spiritual change in the Church, and through the Church in the world, then it is not unreasonable to expect massive calamities on the face of the world. The outer shell is there to be seen, but what of the inner life? We have become accustomed to living what is no more than a charade of the vital living mystical spirituality that was inspired and set up by Jesus himself. In those days tens of thousands would choose to suffer indescribable torture and die appalling and degrading deaths rather than deny or dilute the faith. Remember faith does not primarily mean believing in a list of dogmatic propositions, but in a person, the person of Jesus Christ. Repentance means turning to him daily in prayer, so that through him we can turn to the Father to love, honour and give him glory. When Our Lady, or Our Lord, find it necessary to appear to appeal to us in one way or another, to avoid impending calamity, if not mass destruction, the message is always the same – repent - and the way to repent is by turning to God in prayer. They do not come to give detailed instruction on how to pray and how to persevere - great saints and mystics have already done that.

Since before the Second Vatican Council there has been incessant talk about the need for reform or renewal and that talk has gone on and on to the present day. There have been myriad courses, seminars and workshops about renewal but still nothing happens that remotely resembles the massive spiritual upsurge that changed the world in the immediate aftermath of the Resurrection. That is why the time for endless woolly talk of renewal is over. The call now is for radical and immediate change of heart, change of life, instant and ongoing repentance, not so much for the sake of renewal, but firstly to avert impending disasters of cataclysmic proportion, which are of our own making. You do not need to be a prophet to see how our failure to live decent Christian lives, that show the glory and the goodness of God to the world, results in the moral malaise that prevails everywhere about us.

Only Christ can triumph over the dejection, the despondency and the disquiet that surrounds us, but only he can do it, in and through those who choose to admit him. The only way that he can be admitted is by continually inviting him in, by the selfsame quality of loving that was generated by our first Christian forebears. That is why I have been detailing their profound and daily mystical spirituality in these talks. I have gone to great pains to do so, and spent very many years studying the sources to do this, because this spirituality comes not from man, but from God, and it was first practised by Jesus himself with his disciples. That is why it should always be the most perfect example of what we must try to embody.

Although I am in no way suggesting that we should end the practice of infant baptism, it can, however, easily blind us to something that was commonplace in the early Church. Namely every prospective candidate for baptism would have to spend a minimum of two years preparing for the sacramental reception of the Holy Spirit. This entailed daily prayer and fasting, instruction and weekly participation in the first half of the Mass to hear the scriptures and listen to speakers, many of whom had known Jesus personally while he was on earth, or known those who had. Many of the candidates knew the Gospel off by heart by the time they were baptised. They prayed at least five times a day as a minimum, just as the other Christians did whose community they were preparing to join. It seems to me that serious attempts should be made to recreate something of this deeply spiritual preparation for baptisms for those already baptised, to facilitate the effective indwelling of the Holy Spirit who brings Christ to birth in us. Naturally the home would be the place to lay the foundation for what would be developed at further depth in school. But sadly, syllabuses are all too academic and anyway it would demand deeply committed and practising teachers who are sadly thin on the ground today. I do not say this as a recipe for doing nothing, but to pinpoint the problem honestly, which is always the prerequisite for the decisive action that must follow.

It was not only candidates for baptism, who spent a considerable time learning how to turn to God each day in prayer, but others too. The Apostles themselves did the same in Jerusalem after the first Pentecost Day. After his dramatic conversion on the road to Damascus St Paul retired into solitude to begin practising the repentance that would allow the Holy Spirit to bring Christ ever more fully alive within him. It was the prayer that he began to learn there that would enable him to say, he no longer lived, but it was Christ who lived in him. That is still the only way that Christ can reach out today, to heal the sad and sick world that we live in, namely through us. That is why all the great saints, who achieved so much to change the world first went into solitude for a time for the same reason, and continually returned there. St Francis of Assisi spent three years as a hermit learning to repent before he set out to call others to do likewise. St Bernadine of Siena did the same and so did St Ignatius at Manresa. St Catherine of Siena did not have to travel far to find the solitude that she needed for Christ to be reborn in her; she found it in her own home. It was here that she spent three years in solitude preparing for the work that God wanted of her.

Two of my very good friends who in fact invited me to speak to you this week, ran a year's course for young people which was a sort of 'novitiate for life' at a retreat centre in North London. Instead of taking a year off to back pack around the world, they were inspired to give the same time to enter the inner world so they would come to know, understand and change that inner world, so it would become the source of strength and spiritual energy for the rest of lives. They called their little group 'The Cana Community'. The name instilled into each one who joined them the profound truth that St John wished to instil into his readers at the beginning of his Gospel. It was that, thanks to the Love of Christ, human love can now be suffused and surcharged with the divine. This means that in the sacrament of marriage the bride and the bridegroom, through their human loving imbued with the divine, transmit God's love to each other. This is not just true on their wedding day but on every day when they try to love each other with their minds and hearts, with their bodies and souls, not just until death do they part, but to eternity. In the other sacraments, the minister is normally a priest and therefore access to the grace of the sacrament is limited, unlike the ministers of the sacrament of marriage. They are always on hand to love and cherish each other and in so doing continually recharge and replenish one another with their human loving that is permeated with the divine.

No one doubted that marriage was one of the great mysteries or sacraments that helped draw the participants ever deeper into Christ, and so it was never deemed necessary to define the obvious. However, as heresies gradually infested Christendom and taught that the body God created and said was 'good', so good that his own son was 'made flesh,' was in fact evil, called into question what had never been questioned before. That is why it was as late as the Council of Trent before marriage was officially defined as a sacrament – not that it had just become one, but it always had been. If the baptismal pool is the womb of the Church, then married love is the mystical nursery in which God's love continually supports, sustains and succours newborn Christians. This therefore, is the place where, if all else fails, the saints, the mystics, and the spiritual leaders that the church needs, are formed, not just for its survival, but for its future wellbeing and success. If therefore, for whatever reason, Christianity falls into moral decline, as it has done from time to time through the centuries, then help is at hand. If a corrupt or spiritually inept leadership in the Church brings the Barque of Peter to a standstill, then the breeze of the Holy Spirit that is breathed into young Christians through the love generated in marriage can always set it back on course again. It is the love generated in marriage then, that gives the hope that 'springs eternal' with every new generation, formed by new couples' mutual loving.

It is for this reason that it can be said that all major renewals in the Church have come through laypeople; not just through the great leaders who are remembered in history, but through the parents who helped form the people they became. They might end up as popes, cardinals, bishops and abbots, but almost all of them were formed in the same nursery where human and divine loving combined to inspire them with the inner security and love that would enable them to do and achieve what could not otherwise be done. In the history of renewal and reform the rise of a Christian Renaissance always comes, not primarily from the top down, but from the bottom up, where parental loving infused the love of the Holy Spirit into future spiritual leaders. The Christian Renaissance that is so desperately needed must encourage, not just the mystical theology to regenerate clerical and religious life, but married life too, because both are indispensable for the 'new spring' I believe is about to dawn. I will not attempt to detail the place of mystical theology in married life because that has already been done in the book, *Wisdom from the Western Isles*. However, I would like to encourage all to do whatever you can, to deepen your own daily prayer life to enable the Holy Spirit to work in you to bring about the Christian Renaissance that he can only bring about through those who choose to admit him.

St Catherine of Siena could find a place, far from the madding crowd, in her own home. Sadly in this world of noise that now prevails we might not be able to do the same, however, the local church could be our refuge. If it is locked ask the parish priest to give you a spare key and it should be a great joy for him to see that at least one of his parishioners is set on doing what all the others should be doing too. If it is thought to be too dangerous to leave the church open during the day, then arrange for a rota of parishioners to ensure there is always a presence there. This venture would give the parish priest the opportunity to arrange for talks to teach people how to pray in the time they have given. Admittedly it was during, and in the immediate aftermath of World War II, but whenever I went into a church during the day, there were always others who had come in to pray, and the city churches were often more than half full.

After my mother died I would always spend a few weeks with my father until he died. To give him a little respite from meals on wheels I would do the shopping and cook for him. In the course of time I became very friendly with the girl who served at our local supermarket, because she seemed so transparently kind and understanding. When she found out what I was doing, and why I could not be at home all the time as I would have wished, she promised to pop in to see my father every few days and keep me informed. She and her husband would also invite him for Sunday lunch. She was an Australian girl, so on my last visit to the shop I asked her whether or not she and her husband had seen the magnificent programme that my father and I had watched on the Great Barrier Reef the previous evening. She said that they did not have a television. They were both committed Christians who went on retreat twice a year to a retreat centre near Hereford. They spent their evenings reading books and meditating. So that was the source of her inner strength, I thought.

No, I am not suggesting that the television should go, but when you read, as I have read only today, that the average viewer watches over thirty hours of programmes a week, surely something could be done to save our sanity. Reducing that time by a third would give us more than enough time to start doing the only thing that can permanently change our lives for the better. One way or the other, if we are going to be serious about finding time for prayer, we will have to find what Montaigne called, "a little back shop for ourselves, all our own, untouched by others, in which we establish our true freedom and chief place of seclusion and solitude." You do not need this so much for the daily prayer that I have been explaining to you so far, but for a deeper form of prayer, that will underpin it, where the closeness that you have at times experienced will develop through Christian meditation to profound mystical contemplation. It is this that leads to the most important prayer of all, prayer the first Christians called 'the prayer without ceasing'. It is this that I will speak about in my next talk.

Chapter 9

From Meditation to Contemplation

(Peter's eighth talk)

When our Bishop slipped and broke his nose, he cancelled his pilgrimage to Lourdes and decided to grace our school with his presence for speech-day instead. It was customary to put on some sort of entertainment when he was presiding over the proceedings, but nothing was prepared, so it was decided to produce a Shakespearean anthology at the last minute.

It would comprise two comic scenes sandwiched between three serious ones. There were no budding actors in my class so we all drew lots to decide who would play the part of Henry V, and the lot fell on me. Day after day I practised extravagant gestures in front of my mother's full-length mirror, as I recited his famous speech before the final assault on Harfleur. "Once more into the breach, dear friends, once more..." At the dress rehearsal I received far more laughs than the grave digger from Hamlet and the porter from Macbeth put together. I put it down to the dramatic tension that I was able to generate. Had they never seen great Shakespearean acting before?

Time was short, so the English master said nothing until a matter of moments before I stepped on stage. Then he took me by the arm and said. "Now listen here boy, forget about that pathetic little performance last night. If you act like that today, Reverend Mother will take you back to the convent school and make you head girl. You're supposed to be a warrior king. not a fairy queen! This isn't a stage, it's a battlefield. They're not fifth formers, they're your men who are tired and exhausted. They've been storming the town all day, and they're getting nowhere. They've seen their friends falling at their side, they've heard the cries of the wounded, the screeching of the horses and they're all but defeated. Get out there, rouse them up, and rally them for one more attack before it's too late."

Then, with those words he pushed me onto the stage with one hand and pulled back the curtains with the other. To this day I do not know what happened, I just remember saying, "Once more into the breach, dear friends, once more...." but I cannot remember what happened next until that thunderous applause at the end that I will never forget. Even my worst enemies thought it was a fairly reputable performance. The Headmaster thought I was drunk and the Bishop wanted to sign me up for the Diocese. "Put him in a pulpit," he said, "and he'll collect enough money for me to build a new Cathedral that will dwarf that glorified wigwam they've just built in Liverpool." Everyone seemed to think it was a great performance. But they had it all wrong. It was not a performance at all. I was not acting - it was for real. Somehow the English Master had managed to inspire me with the spirit of the man who trounced the French at Agincourt. I was famous for fifteen minutes, not because I was a good actor, but because for fifteen minutes I became a living reincarnation of the greatest warrior King in English history.

I have always seen that performance as a key moment in my life, because it gave me the most important spiritual insight that I ever had. I may well have known that Jesus was Mr Loving since I was a very small boy, but I was too busy learning my lessons in school and playing with my friends out of school to ask the next question, until Shakespeare suddenly stopped me in my tracks. Thanks to him I was able to see that you can only really become like someone else, act and behave as they do, by being inspired by the same spirit that inspired them. I may well have been able to see that Mr Loving never stopped loving me, but that would never change me unless his loving could enter into me to make me more and more like him. If you try to copy someone else, as I had initially tried to copy Henry V, then you will certainly end up caricaturing them, and people will laugh and call you a ham. But if you try to copy Jesus Christ in that way, they will probably call you a sanctimonious hypocrite, and they will probably be right.

There is only one way to copy Jesus and that is not by trying to copy his outward behaviour, but by trying to allow the same love that continually animated him to flow into us to animate and inspire us and all we say and do. After all, this is what he did. Throughout his life on earth he continually opened himself to be inspired by his Father's Love, the Holy Spirit who conceived him in the first place, and then continued to inspire everything he said and did while he was on earth, and filled him to overflowing when he returned to heaven.

The love that continually flows out of Mr Loving now is the same love that flowed into him throughout his life on earth, the same love that was brought to perfection after his death, and the same love that reunited him with his Father, enabling his Father to send that love out through him onto and into us. The spiritual life is the expression used to describe a new way of life, organised by someone who wants to start turning towards God regularly, in order to receive his love or his Holy Spirit that comes to us through Jesus. First and foremost, this means building a prayer life that leads through meditation to contemplation where a person is more open to receiving God's love than ever before. However, to begin with it is necessary to set aside quality space and time each day as Jesus himself did in order to practise turning to God regularly. In order to do this, I decided to set aside a full half an hour every day of my life, not just for my daily prayers which were said three times a day with the other boys in the Chapel at the school where I was a boarder. Then each Monday I went to a seminar on prayer given by the school spiritual director, Fr Handley. He told me to begin studying the scriptures in a new way, to discover what Jesus did to enable the Holy Spirit to fill him with the supernatural life and love that animated and inspired everything he said and did.

Here is the key to the spiritual journey to which we are all called. It is to be found in the way in which the helpless child who was born of the young Jewish virgin, Mary, grew into the masterpiece of God's creation. As the years passed by, the growth of Jesus' human body was paralleled by the growth of his inner spiritual being. Just as the exercise of the muscles of his body facilitated the growth of his body, so the exercise of the spiritual muscles of his mind and heart facilitated the growth of his soul. St Luke draws our attention to this spiritual journey when, after recording the finding of Jesus in the temple, he wrote that on returning to Nazareth with his parents, "Jesus increased in wisdom, in stature, and in favour with God and men" (Luke 2:52). The way in which he could discuss and dispute theology with the experts for several days in the temple as a twelve-year-old, showed how far he had already developed.

He did not meditate, as I was taught to meditate, because his daily vocal prayer put him into direct daily contact with his Father. For instance, the moment he said his *Shema* to commit himself to love his Father with all his mind and heart and body and soul, then that prayer led him on and into direct contact with his Father, loving, praising, honouring, thanking and glorifying him in an act of pure and simple contemplative loving. Over a thousand years later St Thomas Aquinas defined contemplation - if I may paraphrase him - as a pure and simple mystical gaze upon God, accompanied by loving adoration, and awe. Jesus did not need to meditate in order to be lost in contemplation, the wordless form of prayer that kept his gaze fixed upon his Father throughout his day. As D H Lawrence once put it, "Speech travels between the separate parts. But in the perfect One there is a perfect silence of bliss." This profound form of prayer not only enabled his love to rise to his Father, but his Father's love to descend into him. This gave him the inner power and strength to love his neighbours as himself, and to become the most secure, the most mature and the most loveable human being who has ever walked on the face of this earth. Later, through his love sent down upon and into them on the first Pentecost, his disciples and his followers were not only able to pray with him, but in, with and through him in a way that was quite impossible for the Jewish community who had rejected him.

In an attempt to make themselves more acceptable to God, instead of trying to deepen their prayer the Jews multiplied their prayers. There was a prayer for virtually everything and for every occasion, before rising in the morning, before washing, before leaving home, before going on a journey, before entering a house, before starting work, and these are, of course, in addition to all the other prayers they said each day. It was as if quantity could make up for quality. It was exactly the same with all the rules and regulations that governed every moment of the day. Once love is lost then the law takes its place and religion is on a steady downhill slope to oblivion. By the time Jesus was born there were in addition to the Ten Commandments over six hundred petty rules and regulations that a good Jew must observe. The laws for keeping the Sabbath holy are a case in point. Travel was curtailed by restricting the number of paces they could take, and if they used a donkey to visit friends they had to sit side-saddle, for the extra work involved in sitting astride would infringe the law. If on arrival bread was offered, it could not be eaten if it was cooked that day, as lighting a fire was prohibited on the Sabbath. And if the food included an egg it was imperative to enquire whether or not the hen had laid it on the Sabbath. And all this is nothing compared with the rules and regulations surrounding the sacrifices made in the Temple at Jerusalem. When Jesus saw Jerusalem for the last time, he wept for what had happened to the people his father had called to inaugurate a new world order to govern the world with the law of love. As Isaiah made clear many years before, "This people honours me only with lip service, while their hearts are far from me. The worship they offer me is worthless: the doctrines they teach are only human regulations" (Mathew 15:8-9 Isaiah 29:13). The destruction of Jerusalem in AD 70 marked the end of a people who had been weighed in the balance and found wanting.

However, the world order and the new law of love that was first brought to perfection in the risen and glorified Christ was now open to all. The simple and pure act of contemplative loving that bonded him to his Father while he was on earth, was brought to perfection after his death. Through love everyone could now, not only enter into the Risen Christ, but into his profound contemplative prayer. However, for newcomers it would not be as easy to love Jesus as it would have been for the Apostles and the first disciples who had known him while he was on earth. To facilitate this, a new form of prayer was developed for the first time that came to be called Christian meditation. In order to come to know Jesus and to develop the love that would enable them to enter into him, as he is now, beginners would have to come to know and love him as he was on earth. This was the whole point and purpose of Christian meditation. Through meditation they would be led on to generate the love that would enable them to come to know and experience the profound contemplative prayer that enabled Jesus to remain permanently at one with his Father. When this finally takes place, meditation will no longer be necessary, as it was not necessary for Jesus.

Contemplation is the best possible form of prayer for a Christian, as it was for Jesus before the Resurrection. It meant that he was at all times open to the love of God while simultaneously channelling it to others. It was for this reason that, when in the middle of the thirteenth century the new apostolic orders were criticised and asked to explain what they were doing, St Thomas Aquinas gave them his famous answer. Their *raison d'etre* was firstly to learn how to contemplate, and then to share the fruits of contemplation with others, as Jesus had done before them. This was the ideal prayer for the first Christians too, participating in the contemplation of Jesus that enabled them to receive and embody the very presence of Jesus working in and through them. This was how Jesus was made seeable, touchable, and loveable again to the pagan world in which they lived.

However, only those who were able to come to love Jesus would be able to enter into him and into his contemplative loving, and the way to generate this love was through the new form of prayer, Christian meditation. In order to teach new Christians how to meditate, they were given set events in the life of Jesus to meditate on after they had recited their version of the *Shema* at the third, the sixth and the ninth hour that was reserved only for vocal prayer by the Jews. In addition to this they were encouraged to get up at midnight to meditate on the death and Resurrection of Jesus that was traditionally believed to have taken place at midnight. Today this might be seen as expecting too much, but in those days when most decent people went to bed shortly after sunset and arose at sunrise it was not such a terrible imposition, and for many it became the favourite time for prayer, when all was still and quiet.

This new method of prayer was far more alive, far more vivid than the meditations many of us remember that were inspired by the meditation manuals of the past. Ancient peoples had prodigious memories. Voluminous works like the Iliad and the Odyssey for instance, were handed on for centuries by word of mouth long before they were written down for posterity, as were major parts of the Old Testament. When Jesus preached, even the least educated of his listeners would have understood his continual allusions to it, much of which they had not only heard from their regular attendance at the synagogue, but committed to memory too, with so many other stories and family reminiscences that were told and retold, as they gathered around the fireside. Before literacy was commonplace, everyone's memory was a personal library from which wisdom could be drawn.

The first part of the Mass, called the *synaxis* by the first Christians, was based on the old synagogue service where readings from the Old Testament would be followed by readings from the New Testament, showing how the New Testament fulfilled the Old. In the first century congregations would be enthralled, listening to speakers who had known Jesus personally. It might even be an Apostle who would fire the imaginations of his listeners, and whose words would be stored away never to be forgotten, and used to inspire future generations who had not known Jesus personally. A saint and martyr like Polycarp for instance, who had known St John personally and listened to his recollections of Jesus, handed his reminiscences on to the faithful in his sermons until his death in AD 155, well over a century after the death of Jesus. And these were in their turn handed on into the following century by his pupil St Irenaeus. And there were very many others too, who were heirs to the oral tradition about Jesus, whose words lit up the scriptures with pictures of the man who fulfilled them. They inspired ordinary men and women and transformed their meditations with vivid heart-felt aspirations and desires to love ever more deeply and enter into communion with Jesus and into his profound contemplation of his Father.

Even in my own experience, I remember listening to my two ninety-year-old aunts in the 1940s when I was only eight or nine. I have never forgotten the story they told me of two old men in their village who told and retold their memories of the battle of Waterloo in 1815. They were shocked by the pillaging of those lying dead on the battlefield, not just by common thieves, but by fellow soldiers too, and dentists who extracted the teeth of the dead to make homemade dentures for their wealthy clients. If these vivid memories have come down to me over two hundred years after they occurred, how much more did the well-practised and sometimes prodigious memories of the first Christians, hand on to successive generations what they had seen and heard. These stories helped bring alive the sacred words of the scriptures which most of them had committed to memory, enabling them to come to know and love, ever more deeply, the Jesus who rose from the dead and lived on continually amongst his people. As he promised shortly before he ascended into heaven. "And know that I am with you always; yes, to the end of time" (Matthew 28:20).

His continual presence after the Resurrection helped create an electric atmosphere amongst the early Christians as they heard stories, not just of Jesus speaking to, and converting known bigots like Saul, but endless stories of other conversions too. There were stories of once influential pagan rulers and administrators, or one-time torturers and executioners who saw for themselves a quality of love in action they had never seen before. Read the ancient *Acts of the Martyrs* to find story after story of Christ making his presence visible, not just through the superhuman heroism of the martyrs themselves, but in the way it moved onlookers too who were inspired to seek out the source of the supernatural love they had seen at work.

These stories and these sacred memories would be told and retold to the faithful at the end of the scriptural readings, when it was the custom for more than one speaker to set the congregation afire with stories of what Jesus had said and done, and what he was still doing in the world that he wanted to transform through them. Often visiting speakers would have the congregation on the edge of their seats telling of how the branches of the mustard seed were spreading and bearing fruit in every corner of the then known world. But of course, what was most important of all, was reading and listening to the scriptures in the light of the inspired stories of those who had known Jesus personally. It set the first Christians alight, with a deep and personal longing to come to know him personally too, and to come to know and experience the love that inspired and animated him throughout his life on earth.

This deep and prayerful longing that was inspired by their daily meditation would lead them on to desire the personal intimacy and eventually the union that love ultimately desires. But, this union was now no longer directed to the Jesus who once lived on earth, but to Jesus as he is now, risen and glorified. In short their meditation led them on and into the contemplation that Jesus experienced throughout his life on earth which was brought to perfection at his glorification. However, this new direction in their prayer life was not as thrilling or as exhilarating as the meditation they once turned to with such delight. Let me explain why.

Like his mother before him, Jesus was immaculately conceived and, as he never succumbed to the sin and selfishness that affects us, there was nothing to prevent his continual mystical contemplation of his Father. Our sinfulness, however, means that although we are in the process of being drawn up into the glorified Christ, we cannot be fully fitted into his continual contemplation of his Father. Those first Christians who were inspired by meditation found themselves in a spiritual limbo land where they found that although the pull towards God prevented them from returning to meditation on the Jesus who once was, could not go forward into the Jesus as he is now, and into his contemplation of his Father. However, they were fortunate because they were surrounded by fellow travellers who knew precisely what was happening to them and who were able to act as spiritual mentors. There was no going back but only forward into the Risen Christ and into his contemplation of his Father where he continually praised, thanked, loved and glorified him. This going forward involved two things, firstly persevering in following their desire for the contemplation of God that drew them out of meditation. This meant giving more, not less time for prayer than before. Secondly it involved the continual endeavour to persevere in the inner spiritual purification that would gradually free them from the sin and the selfishness that prevented them attaining their heart's desire. The desire to join Christ in his contemplation of the Father remains throughout mystical purification, but it gets weaker at times when, what St

John of the Cross later called 'The Dark Night of the Soul,' gets blacker. However, it becomes ever stronger with the grace that perseverance brings and with the ongoing endeavour to come to terms with the sinfulness and the selfishness that is laid bare. It is this spiritual cancer that prevents the union that is desired more than anything else. Perseverance is the mystical ladder that enables our love to rise up and into God and God's love to descend into us.

In time, what can only be described as Obscure Contemplation at the beginning, gradually becomes clearer and more tangible, as the love of God begins to touch them, albeit briefly at least to begin with. The expression sober or spiritual intoxication or similar phrases were used to describe these moments when their contemplation in Christ enabled them to be touched by the divine. At first, the experience of this mystical life, that was also described as spiritual inebriation, with all the good and none of the bad effects of alcohol, was something predominantly spiritual. It was all in the mind rather than in the body. However, the ultimate experience supersedes what was likened to sober or spiritual intoxication, for now it is far more complete, far more completely human, as it begins to spill over from the mind or the head to penetrate the whole body, awakening it to a new mode of being. It is as if the body and the emotions, once so active in 'first fervour', had been frozen in winter without knowing it. But, as the Holy Spirit progressively surges out and into the body, it is as if a great thaw is underway that heralds a new spring in which the believer will be united heart and mind, flesh and blood, with the Jesus who rose on the first Easter Day. This experience makes it clearer than ever before to the recipient that the end of the spiritual life is not to be found in some obscure disembodied experience of ecstasy, as Neoplatonists and those influenced by them would have us believe, but in the full-bodied experience of union with the Risen Christ. This union is often called Divinisation or *Theosis* by the early Eastern Fathers, and the Transforming Union or the Mystical Marriage by the later Western Fathers of the Church.

If you read the historians of early Christianity and most especially those theologians whose exemplary work enabled the second Vatican Council to take place, great emphasis is placed on the public liturgical worship, that is for them and indeed for us all of great importance. However, this emphasis has often been to the detriment of the personal and daily piety of the believers who were steeped in a profound Christocentric spirituality that enabled them to participate in the liturgy with such effect. This aspect of early Christian spirituality, however, is regrettably too often dealt with as a footnote, or as a brief appendage under the heading of daily devotions of the early Christians or some such title which is viewed as incidental to the main matter in hand. It is quite evident that otherwise well-meaning scholars have failed to grasp the crucial importance of the personal spiritual endeavour of ordinary Christian men and women. And what is so deeply regrettable is that this failure prevented the Second Vatican Council from emphasising something so important, that it has undoubtedly contributed to its partial rather than its complete success.

Before the Vatican Council, the faithful were often caricatured as groups of hermits, as they made their way to Mass, in contrast to their early Christian forebears. In the early Church the liturgy was the supreme communal expression of brothers and sisters, offering themselves together through Christ, to their common Father. But the emphasis on the liturgy as a communal act of worship was such that the new breed of liturgists, like their mentors, failed to realise that it depended for its efficacy on the quality of the personal spiritual life of every single individual participant. Let me make my point by quoting from one scholar, who did not make the mistake of many of his peers, perhaps the greatest liturgist of them all, Josef Jungmann SJ, whose words have fallen on deaf ears.

"In the present day liturgical movement, primitive Christianity is often held up before our eyes as a model, an exemplar of liturgical observance. We are to believe that Christians of old, contrary to the tendency of modern individualism, knew no other, or scarcely any other form of prayer than liturgical prayer.... Unfortunately, this ideal is not correct. The idea that the life of the primitive Christians revolved exclusively around the liturgy is not correct. And it cannot be correct, simply because it would be unnatural and in contradiction to the Gospels. How could the Christian life exclude private and personal prayer? It is a gross exaggeration to restrict the prayer of Christian antiquity to liturgical prayer alone."

The early Christian liturgy was deeply inspiring, vibrant, and spiritually re-energising, not because it was rubrically correct in every detail, or verbally faultless, but because it depended on the daily personal prayer of the faithful, and the profound mystical spirituality that it generated that transformed all and everything they said and did into 'the prayer without ceasing'.

Even from the brief synopsis that I have outlined, it should be evident that the daily personal spirituality of the first Christians was intense and all-consuming. It contained one vital ingredient on which the whole success of Christianity depended, and still depends for that matter. Whether the believers were at prayer, as they were, at least intermittently throughout the day, practising regular fasts, or serving the poor, they were essentially turning away from self and towards God. They were doing this as they turned to him directly in prayer and indirectly through the neighbour in need. In doing this they were practising the repentance that St Peter had called upon everyone to practise on the first Pentecost Day, so they could receive the Holy Spirit whom he and the other Apostles had received before them. The message was simple; henceforth the Holy Spirit who raised Jesus from the dead, promised to raise everybody from the dead and into Christ's life, to experience there the endless loving that flowed to and fro between him and his Father for all eternity. But this promise depended on a continual human response. This would infallibly happen, so long as personal and daily repentance, practised both inside and outside of prayer, embodied the desire to receive him.

* * *

There was a change in plans after the Thursday talks, as Peter accepted the parish priest's invitation to stay overnight. I think he wanted to speak to Peter alone. Peter was delighted to accept the invitation because it enabled him to visit the Tower of London the following morning where several of his recusant ancestors were imprisoned. He then made a pilgrimage to Tyburn, near Marble Arch, where they were executed, and spent the afternoon at prayer in Tyburn Convent, built as a memorial to the heroic sacrifices of the English martyrs. When we arrived for the evening talks on the Friday, it was to find that an enterprising parishioner had fitted up a large video screen in the hall beneath the church for the overflow who could not fit into the Church. It was needed!

Chapter 10

A Matter of Life and Death

(Peter's ninth talk)

When he was only twenty-eight the Russian novelist Feodor Dostoevsky was condemned to death. It was the spring of 1849. He was condemned to death for reading subversive literature and frequenting suspect gatherings of anarchists. There was nothing in these charges but at the time the Tsar, like other monarchs who had survived the aftermath of the French revolution, was still paranoid. Two days before Christmas he was taken to the place of execution. The prison yard where he was to meet his death, was arranged with funereal decorations to suit the occasion and strike further terror into the condemned. The whole thing was a farce, a pantomime ordered by the Tsar. It seemed to appeal to his obscure sense of theatre. As the executioners raised their rifles the procedure was suddenly interrupted by a messenger from the palace with a reprieve - the charade was over. The sentence was commuted to eight years' hard labour in Siberia. Later, Dostoevsky said that day, 23 December 1849, was the happiest day of his life, for on that day he experienced both death and resurrection. It influenced him for the rest of his life.

It was the same for those first Christians who came out of the pool where they had died with Christ, died to their old selves and to the world they now rejected. It was this death that enabled them to enter into a new life in Christ to whom they totally committed themselves, as they were signed with Chrism. When Jesus rose from the dead he was wearing a shining white garment. To express their new identity, after their anointing the newcomers were clothed with a shining white garment too, which they would wear for a week and then reverently retain to remind them of the new life they received from the Risen One.

His glorified life did not cease to flow onto and into them after the ceremony. It continued, not only on every day, but at every moment of their lives. Now they were dead to their old selves and to their old life they were free to live for the truth and to bear witness to the truth as never before.

Some years ago I saw a film, called *Last Holiday.* The protagonist in the film played by Alec Guinness, was a salesman for agricultural machinery. On being told that he only had three months to live he sold his home, cashed in his insurance policies and went to spend his final days in a five-star hotel on the South Coast of England. While putting on the first dinner jacket he ever bought he suddenly became frightened. He had never stayed in a place like this, never mixed with the great and the good before. He felt socially inferior. He was just about to pack his bags to leave when a thought struck him. What did it matter anymore, he was as good as dead, dead to the world of social class, and dead to all that previously intimidated him. He not only mixed with those he would once have considered his social superiors but he spoke to them bluntly, telling the truth to those who never heard it before. He prevented the divorce of newly married aristocrats by telling them to stop acting like spoiled children. He saved the livelihood of a business tycoon by telling him the design of his new combine harvester was flawed and he saved the job of the bar man by telling him how he should stand up to his boss. Because he was all but dead he could speak the truth as never before and do more good for others in a couple of weeks than he did in his life time.

This was the experience of the first Christians. They had died with Christ and to the world that intimidated them before. Their mystical dying enabled them to speak the truth loudly and clearly to all who would listen to them, and even to those who would not. If they were to pay for this with their life, what did it matter? They were dead anyway. There was only one death that really mattered to them, that they dreaded more than anything else, and that was the death that came from the separation from Christ into whose life and love they had been baptized forever.

In the first three centuries, wave after wave of persecutions meant that tens of thousands of believers became martyrs so that martyrdom came to be seen as a sacrament. They believed that in their dying the Risen One would in some way rise up and manifest himself, not just to the martyr, but to onlookers too. It might be through the smile on an old man's face, like St Polycarp as he slowly burned to death, or the ecstasy of the slave-girl Blandinia when, after being whipped and scalded she was thrown to the beasts in the arena. Carpus the deacon was actually laughing and smiling as he was being nailed to the cross. Many pagans who came to scoff were so moved that they too became believers and later martyrs themselves.

Perhaps the attitude to martyrdom amongst the early Christians can best be summed up in the story of St Perpetua and St Felicity. When the soldiers were about to throw them to the beasts, they saw that Felicity was pregnant so they held them back for another day lest the crowd were moved to compassion. When later, the jailer heard Felicity crying out with pain as she was giving birth he said, "If that is how you carry on now, what will it be like when they throw you to the wild beasts?" Then came the famous reply. "Now", she said, "It is I who suffer, then it will be another who suffers in me." Although they were both cruelly tortured before they were thrown to the wild animals to be torn to pieces they did not say a single word, deeply moving those who had only been moved by hatred before.

Not all were martyred, and these others came to see that there was another way of bearing witness to the truth and therefore dying with Christ each day. It was through what later came to be called white martyrdom, to which all Christians were called. It was the daily dying to self of those who tried to follow Christ day after day through turning to God both inside and outside of prayer, taking up and carrying their daily Cross with Jesus.

Their initial enthusiasm for their faith in the Risen Christ enabled them to pass through what later came to be called their first fervour or first enthusiasm in a comparatively short period of time, and then into what later came to be called the 'Dark Night of the Soul'.

Two things are necessary for prayer to grow beyond the stage of set formulas and petitions to the stage when it becomes a personal encounter with the most loveable man ever to walk on this earth. The first thing is to find space and time in which to stop being busy about many things so there can be time to come to terms with Christ's death, and to celebrate his continuing life and love. The second thing needed is to read and re-read every word that has been written about him in the Gospels and to read everything that he said, because what he said is addressed to us personally. These sacred words are precious so they should be read slowly and carefully to experience their impact, as you would pore over poetry to penetrate its meaning. Gradually in time and under the influence of the Holy Spirit, the faith that once seemed solely cerebral will deepen, as hearts and minds that were like stone before, soften and become porous to receive and experience the love of Christ ever more deeply.

When this happens the feelings and the emotions react as the whole personality begins to respond in a perfectly human way to the most perfect human being of all. Prayer begins to grow, to develop and deepen as in any loving relationship. It expresses itself in the language of love as it responds to the One who now seems to rise out of the sacred texts, out of history to enter into the heart and mind of the person who has persevered in prayer beyond first beginnings. As love grows and deepens into union, words finally fade away as they give way to a profound and pregnant silence. Meditation gives way to contemplation - the still, silent and loving gaze upon the One whose life we now experience within us because we have finally come to terms not only with his death, but with his Resurrection.

This period of my own spiritual development was deeply moving, and what some spiritual writers have called Acquired Contemplation, enabled my mind, my heart and my emotions to be drawn into a profound love of God that enveloped my whole being. Then, after a matter of months this new form of prayer that exhilarated me and inspired everything that I did suddenly came to an abrupt end, as it always does for those who persevere in it both deeply and daily. St Teresa of Avila said that this form of heartfelt contemplation is a brief anticipation or foretaste of what she calls the Spiritual Marriage which is for her the summit of the mystical ascent. It involves the fulfilment of the feelings, the emotions as well as the mind and the deepest spiritual desires that have inspired us from the beginning, as we are united with Christ and with his contemplation of the Father. The completion of the Christian life then, involves a union with Christ that includes, not just the mind and the soul, but the body too, encompassing the heart and all human feelings and emotions. It is far from the disembodied consummation that has been taught and sought by Gnostics and the Neoplatonists down the centuries, whose teaching has always threatened and often succeeded in distorting true Christian mystical theology.

However, before this union with God, in Christ, can take place, all these feelings and emotions, all these intellectual and spiritual desires and yearnings must be purified of all that sin and selfishness has done to corrupt and distort them. This is why, after the emotional thrills of Acquired Contemplation, a new stage takes place when those who have abandoned themselves to the mystic way are led into the dark night. Some mystical writers call this Obscure Contemplation where saints are made from the sinners who enter it. It was only after I finally retired into solitude that I made a grand entrance into this dark night.

When, after my degree I became a qualified teacher, I taught for several years at Daliburgh School on the Isle of South Uist in the Outer Hebrides. This enabled me to save enough money to try my vocation as a hermit on the remote Isle of Calvay. This was almost fifty years ago. Everything went well, better than I expected and after restoring an old house on the Island I started my first year of complete solitude. I was proud of myself and of my spiritual growth in the first few months that made me sure I had done the right thing. It was then that the bombshell hit me. The bombshell arrived in the person of my older brother. He had just arrived home from South Africa and the first thing that he did was to come out to visit me with his good news. I rejoiced with him when he told me that he was about to get married and that he wanted me to be his best man. It was when I asked after his future wife that the bombshell exploded in my mind. She was a black African, a Zulu. He admitted that our parents were not too pleased. I tried to show no surprise at all nor give any indication that I was just as shocked as they must have been. After all I was a hermit now, immersing myself in the spiritual life. How could there be any prejudice in me?

That night I didn't sleep a wink. I was appalled at my own reaction to my brother marrying a Zulu. I had written and spoken out against the hideous regime of apartheid in South Africa. I had marched with my fellow students to protest against the imprisonment of Nelson Mandela and I had boycotted the Springboks when they came to play rugby in Paris. Yet the truth was, deep down there was a racist hiding behind the facade of a white liberal. Then I had to ask myself if I was prejudiced against other races. What if he wanted to marry a Chinese or Japanese girl, an Indian or a West Indian girl? I was horrified to find just how deep my racism went. One of the advantages, or rather the disadvantages of choosing to live in solitude, is that there was nowhere to go, nowhere to hide, and nothing to do to avoid facing the real man that was hidden beneath all the religious fervour that had blinded me to the truth. If there was some place to hide, I might have been able to avoid seeing that I was not just prejudiced against other races, but other classes too, and other religions and… the list went on and on.

I was forced to see the truth about the man to whom others were beginning to write, to ask help in their spiritual life. How could I possibly keep the second commandment to love others as Jesus had done and still does? St John said, "A man who does not love the brother that he can see, cannot love God that he has never seen," so what hope would there be for me. He even went further saying, "Anyone who says, 'I love God', and hates his brother, is a liar" (1 John 4:20). After my brother left things got worse when I was forced to confront the murky world of my miserable motives, past, present and to come, together with the sinfulness and the selfishness that not only determined how I behaved towards others, but how I behaved towards God too. Was I fooling myself? Was I wasting my time pretending to be a man of God when I was no more than what Jesus had called a whited sepulchre, all white and wonderful on the outside, but full of corruption and decay within?

I was ready to pack and leave rather than remain to be no more than a hypocrite. But first I thought I owed it to my spiritual director to let her know why I had decided to go; after all she had been supporting me for many years while I was teaching and trying to maintain the semblance of the spiritual life to which I aspired. Agnes was almost thirty years older than I and she had been teaching at the same school where I had been teaching. She was simply a living saint who lived in a caravan on church land so close to the church that many people called her an anchorite. I already had several spiritual directors before, but none like her. Strangely enough I met her in passing, years before when a mutual friend introduced me to her in the Basilica of Santa Maria degli Angeli in Assisi. My friend told me that she was a spiritual daughter of Padre Pio and would go to him twice a year to receive his spiritual direction, a privilege reserved for only a chosen few. She told me that she was a teacher in Scotland, but not that she taught in the Outer Hebrides. Imagine my surprise when she was the first person that I bumped into after giving my first French class. Although her bi-annual trips to Italy were well known, nobody knew where she went, nor why they suddenly came to an abrupt end in 1968, the year Padre Pio died. Although I was the only one in the school who knew, I did not tell anyone, as she obviously wished to keep it secret, nor did I ever mention it to her, although I grew close to her as my spiritual mentor.

When I told Agnes, what happened to me and why I decided to go rather than to remain and become a hypocrite, she laughed at me before apologising for her unprofessional behaviour. If everyone decided to give up the spiritual life when they saw the truth about themselves, we would never have the great saints and mystics who have inspired us for almost two thousand years, she told me. She insisted that what I saw within myself was inside all of us, even though the vast majority of people are unable to see this, and spend their lives treating others by their own inbuilt prejudices rather than the content of their character, as Martin Luther King put it. The whole point of the spiritual life is to let the Spirit in, which is the love of God that fully resides in Jesus. She told me how so many saints and mystics insisted that God gave them a glimpse into hell that horrified them. Where did God take them to show them this infernal place? Where was it? Was it in this world or was it in the next, in this dimension or some other, in this universe or in some parallel universe? The truth of the matter is that it was in no other place than within themselves. If you remember, that is why St Catherine of Siena said, "The trouble with the world is me," because she knew that the hell she had been shown was actually within her. The ancient theme of the 'Harrowing of Hell' describes how, after his death, or his glorification as St John called it, Jesus began the work of defeating the same power of evil that had attempted to destroy him, in others, both those who had preceded him and those who were to follow him.

The prolonged and unprecedented eclipse of the sun that plunged the world into darkness during Christ's terrible death on the cross, replicated the inner blackness that plunged his heart, his mind and his soul into pitch beyond pitch of anguish, grief and unutterable agony. No other will experience the hideous horrors that he experienced as the power of evil engulfed him and forced out of him that primeval *cri de coeur*, "My God, my God, why have you forsaken me?" It received an immediate response that raised him from the malign maelstrom that lay siege to every part of his being, and into the world where the goodness of God's glory enfolded him, obliterating the evil that threatened to destroy him before.

The very moment after this evil threatened to obliterate him, was the moment when he descended from the heaven that he so recently entered, into Hell. Now, the love that had done to death the evil that so recently threatened to annihilate him, could also annihilate the evil in those who went before him. This is the meaning of the descent into Hell as depicted by the earliest icons. The Aramaic word *Sheol* was used to describe the place where those who preceded Christ, waited for his coming. Misunderstandings arose when the word Hell was used in translation to describe this place of waiting. The Jews used the word *Gehenna* to describe the place of eternal punishment that was full of flame and fury. It took its name from a valley near Jerusalem where some early kings of Juda were said to have burned their own children in sacrifice. The custom of misusing the word Hell to describe *Sheol*, has created an ambiguity that has prevented us from understanding fully the meaning of Christ's descent into Hell to bring salvation to the decent, the good, and the just, who preceded him. The whole purpose of his descent was to infuse into them the love that he now shared with his Father, so that they could rise in, with and through him to enjoy what God created them for in the first place.

However, Christ's descent into Hell has a further mystical

meaning that is relevant to us all here and now in our daily spiritual lives. For Christ is at all times poised to release that same love, to do to death the evil that is within us, now. This is the fuller and mystical meaning of the descent into Hell, and of the icon that can remind us of it. It reminds us too of our responsibility to respond to the same love that destroyed the power of evil that once threatened to destroy Christ. What was done in him, will also be done in us, if we are only patient and persevere in the mystic way for long enough. Here we are gradually purified sufficiently to be taken up in, with and through him, into God's glory, beginning in this life and continuing in the next.

When we look on the icon of Christ's descent into Hell, then, we are not just reminded of what once happened to those who preceded Christ, but what will happen to us now if we allow his love to do in us what has already been done in them. It is in this way that the prayer that we make to be delivered from all evil is answered. This icon is the best possible reminder for all who are travelling on the mystic way, of how we receive from Christ all the divine love that is necessary for the power of evil to be destroyed within us. Then, how our weak human love is infused with the divine to enable us to travel in, with and through him to the Paradise that Jesus promised to the good thief moments before he died. I refer to the good thief because it is never too late to start again, no matter how many times we have failed, no matter whether it is the last second of extra time, or whether we have our whole life before us. Agnes told me that I had my whole life before me to journey onwards toward the heaven that, as Dante insists in his *Inferno*, passes through Hell. She gave me a copy of an ancient Icon depicting Christ and his Harrowing of Hell that still hangs on the wall of my hermitage. But before I left she explained the difference between the descent into Hell that immediately followed Christ's death, and his continual descent into the Hell that is within us all. This second descent began after the Ascension, after the sending of the Holy Spirit on the first

Pentecost, and it is ongoing.

Christ was only able to descend into Hell to bring salvation to those who died before him, because the evil that assailed him throughout his life, and most particularly as he was dying on the cross, was completely obliterated by the power of love that then completely possessed him. Now the evil that Christ had fought against and defeated, did not come from his lower nature like ours, but from our fellow human beings who hated him and who were bent on destroying him in the most humiliating, degrading and painful way possible. When you look on his lamentable and lacerated body on the cross you are looking at what evil can do to goodness. But that is not all, because his sensitive body became porous, permeable as it were, so that the evil visited on him, entered his mind and heart so that he had to experience a more terrible dark night than anyone else before or since.

"When we first encounter the Holy Spirit after our first baptism, he fills us with joy, with a spiritual *joie de vivre* to set us on our way and sustain us, up to and into the second baptism of fire. This baptism of fire, to which St John the Baptist referred, "He will baptise you with the Holy Spirit and fire" (Matthew 3:11), is an ongoing baptism given to destroy the evil that is within us, the evil that comes from the Hell within our inmost being. When his disciples wanted to enjoy the rewards of the Kingdom that Jesus proclaimed, he said, "You do not know what you are asking" (Matthew 20:22), and he went on to ask them if they were prepared to be baptised with the baptism of suffering that he had to endure, the suffering involved in carrying a daily cross. They had to think again. The suffering involved in this second baptism is the suffering that must be endured as a spiritual teenager learns to grow up and face the truth within that would prevent the maturity to which he or she aspires. Deep down within us and determining all we say and do, without us realising it, are powers initially meant for our good that have been perverted: The power to possess, to procreate and protect, the power to own and to make a home, the power to belong to, to share, and to care, and so many others. Hell is born within as these desires are perverted by a warped and self-centred nature, becoming an inferno when they are allowed free reign. This is the Hell that needs to be harrowed by the Holy Spirit as we allow Christ to descend within us and through his love, to destroy the evil within, so that we can finally be victorious as Christ was victorious on the first Easter day.

"This is the theological explanation of what is happening to you," Agnes insisted, before going on to explain how I must continue and persevere in prayer despite all that would happen to me in the purification of the second baptism that was just beginning. "When perseverance stops so does purification, and when purification stops you don't just stop going forward, you start going backwards!"

It was then that she gave me what she called the great secret of the mystical life that the first Christians learnt from both the teaching and example of Jesus. Like all first principles it is deceptively simple, but because it has become a pious platitude, its profound significance is rarely taken as seriously as it should be. It is simply this: *It is in giving that we receive*. The whole of Christ's life involved a continual giving, living and loving for others. This was made possible by the help and strength that he received in prayer. It was this that enabled him to sustain the other-considering, single-minded mindset that opened him at all times to receive the mystical life and love that comes from God. To follow him, the first Christians tried to build up a daily sequence of spiritual exercises. Their day began by making their morning offering to sacralise all they said and did each day, so that like Christ before them, they would practise their priesthood in and through all they said and did. To sustain this new worship, "in spirit and truth" (John 4:23), they would seek the same help and strength that Jesus had sought through both brief and more prolonged periods of prayer, to help them procure the 'prayer without ceasing' that characterised his life. It was this that enabled them to do ordinary things extraordinarily well, because they were all done, not just by human love alone, but by a human loving that was surcharged by the divine. This is the meaning of the mystical life. It is this life lived at all times within the mystical body of Christ, practising that mystical giving, living and loving for others, that characterised Jesus' life in the past, to enable them to enter into his mystical life in the present, and to enjoy his glorious life in the future. It is here that all will be seen, all will be understood, and all will be loved in the place where, "All shall be well, and all manner of things shall be well" (Julian of Norwich), as they were never well before.

"So far", said Agnes, "I have been encouraging you to come to know Jesus as he once was before the Resurrection. This activated within you a love for him that yearned for union, the union that everyone desires with the person they love. Now it is this love that enabled your spiritual journey to change course, because, although you may be able to love someone who once lived on earth, you cannot be united to him no matter how strong your love for him might be. That is why in the last few months your love has been redirected to Jesus as he is now, the Jesus who became his full and complete self after he was reunited with his Father. Now it is this love, transformed into human loving in the Glorified Jesus that has been trying to enter into you, to descend into you, to purify you of the evil that prevents the union that you desire more than anything else. I have been trying to explain to you that this is the reason why the emotion-filled meditations that you once enjoyed have gone. It is because your desire for union with Jesus has been transferred from the Jesus who once was in history, to the Jesus as he is now in glory. The deep feelings and emotions that once supported your desire for union before, support you no more. Now it is directed to Jesus as he is now in a pure and simple desire called contemplation, or mystical contemplation.

"To begin with, this contemplation brings a certain profound contentment, until it successfully enables the Holy Spirit to reach out to you from Jesus where he resides. He then begins the process of trying to draw you up into him. But first he meets opposition from the person St Paul calls the 'old man' who still lives within you. It is now that the light of the Holy Spirit highlights in you all that prevents you from entering into union with God. To begin with the light of the Holy Spirit brings only darkness, the darkness of seeing yourself as you really are. That is why St Gregory of Nyssa calls this light a ray of darkness, and why St John of the Cross calls this state the dark night of the soul. In this darkness, you have to see yourself as you really are, and that is why St Catherine of Siena calls it the house of self-knowledge. In other words, now is the time when, in order to progress in the spiritual life, you have to be purified.

"Martin Luther King once said, 'Life's most persistent and urgent question is, what you are doing for others.' We cannot do anything for others that will permanently change their lives for the better until we have been changed ourselves. That is why the great saints could change the lives of others, but only after they were themselves changed, in the purgatory on earth to which you are now being called. I knew that the heaven on earth that you expected to experience in your solitude would turn into its opposite, but I didn't expect it to begin so quickly and so dramatically. But then I did not expect your brother's visit and the effect that this was to have on you any more than you did yourself. However, it has happened, enabling you to see in a matter of moments, what usually takes place in many months or even years. Thank God for it, because it means that your purification has begun and begun in earnest. Please take heart, it means that you are on the right path. Go back and allow the Holy Spirit to continue the purification that he has already begun, or else you will never be changed, and if you are not changed, what can you do for the world that you have been called to change in your solitude? The Desert Fathers used to insist that you do not go into solitude for yourself alone, but for the world that you have left, only to return to it through the love generated by your prayer. The ancient hermits used to say that one wall of their hermitage must remain open to the world they have come to serve though their solitary prayer.

"You see the evil that we read about daily in our newspapers or see on our television screens is but the outward projection of the evil that is firstly conceived and spawned within the human heart and mind. That is why, as I have just said, St Catherine of Siena insisted that, 'The trouble with the world is me'. It is all too easy to blame God or ask why he does not prevent evil when it tears our lives apart or the lives of the innocent for whom we can do nothing but offer sympathy. The truth of the matter is that God is at all times poised to possess anyone who is open to receive the love that only he can give. It is this love that brings the profound inner peace that Jesus promised on the night before he died, so that it can be shared with the world that will always be at war without it. However, love cannot be forced on anyone who does not freely choose to receive it. If we are eaten up with hatred or jealousy, or possessed by pride or prejudice it is we, not God who are responsible for destroying the peace and harmony that he wants to bring to the world through us.

"St Catherine of Siena saw so clearly what she should do to enable God to make her into the greatest politician for peace in her time. She went into the inner room to give prolonged periods of time to prayer, to enable the love of God to purify her of all the evil that could prevent her receiving the peace she was able to share with the world around her. The message is so simple that it needs the simplicity of a child to see what cynics can only scoff at. We are not helpless, we can do something to combat the evil that we see in the world around us, if we are only prepared to go like St Catherine into the inner room, into solitude. It is only here that we can seriously turn to the only One who can first bring to us what he would bring to the world that he now chooses to serve through us. The trouble is, arrogant human beings believe they can change the world themselves, if only people would listen to them, and they become angry when no one does. That is why, as E F Schumacher puts it in his book *Small is beautiful,* 'People become angry when they are told that the restoration of society must come from within and not from without'.

"St John of the Cross said that ninety percent of those who come to the point of purification in the spiritual life pack up their prayer life and sometimes even their faith. This was not the case in the early Church, because those who went into the night, and that was the vast majority of them, were surrounded by many mentors. They knew the way ahead from their own experience and so were able to explain to them what was happening, encouraging them to keep persevering in carrying their daily cross in prayer. Their prayers and their deepest desires were answered and the Holy Spirit was drawing them up into the Risen Christ, where they were not only being fitted into his life, but into his contemplation, into his mystical loving of his Father."

Agnes encouraged me to go back and begin again, allowing the Holy Spirit to continue the inner purification without which my deepest desires and longings could not be satisfied. She gave me two books to help me. One was *The Dark Night of the Soul* to help me understand what was going on within me, and why. However, she told me that I must only read the first part, *The Dark Night of the Senses* until she told me otherwise. The other book was *The Cloud of Unknowing,* to help show me how to pray in the dark night.

When I returned to my hermitage I sat down and reflected on all she had said to me. My mind went back to an event that happened several years before when I went to confession to Padre Pio at his friary in San Giovanni Rotondo. His words that I forgot in all the turmoil that afflicted me, came back into my mind with absolute clarity. "God has called you to become a prophet, Peter. It is a great gift, a great privilege, but it carries with it a great and grave responsibility. A prophet must speak to a world that would rather not hear the message that he brings. All prophets have first to be purified themselves before they can help others. Like the One you wish to follow, you must spend many hidden years where all the prophets are prepared before they return to the world. One day in God's good time, not yours, when he thinks you are ready, not when you do, there is a work for you to perform. God will do his part if you do yours, and your part is to pray, trust and not to worry."

Before I left him I asked him to pray for me and he said he would. I believe that prayer of his for me was answered and was embodied in Agnes, his spiritual daughter. She not only helped me at the most crucial moment of my life, but for very many years to come. It was Agnes who made me realise that for the first Christians, knowledge of this mystical purification was not the preserve of a few, as it was to become later. It was commonplace knowledge once Christianity had spread and gradually deepened with the years. It did not need to be written down in mystical tomes and hidden from all but the few, it was open to all because all needed it, if their hearts' desires were to be fulfilled. Nobody wrote about it at length, as they did later, because it was assumed. That is why I have to use the writings of later mystical writers to show how these first Christians were fully fitted into Christ and into his contemplative loving of his Father. It was precisely because they were surrounded by fellow travellers that they made speedy headway in the dark night where the symbolic dying they underwent at baptism was transposed into reality. This dying process and the transformation this brought about, eventually enabled them to say, as St Paul said before them, "And I live now not with my own life but with the life of Christ who lives in me" (Galatians 2:20).

I would like to explain how this new mystical identity in a

believer is brought about, so there can be no misunderstandings. All that God does though Jesus is to love. It is this love that first brings about the destruction of all that is bad in a person, so that he or she can be filled by all that is good. The result is that a new person is born, the person who was once symbolically made at one with Christ at baptism, becomes at one with him in reality and for all to see. Everyone did see, and that is why a pagan kingdom was converted into a Christian kingdom in such a short period of time. Secular historians are still baffled and perplexed about how such an obscure heretical Jewish sect could grow so rapidly to transform the greatest pagan empire the world has ever known, into a Christian empire and at such speed. They are baffled and perplexed, because they only see and understand external historical causes and effects. The real cause lay beneath the surface, in a strange mystical crèche where other Christs were formed.

Before new converts were led into this crèche however, they usually went through a phase of high octane spiritual awareness as I did. Their feelings and affections were set alight as the experience of The Mysterion – God's secret plan, embodied in Jesus – struck their emotions and generated powerful heartfelt responses. Christian meditation on the life of Jesus and his personal love for us that generates acquired contemplation usually takes place behind the closed doors of a personal prayer life and came to be called first fervour or first enthusiasm. In more modern times this stage of prayer for beginners has manifested itself, not just behind the closed doors of a personal prayer life, but out in the open, as Christian groups gather together for communal prayer.

Those who practise this new form of highly charged prayer have come to be called charismatics, belonging to what is called the Charismatic movement or renewal. The movement in modern times dates back to the beginning of the twentieth century to Pentecostalists in the USA. However, it moved through the Anglican into the Catholic Church, at least in England, in the late

1960s, where I experienced it for myself. I remember my brother taking me to a Charismatic prayer meeting in North London to hear people speaking in tongues, being slain in the spirit and receiving healing, although I have never come across the sort of miraculous healing that you find in the Gospels. I found the whole phenomenon very interesting and the experience led me to reread Monsignor Ronald Knox's book *Enthusiasm*, which he considered his life's work. It comprised a study of emotionally charged movements since early Christianity, and should be read by anybody interested in understanding this subject. The claim of modern charismatics is that they are but a contemporary embodiment of similar groups that were to be found in the early church. However, what happened to them, because they suddenly disappeared without a trace? Did the Holy Spirit suddenly decide that enough was enough and deserted them? On the contrary he decided that they were *bona fide* Christians yearning to be united with Christ. That is why they disappeared from view. They did not disappear because the Holy Spirit deserted them, but because he led them on to be purified of all the sin and selfishness hidden beneath all the spiritual euphoria that blinded them to what had to be stripped away so they could be more fully united with Christ They were described as the saints in the letters of St Paul. Their need for purification is detailed in the first nine chapters of *The Dark Night of the Soul* by St John of the Cross, made a Doctor of the Church for his unparalleled spiritual insight into this mystical purification.

Although modern charismatics are still inspired by the Holy Spirit, their spiritual development can be prevented for two main reasons that were not experienced by their early antecedents. The spiritual enthusiasm of those first charismatics was not just ignited at community gatherings, but further inflamed every day as they practised the intense daily prayer that was given to them by Jesus. Their desire for union with him was therefore intensified and brought to a spiritual high point sooner rather than later. In its recent manifestation of charismatic renewal, many tend to depend almost exclusively on weekly or monthly meetings to generate the fervour that is rarely supported by the ardent daily prayer that was commonplace in the early church. The second reason why their journey can be halted is because mentors or spiritual directors who were commonplace in the early Church are no longer as commonplace today, indeed they are a rarity. The result is that, as St John of the Cross put it, ninety percent of those who go into the dark night run away because of ignorance of their predicament as nobody to whom they turn seems to understand them. The first experience of a person led into the night is that the love that led them there highlights all that separates them from the one to whom they crave to be united. They believe therefore that the Holy Spirit has deserted them, and they either return to being just the nominal Christians they were before their charismatic fervour, or even pack up their faith altogether to become agnostics, or worse. Before any deep and lasting renewal can take place in the Church these problems must be addressed, not just for charismatics, but for the silent majority who are also led into the dark night through personal and private prayer where they experience an unsettling and inexplicable malaise that nobody to whom they turn for help seems to understand.

When a person has undergone a sufficient purification to experience the love that has been purifying them, they begin to experience moments when that love becomes tangible. To begin with, sin and selfishness only enables that love to shine dimly, but gradually it becomes strong enough to lift a person up to experience the first touches of God to reassure them of his presence. Then they can be lifted up to an ever deeper absorption into God to the point of ecstasy and beyond, to what mystical writers have called the Mystical Marriage or the Transforming Union in the Western Christian tradition, or Divinisation or *Theosis* in Eastern Christianity. As love raises a person to ever deeper experiences of the love of God, it also fills them with wisdom and with all the virtues that you find so perfectly embodied in Jesus while he was on earth.

When I was learning how to become a Franciscan hermit, I met a real hermit in Franciscan Italy who had been a university Professor in Nuclear Physics. He gave me many good examples that shed light on the spiritual life. I remember him explaining how the love of God is like a shaft of light. Isaac Newton discovered that although light is colourless, it contains within itself all the colours of the spectrum. They remain unseen until they strike a prism that reflects and refracts them in such a way that all the colours of the rainbow are clearly visible for all to see. It is the same with the love of God. When that love is allowed to shaft down into the human heart, it first purifies it, and then it refines it into a prism that refracts and reflects God's love into every part of the human personality, becoming visible to onlookers by the way it manifests itself in human behaviour.

The Christlike care and compassion, the superhuman quality of selflessness and sacrifice, and the heroic virtues that are generated, are but the outward expression of the divine life possessing them from within. The exercise of the human heart in prayer allows the divine life in, so that it is transposed through human being, into human acting. Not only does this love further strengthen the muscles of the heart, but it opens that heart out from the inside to receive even more of the love tit has already received. In this way true Christians are fashioned, enabling them to return the love received in kind to the One from whom it came in the first place, as they are being fitted into the Risen Lord. The profound interchange of love that takes place here bears fruit in all they say and do, for the world that God is now able to reach by transforming them into other Christs.

It is only as weak human love is suffused and surcharged by the divine, that we are now able to love God with our whole heart, with our whole mind and strength, and to love our neighbour as Jesus loves them. In this way, by keeping the greatest, they keep all the commandments, that a promise can be kept. The promise was made by Christ at the Last Supper, when he promised that whosoever keeps these commandments would be loved in such a way that the Father, the Son and the Holy Spirit would make a home within them, so that the community of God's own life can dwell on earth in the person who is redeemed by love.

As this whole process of transformation, or Divinisation is taking place, the mystic begins to experience the love they are receiving, sometimes to shattering degrees of intensity, and with a regularity that finally becomes permanent, as the Trinity of love which is God is finally homed within them for good. This is true contemplation, a pure gift of God that cannot be generated by any man-made methods or techniques from the East or from the West. Those who suggest otherwise are simply deceiving you, as they have been deceived themselves. This is how those first Christians were reformed into the living image and likeness of Jesus Christ, so that all who met them, met him through them. It was in this way that the ancient pagan world was introduced to Jesus Christ, in and through those who followed him in life, and those who followed him in death too. If what was done then, is done now, then the pagan world that we live in today can be converted too. But this conversion can only happen when those who call themselves Christians are themselves converted into other Christs in the same crèche that converted their illustrious forebears.

In the first Christian centuries no one sought to live for themselves, but for God and for his honour and glory alone. All authentic prayer ends up here, as did the prayer of Jesus. That is why the first Christians learnt to seek God for himself alone, not for what they could get out of him which was an unfortunate development which came later, most particularly thanks to the influence of a Greek form of esoteric spirituality called Neoplatonism. However, as I have already mentioned, you do find expressions like 'sober inebriation' or 'spiritual intoxication', used by the early Greek Fathers, which express the profound spiritual feelings experienced when a believer is being drawn up into mystical prayer. Words like *Apatheia* or *Ataraxia,* borrowed from Stoicism are also used, to refer to the inner peace and tranquility experienced at the outset of pure contemplation. The Greek fathers also used words like 'spiritual transportation' to refer to ever more intense and ever higher experiences of God's love, like that described by St Paul when he tells how he was lifted into a mystical trance where he encountered Christ (Acts 22:18). He also writes about, "The visions and revelations that I have had from the Lord," and how he was raised up into what he called the third heaven, and, "was caught up into Paradise and heard things which cannot and must not be put into human language" (2 Corinthians 12:1-52). These are some of the first written attempts to describe what were later detailed by St Teresa of Avila in her masterwork *Interior Castle.* However, I have only mentioned them to make the point that they were only very rarely used. Why? Because the whole emphasis of early Christian spirituality was not on oneself, but on God, and on his good pleasure, not one's own. The faithful did not seek out mystical experiences to give themselves pleasure, they sought out God to give him pleasure. Their whole aim and the whole object and direction of their spiritual life was not to seek their own honour and glory, but the honour and glory of God. It was in doing this that they, like any lover who lives for another, forgets themselves. Then, freed from self-absorption and the misery that this brings, they experience the joy of living for another.

Whenever individuals seek pleasure for its own sake or rather for their own sake, then the happiness that they hoped it would bring usually eludes them. This is what eventually began to happen when, after several centuries of seeking God for himself, the influence of Neoplatonism began to encourage believers to seek mystical experience for its own sake or their own sake, for their own personal pleasure and gratification. When this insidious trend began to infiltrate Christian prayer in subsequent centuries, otherwise good and well-meaning believers were encouraged to adopt alien forms of prayer, culled from philosophies from the Far East which they believed were in perfect conformity with the Christian mystics whose teaching they misinterpreted.

In her book *Praying with the Mystics,* Annetta Maguire writes how, for years, she became a spiritual tourist going nowhere. "I spent many years studying Eastern philosophy, practising Transcendental Meditation and reading literature from the Vedanta tradition. Despite this study I found that I was, in fact, just going around in circles." Finally, when she discovered the Christian mystics, she was able to free herself from the roundabout that was leading her nowhere. "Through their writings they have left a map which led them to union with God. Reading their words made it possible to appreciate that their step-by-step directions were as relevant today as they were then." Unlike so many others over the last thirty or more years, she found her way back to the authentic Christian tradition.

Sadly, there are many modern examples of seeking to Christianise Eastern forms of meditation, which I call the mantra movements. Some time ago I visited one of their centres. After listening to several talks and asking questions of both members and speakers I became disturbed to find otherwise good and committed Christians believing that simply by reciting what was called a mantra they could be taken up virtually instantly into mystical contemplation. By contemplation I mean the contemplation described by St Teresa of Avila and practised from the earliest days by the great Christian mystics. For them mystical contemplation meant being taken up and into the same contemplation that Jesus experienced while he was on earth, and which he now continues to experience in heaven. That this sublime experience is possible, is one of the most astounding, astonishing and awe-inspiring mysteries of our faith. However, from the very beginning it has always been taught that it is a gift of God, given to those whose perseverance and constancy has been tested in many years of deep spiritual purification. The belief that man-made methods or techniques can instantly lead a person into such sublime experiences would be simply risible, if it was not so spiritually perfidious. Sadly, many hundreds of thousands of decent and sincere Christians have been deceived into believing that this is the way to mystical contemplation as experienced in the Christian tradition from the beginning.

My sister-in-law, a doctor and psychiatrist, has for many years used techniques similar to those used by these movements in her work. They are a great help to enable patients to attain a certain inner peace and repose. These effects can be attained by anyone who needs a psychological technique to slow down, to become still and to experience mindfulness or inner recollection. However, if those who use a mantra, whether it is a Christian or Buddhist mantra, believe that the inner peace that this generates is mystical contemplation, then they are being deceived. Sadly, they are being deceived by priests, religious, and monks whose own ignorance underlines the present malaise in the true understanding of the spiritual life. I spoke to many people who have been saying their mantras daily for over twenty years, one for over thirty-five. They were all sure that it helped them and still does, and I believe them. It has certainly helped their mental equilibrium and that is undoubtedly good, but it has not helped them to advance on the mystical journey. To believe that endlessly repeating a mantra will almost instantly lead a person into mystical contemplation is to believe in magic, or in the old heresy of Pelagianism.

I was given a book by the promoter of one of these movements. The author learnt his method of meditation when he was working for the British Colonial Service in the Far East. In his own words the essence of his teaching is this. "When we begin to meditate we must say the mantra for the whole twenty or thirty minutes of our meditation. I repeat this to re-emphasise what is essential and perhaps the only advice worth giving about meditation which is simply to say your mantra." When he later became a monk he began to study the Christian tradition of prayer. He did this, on his own admission, to seek confirmation that what he had learnt from his guru was in total conformity with the Christian tradition. Inevitably he took texts out of context, misinterpreting and explaining them to endorse the method of meditation that he found helpful. He does not use the word meditation as used in the Christian tradition, but in the way it is used in the Eastern tradition, as a means to sedate the mind and tune in to the transcendental. Despite protestations to the contrary this is completely alien to the Christian mystical tradition

The Vatican Document, *Jesus Christ the Bearer of the Water of Life – A Christian reflection on the "New Age"* published in 2003 makes it clear that the so called Christian mantra movements have one thing in common. "Their meditations are self-centred, directed towards attaining feelings of inner relaxation, peace and mindfulness, and are totally opposite to authentic Christian prayer."

Another quotation from this document makes it clear that, "Christian prayer is not an exercise in self-contemplation, stillness and self-emptying, but a dialogue of love, one which "implies an attitude of conversion, a flight from 'self' to the 'You' of God" (see also Catechism of the Catholic Church, 2705-2719).

The recitations taught by the mantra movements are not found anywhere in the practice of our first Christian forebears who simply followed the example of Jesus that they put into practice every day of their lives. They continually committed themselves to love and serve God throughout every moment of every day, without any thought of what was in it for themselves. God and God alone was the object of their prayer, not what they could get out of him by way of exhilarating and esoteric experiences.

The byproduct of such selfless giving of themselves to God, was rewarded by God giving himself to them as he did to Jesus. Like Jesus then, they began to experience the love of God that St Paul said surpasses our understanding. We are so used to seeing Jesus depicted on the cross that we forget that he described himself as a man of joy, the joy that he promised for those who would follow him. It was this that enabled them to become infused with the inner peace that at all times possessed him. No wonder people flocked to the early Christians, begging to be a part of the brotherhood and sisterhood that was so alive and vibrant, so full of joy and peace. This joy and peace was the fruit of the deep mystical experience of God's presence that was generated within them, the natural by-product of living and loving each day for the honour and glory of God. It was an intimate and private matter, as is the love that bonds a husband and wife together. The experience of true love is only ever given, not to the person seeking pleasurable experiences for themselves, but to the person seeking to give pleasure, fulfilment and happiness to the one they love. The great mystery of God's love for us is that, although he demands that we love him by giving him praise, thanksgiving, blessing and all honour and glory, it is not for his benefit but for ours. It does nothing, nor can it ever do anything to further his own happiness, his own fulfilment or his own honour and glory. And herein lies the secret of God's selfless plan for us all. For it is in encouraging us to love him, although he gains nothing for himself, that we receive everything that we could possibly hope or dream for, "The height and the depth; the breadth and the length of God's love that is beyond all understanding" (Ephesians 3:19).

Chapter 11

The Primacy of Love

(Peter's tenth talk)

A most unusual idea inspired by the English actor, Alec McCowan, hit the London stage in 1978 when, in a personal *tour de force,* he devised and delivered a solo performance of the complete text of St Mark's gospel. Against all predictions he performed to a full house night after night. When the same thing happened in New York, where it was performed at the Marymount Manhattan and Playhouse theatres, a Catholic impresario had an idea. He approached Kieron Moore who had made a name for himself playing Count Vronsky in the film version of Anna Karenina opposite Vivien Leigh. He asked Moore, who was a devout Catholic, if he would star in a similar stage production, but this time in a rendering of the final discourse of Jesus at the Last Supper. "It cannot be done," said Moore, "and it most certainly will not be attempted by me. Only one person could utter such deep and profound mystical truths, and that is Jesus himself, and when they are read they can only be read and understood by those who are inspired by the same Spirit who inspired him. It would be all but sacrilegious to turn it into a theatrical production for financial gain."

The sublime and awe-inspiring plan of God for all of us to share in his glory was not detailed fully by Jesus during his life on earth. He only had less than three years to explain to his compatriots the revolutionary transformation to their religious beliefs that God had sent him to bring to fulfilment. At the same time he had to instruct the Apostles to bring his work to fruition after he had gone. That he was going to leave them he knew well, but there is evidence to show that even he was surprised at how quickly the powers of evil were organised to destroy him.

The way in which so much esoteric and mystical teaching was crammed into the discourse that Jesus gave to his closest followers at the Last Supper seems to support this theory. Knowing that his time had come, and that he still had not finished their training, he promised to send the Holy Spirit after his death to make everything plain to them. Now the Holy Spirit does not only transmit the love of God, but his truth too, the fullness of the truth that the untimely death of Jesus prevented him from explaining as fully as he would have wished. That is why it is only later that the full plan of God for humanity is understood by the Apostles, and explained in their teaching and in their writings, although almost everything is to be found in the sublime teaching given at the Last Supper.

When I first started to meditate on the scriptures I began with the synoptic Gospels, reading the story of Christ's life, and his teaching about his Father's love for us. I came to understand the awesome and awe-inspiring truth that by allowing the Holy Spirit to permeate and possess me, I could be taken up into the body of Jesus here and now. It would be here and here alone that I would come to experience, even in this life, something of the mutual loving that bonded him to his Father, as a foretaste of what was to come in the next. Once these sublime truths began to register deep down within me, I could not but keep turning to the profound mystical teaching of Jesus at the Last Supper, reading and mulling over these elevated, exalted and ecstatic truths again and again. In the end, I found that all I wanted to do in my meditation was to pore over those last chapters of St John's Gospel beginning with Chapter thirteen.

It was in slowly and prayerfully pondering on Jesus, and the profound mystical teaching that he gave to the Apostles at the Last Supper, that my whole being was filled with an otherworldly love that enveloped me time and time again when I came to prayer. This led to a simple contemplative gaze centred on God. If a relationship is to deepen we need to learn to stop talking and listen, to be silent and to be loved. I wanted to be silent and to listen, to be still and to bathe in the love that permeated and penetrated my whole being. This lasted for many weeks. Then one day when I came to prayer once more, eager to experience what I had come to believe would be my prayer for the rest of my life, it suddenly came to an end. At the time I had no idea what happened to me, but I had every reason to believe that my prayer would be back to normal in the near future, but it never was. I did not know what had happened to me at the time, and I could find no one who understood the strange predicament in which I found myself.

Several people said I had just come through my first enthusiasm, or my first fervour as they had done years before. When I asked what I was supposed to do next, they just said I should get on with life. All marriages go through a similar stage I was told, but when all the emotions and feelings fade away, you have just to get on with living your life. But how I was to carry on in prayer instead of just abandoning it as others seemed to have done I had to find out for myself, the hard way, because I had no one to support me and tell me what I had to do, at least before I met Agnes.

One thing that she insisted upon if any progress was to be made, was that I must give the same amount of time, if not more to prayer than was ever given before, because it is easy to pray when all is sweetness and light. At this point it is impossible to tell whether a person is giving their time to God for himself or rather for what they get out of him. That is why when sweetness and light in prayer is replaced by darkness and gloom it is the time when the boys are separated from the men, the girls from the women. This is the point at which cupboard lovers' pack up serious prayer. Before talking about how to pray in this strange new world, let me be clear why a person finds themselves there. They are there not because their prayerful reading of the scriptures has failed, but because it has succeeded. It succeeded in filling them with love for Jesus Christ. It is this love that makes them yearn to have an ever deeper intimacy with him. However, Jesus Christ who once lived on earth, the Jesus Christ on whom they have been meditating, is no longer on earth but in heaven. He has been glorified and taken up in an infinite act of contemplative loving of his Father. Like Jacob's ladder this enables both the love of Jesus, and those who have entered into him, to reach out to the Father while simultaneously enabling the Father's love to reach out and into all who are in him. It is this love that draws a person away from meditating on Jesus, as he once was, and into him as he is now.

It is for this reason that the love generated while meditating on Jesus as he once was, is subtly redirected to loving him as he is now. What I am trying to explain with much difficulty to modern Christians was known and lived by the first Christians as something that was commonplace; it was a profoundly mystical but normal part of their everyday spiritual lives. When they were led, as I was, into the place where meditation ends and true contemplation begins, they too would have found themselves, as I did, alone and bereft of the highly charged and emotional prayer they were beginning to think was the norm. Fortunately for them however, they were not as alone as I was, because they had fellow travellers around them who could guide them onward into the Risen One and into his mutual loving of his Father. Although they could no longer use their memories, their imagination and therefore their feelings and emotions as they did before, they could still hold on to one thing. That one thing was their intense desire for God, for all else had left them. The only way to enter into another is through the love that begins with such a desire, so it is important to sustain it, to support it and to keep it fixed on the one to whom it is directed, in, with and through the Risen Christ.

To do this, they would take a very brief prayer, or even a single word to help them keep their hearts' desire fixed on God.

It might be a word such as God, or Father, to whom their love was directed, or the word Jesus, in and through whom their desire would rise to their maker. This task was not easy, as it was for Jesus, for he was born without sin nor was there any selfishness in him that could prevent the continual mystical contemplation of his Father throughout his life on earth. Unfortunately, this was not true of the first Christians, so it became essential for a purification to take place. Then, as this purification deepened, their desire for God gradually became ever purer. Eventually it became like an increasingly more efficient and effective lightning conductor, through which God's love could become earthed within them, preparing them for the communion for which they craved. How else could they be united with the perfect human being, Jesus, and through him with his Father? How else would they be able to receive the love of the Father to bring the Son to birth again within them?

Those early Christians were led, like me, into what I have called the mystical crèche where saints are made out of sinners, or to use another word, into purgatory on earth. This is the only way a human being can be sufficiently purified to enable them to enter into union with the glorified Christ and through him with the Father. This is not the optional way for a chosen few, but for everyone, for by their very creation everyone has been called to return to and experience full union with their Creator. This is why deep down, like St Augustine, everyone is restless until their hearts rest in him. If we do not go through this deep inner mystical purification here on earth, then sometime between our death and union with God, this purification has to be completed. Unlike things cannot be united. Nor can two persons be fully united together through love until that love has been purified. The difference between those who are purified before death and those who are purified after death is important. Those purified after death can do comparatively little for others, while those who are purified before death can benefit them enormously.

Take for instance the example and the influence of the saints throughout the centuries, but particularly the saints of those first two centuries who set the world alight with the light of Christ shining through them. They achieved a world-shaking change in the Roman Empire, and in such a short time that it has left secular historians baffled for centuries.

The way for Christians to follow their example today is to pray the Christian way, by meditating on the life of Jesus and on all he said, did and promised. For this to have the desired effect, this meditation must be regular and concentrated, preferably daily. If you say there is no time, remember how many hours are spent in front of the television, surfing the net, following social media or in idle gossip. The more regular this meditation is made then the sooner the love is generated to take us up and into Christ on the next stage of our journey. If this form of fervent prayer is only irregular, and what is worse, only when we are in the mood, when we feel like it, then it will never have the desired effect even in a lifetime. So a person can remain a spiritual adolescent for their whole life. If the participants in Charismatic prayer only generate their praise, thanks and glory to God when they come together for their weekly or monthly meetings and do very little in-between, then they will get nowhere beyond the next emotional high generated by the group. They will only progress if they also pray daily and deeply through Christian vocal prayer and meditation. Those who do this will progress, those who do not, will not.

That the Charismatic movement is a good beginning is beyond question for those who find it spiritually helpful. But in 1971, the Vatican, who had been in dialogue with classical Pentecostal movements, agreed that, "It is not a goal to be reached, nor a place to stand, but a door through which to go into a greater fullness of life in the Spirit." For those, who are inspired to make their whole lives over to the Holy Spirit, not just at group meetings, but through the rest of their daily lives, then the Charismatic movement will become the door into the mystical crèche that I have been speaking about. At best it is a door that can lead to the place where a person is deeply renewed and then transformed into the Risen Christ by undergoing the deep purification that all genuine Saints must undergo.

The best-known analogy to describe this place was used by St John of the Cross who called it the dark night of the soul. St John was writing for his sisters in the Carmelite order who had already come through what I have called first fervour to find themselves in purgatory on earth. He makes it clear that his writings begin precisely when first fervour has fizzled out to help his readers move on, into and beyond the mystical purification that fits them more perfectly into Christ. He wrote to explain to them why they had found themselves in such a predicament, and to detail all the pride and all the arrogance that was to be found in their spiritual adolescence. It was festering beneath the religious euphoria that deceived them about their spiritual progress. He detailed all the faults and failings that always characterise beginners in the spiritual life in the first nine chapters of *The Dark Night of the Soul*, to show why they must undergo purification before their longed-for union with God could take place. St Teresa of Avila who looked to him as a spiritual father, even though he was much younger than she, also had to undergo her dark night before she could experience the profound mystical experiences that she detailed in her masterwork, *Interior Castle*.

Several centuries later another young Carmelite, St Thérèse of Lisieux also found herself in the dark night. She described her predicament there as trying to gaze upon God, but finding her vision obscured by a massive cloud and her prayer obstructed by legions of distractions. She insisted that by faith she knew that God was on the other side of that cloud, but she experienced nothing of the love for which she craved. Four or more centuries before, an English mystic, possibly a priest educated at Cambridge who was living in the Midlands, used a similar analogy in his book, *The Cloud of Unknowing*. This remarkable little book offers practical advice that no single book offered before.

The common theme you find in all those who are led into the mystical crèche where purification begins is this. Although all else is lost that once supported them in prayer, one thing remains. This one thing is their desire for God that makes them yearn for the One who seems to have hidden himself behind the cloud of unknowing. The author of *The Cloud of Unknowing* suggests that a person in this predicament choose a word, preferably a single word, like God, or love for instance, that embodies what they desire most of all, and that it should be repeated over and over again. In the early Church and in the teachings of the Desert Fathers other words were used like Father, or Abba, or Jesus, or simply help, or mercy. The point of this exercise is to help keep our heart's desire fixed on God in naked intent while simultaneously trying to silence the distractions that he says must be placed under 'a cloud of forgetfulness'. This gentle, but active waiting on God, is how so many of the saints have been depicted - waiting on him at the foot of the Cross. There they waited for the love that will, in God's good time, not theirs, come pouring out from the side of Christ. What happens then is described in detail in St Teresa of Avila's book, *Interior Castle,* which I have mentioned several times.

If we persevere for long two things will most certainly follow. Firstly, as the prayer is answered, the fire of God's love begins to draw out all the sinfulness and all the evil that separates us from God. It happens in such way that we see the person that we always were, the person once hidden beneath the fervour generated in spiritual adolescence. When the *Curé d'Ars* was once asked what he found most difficult in the spiritual life he answered simply, 'depression'. Is it any wonder? That is why so many flee from the prayer of darkness, where they have to face the truth about themselves in what St Catherine of Siena called the House of Self-knowledge. However, for those who persevere there are moments of light detailed in *Interior Castle* when a person is drawn toward God, as to an irresistible magnetic force and sometimes with a speed that she likens to that of a bullet fired from a musket. The purification then, involves the experience of light and darkness, presence and absence, joy and desolation.

It is essential to distinguish between the repetition of a word as advocated by members of the many mantra movements, and that of the repetition of a word in prayer as used in the *Cloud of Unknowing,* the Desert Fathers or in the earlier Christian tradition. The mantra movements introduce the repetition of a word immediately and from the outset promising that it will lead to all but instant contemplation, without any mystical purification. Apart from short prayers that St Augustine first called ejaculations, the authentic Christian mystical tradition only recommends using short phrases or single words in prayer after a person has been led into the dark night of purification. It is then used, not to generate inner peace, states of transcendental awareness or mindfulness, but to keep the heart's desire raised and fixed on the God who is drawing us to himself. As the purification continues, this enables God to continue sending the fire of the Holy Spirit to do two things. Firstly, to burn away all the dross that disfigures us and secondly to give us moments of exhilarating joy as we are briefly touched by the love that will ultimately enfold us. Let me tell you a cautionary tale of how a person seeking help, as they travelled on in the mystic way, was seriously disconcerted, even devastated when they fell into the hands of a false mystic who advocated mantras.

Only a few years ago a very good friend of mine, Amelia Tyler, died. She was president of the secular Franciscans for the province of Florence. Shortly after setting up a house of prayer in Tuscany she found herself still deeply in the dark night. She discovered for herself that it was a great help using a single word, as the *Cloud of Unknowing* explains. Unfortunately, she was unable to find a spiritual director who understood her. So when she heard of a monk in North America whose whole spirituality revolved around saying a word or a short prayer, as she had been using, she went to see him to seek his advice. She was surprised to find that he originally came from London, not far from where she had lived with her English husband where she used to run a shop in London selling fashions imported from Milan. Sadly, her initial joy at finding a person who she thought would be her spiritual saviour turned into disaster. When she explained how, by repeating what he called a mantra she did not experience inner peace, inner recollection, or mindfulness, but inner turmoil as her purification progressed, he simply did not understand her. When she explained how despite this she also experienced, moments of light when she felt drawn upward toward God with irresistible force, he was further perplexed. She was in fact experiencing all the features well known to any *bona fide* student of mystical theology about which he was totally ignorant, because he was not on the mystic way, any more than are those who still follow his teaching.

Terrible harm was done to Amelia, because his ignorance was responsible for giving her potentially disastrous advice. As he and his bogus way to mystical contemplation couldn't possibly be wrong, he concluded that there must be something wrong with her. He advised her to go to England to receive psychological help from a psychiatrist whom he recommended in Harley Street. Once cured she could then return to him and he would teach her how to attain mystical contemplation in no time at all, simply by endlessly repeating a mantra.

He, and those who still follow him, some of whom have the best will in the world, are not only ignorant of the teaching of the Christian Tradition, but also of the teaching of the Church. Mystical contemplation is a pure gift of God and to suggest that it can be attained by man-made methods and techniques is heretical. It is the old heresy of Pelagianism. Even if they have been practising for thirty years or more, they will only attain a certain inner peaceful equilibrium that is light years away from true contemplative experiences, as can be seen by reading *Interior Castle,* written by a saint made a Doctor of the Church for her authentic teaching on Mystical theology.

Before she could see a psychiatrist, I met her by chance at a retreat centre run by my brother, where I was giving a course on Christian prayer. She never did see a psychiatrist, but continued to run her retreat centre in Tuscany, where by personal experience she was able to help many others who like her had been deceived by various forms of the mantra movements that are commonplace today. Why are people so attracted to counterfeit mystical theology whilst so repelled by the authentic? I think it must be, not just the promise of instant mystical experience that the first offers, but the fear of the purification that the second offers and the panic at having to face up to the true sinful selves that fester deep down within. T S Eliot said that 'human kind cannot bear very much reality'. I think that this is what so many fear more than anything else, and one must say with so few experienced directors to help them in the aftermath of Quietism, their fear is understandable.

In medieval times the heresy that is clearly intrinsic to the mantra movements would be stamped out with the utmost severity. However, in enlightened modern times when political correctness inhibits the truth being told loudly and clearly, sincere but misguided Catholics can continue for years in error without any official or unofficial guidance coming to their aid. What is worse than a teaching that leads people to turn in upon themselves and away from the love for which they were created? What teaching is more pernicious than teaching people a form of prayer that closes them to the love for which they were created, and away from God's desire to draw them up and into his infinite loving for all eternity, and all for the sake of a little self-generated bogus 'contemplation'. To refrain from denouncing bogus forms of mystical theology for fear of acting uncharitably is to turn the meaning of charity upside-down.

All forms of genuine Christian Prayer are centred, not on self and for self-satisfaction, but on God, to love him with our whole heart and mind and with our whole body and soul. Like all other genuine forms of loving, the delight and joy that a person experiences in doing this is the by-product of selfless giving. If a person spends their time seeking pleasure for themselves, in or outside of prayer, the peace and joy that we all ultimately desire will continually elude them. Remember the words of Jesus, "Set your hearts on his kingdom first, and on his goodness and all these other things will be given you as well" (Matthew 6:33).

* * *

If the Parish Priest had not reserved seats for us at the front of the church on the Saturday evening, we would not have found a place. By the time we arrived both the church and the hall were simply crammed. A place had also been reserved for Peter too, next to us, not just for the Mass, but for the sermon as well. This time it was the parish priest who spoke to thank Peter on behalf of all who had received so much profound spiritual wisdom from him during the preceding week. The applause at the end of his sermon was thunderous and reminded me of the thunderous Amen that Peter had described at the end of the great Eucharistic prayer in the early Church. His final talk did not disappoint anyone, nor did the events that took place later, but here I am getting ahead of myself.

Chapter 12

The Mystical life and the Ascetical life

(Peter's final talk)

Although my handicap prevented me from taking part in athletics when I was at school, I loved the sport so much that I was made president of the athletics club, and accompanied our team wherever they went. We did not do very well at the National Athletics competition at White City in London that year. St John Fisher School from Purley in Surrey swept all before them winning more medals than anyone else. I approached the priest who accompanied them and asked him how a school never renowned for athletics before could do so well. His answer was simply Franz Stampfl. Franz was one of the world's leading athletics coaches of the twentieth century. He was simply a genius, who trained over three hundred and sixty Olympians. If you have ever seen the footage of Roger Bannister running the first four-minute mile on the television, then you will have seen him falling into the arms of his coach, Franz Stampfl, immediately after breaking the tape. How such an ordinary school in Purley managed to obtain the services of such a great man I do not know, but he worked wonders, not just for those pursuing athletics, but for all other sports too.

When I was introduced to him I had the cheek to ask him to come to our school to coach us too. I could not believe my luck when he said yes. When he finally came I never left his side so that I could learn from him. Although I did not realise it at the time, what I learnt from him was to help me immensely in my spiritual life later. After all, St Paul likens true Christians to athletes who should spend their time building up their spiritual muscles through daily exercise, just as athletes spend their time building up their physical muscles. That is why the word asceticism comes from the Greek word for an athlete. There can be no successful mystical life without an ascetical life, so what I learned from Franz Stampfl was to be of immense value to me in the future.

The first thing that I learnt from him was that if something is really important to you, you will find the time for it. If you do not, or you cannot, it just means that, despite what you may say, it is of no consequence to you. He used to say that if you are unwilling to find the consistent and daily time for athletics then please do not waste his time, because you are going nowhere. I can understand someone saying that athletics or sport is of no consequence to them, but how can a human being say that love and loving is of no consequence to them? Life without love is not only purposeless, it is dry, drab, boring, colourless and ultimately utterly worthless. Completely extract it from our life and we will have nothing to give us hope. If love is offered to you everything else must take second place or you will miss out on the most important thing in life

When I was a young man my cousin James told me that his girlfriend suddenly dropped him. It seemed she did not love him anymore. When I tried to discover the reasons why, I found that all his Saturdays were taken up with playing rugby and his Sundays recovering from his efforts. For the same reason he liked to take Monday evening off, sitting in front of the television. On Wednesdays, he went to the gym to start getting back into shape again, and on Thursday evening he liked to treat himself to a night at the cinema. Apparently, she rarely came, because she did not like westerns or war films! Friday night was taken up with pre-match training and of course Saturday was match day, and although she sometimes came to watch him, she rarely saw him for long in the evenings, because he was usually detained in the bar with his mates, especially after away games. That only left Tuesday night, and one night a week is simply not enough. If someone loves you and you genuinely love them, then you must have time together to give and receive what is more important than anything else on earth. It is the same with the love of God. Without daily quality time for God in prayer, we simply cannot receive the only love that can permanently change us for the better. My cousin saw the error of his ways and now he has been happily married for fifty years. God is loving us continually, but if we do not find time for the prayer where we learn how to receive his love then we will get nowhere, nowhere that is, that really matters.

The first time Franz addressed the school at assembly, he said, "If you do what I tell you to do each day, then in less than six months you will be the most feared school in the North. You will not only be beating them at athletics, but at every other sport for that matter." Everybody listened intently and within a week they were seriously engaged in his secret training method. Those who took Franz seriously were taught how they must prepare themselves before their chosen event whether tennis, golf, football, rugby or athletics. They did not just have to warm up their bodies through a series of gentle exercises, but their minds too. At the highest level he would insist, "It is all in the mind. If you want to reach the top you must train your mind." Whenever you watch any sport at the highest level, you cannot but be impressed by the dedication of the participants. It is the quality of their single-mindedness that draws the attention. The moment they begin their preparation, it is as if they enter a time-free zone where they are able to put everything out of their mind so they can live and act fully in the present. If they allow anything from the past to disrupt their concentration, then it must be instantly dismissed. Nor must anything from the future disturb them either. Just a few moments indulgence imagining themselves receiving their trophy, or celebrating with their friends, could mean losing their prize.

I do not think that he ever heard of de Cassaude, but he used to insist that we must learn to enter into what he called the moment or into the zone. It was imperative to carry this attitude of mind from the training ground into the event for which we were preparing ourselves. If we made mistakes, and we certainly did no matter how much we practised, they must be put behind us, instantly cast from our minds, as dwelling on them could ruin the rest of our performance. Stay in the zone at all times he would repeat, never dwell on failures or you will make more and more of them.

It should be exactly the same in our preparation for prayer. We need some sort of countdown to help us drop out from the hectic life that is so often forced upon us, to prepare to turn on and tune in to God. Just as different athletes find their rituals, we need to find our own. It may simply be lying down for a rest, reading some spiritual or inspiring book, exercising, going for a swim, listening to music, exercising gently or whatever helps us to relax. This is all part of the asceticism of the heart and mind that is going to help us enter into that time-free zone when we begin to pray. It is here that we can first begin to enter, as fully as we can, into the present moment, by ridding ourselves of anything from the past or the future that can draw the attention away from fixing our gaze fully upon God.

To sanctify this place and consecrate it to God, the early monks first practised private confession so that no past guilt would disturb them. They even confessed the temptations that might induce them to desecrate holy ground. God cannot be encountered in the past or in the future, but only, as de Caussade saw so clearly, in the sacrament of the present moment. This is the only moment when time touches eternity, and prayer is the offering that makes it a holy place where the human and the divine first meet and mingle before being united. Whenever you turn to God in prayer, whether it is in the set times that you have set apart for formal prayer, in the morning or the evening, or for short prayer during the day, pause for a moment. Realise that it is only now in this present moment that you can open yourself to receive the love of God pouring out through the Risen Christ, now! God does not exist in the past or in the future, but only now in the present moment. God Is. In him there are no befores or afters, he exists outside of space and time in Eternal Life. That is why the present moment is the supreme sacrament; because it is only in this now that you can contact him, receive his love and experience something of the eternal life that will one day be yours forever, here and now in this life.

Another favourite principle that Franz instilled in his pupils he called speed training. The theory is simple common sense. You may be wonderful with the ball at your feet or in your hands, you may have a brilliant backhand and a superlative smash, but if you do not get to the ball in time your skills will be superfluous. Speed training is also of the utmost importance in the spiritual life too. The difference between saints and ourselves, is not that we sin and they do not, but the speed with which they turn back to God to seek forgiveness. Sometimes it takes days, weeks, months or even years before we have the humility to accept that we have fallen, and then seek the forgiveness we need before beginning again. So we waste so much time that could have been saved, if only we had the sort of humility that enabled the saints to begin again without delay the very moment they were conscious of falling. Long before athletic coaches realised the importance of speed training, it was practised by the saints who knew that it was the only way to sanctity. They found, by their own experience, that it is not easy to begin again without delay, without the speed training that they knew could only be learnt in prayer. What they came to realise more quickly than we do, is that it is in turning away from distractions and temptations without delay, inside of prayer, that they learn the speed they need to turn back to God outside of prayer too.

The difference between us and the saints is not that they did not sin and we do. They sinned just as we do. The Holy Father, Pope Francis, has insisted, not just that he is a sinner, but that he has sinned many times over in the past and asks forgiveness for what has shamed him. What distinguishes the saint from the sinner is the speed with which they get up after having fallen. The saints do not waste precious time pretending they do not sin, or making endless excuses, or blaming others for what they know only too well was their own fault. The moment they fall they seek forgiveness and begin again, knowing they have sinned, but trusting in the mercy of God.

St Francis said that the very moment a person sins must be the moment when he or she turns back to God, begging his forgiveness, immediately and without delay. He put it this way in his writings, "A man is faithful and prudent when he is quick to atone for all his offences, interiorly by contrition, exteriorly by confessing them and then by making reparation" (Admonition XXIV).

Herein lies one of the main differences between the saints and sinners like us. Only too often people simply cannot face their guilt so they run away from God and hide, as Adam did in the Garden of Eden. When God called out, "Adam, Adam, where are you?" (Genesis 3:9), God knew exactly where Adam was: it was Adam who did not know where he was. He had lost his way trying to hide his sin and the guilt that shamed him. Sometimes we can spend years on the run because pride will not allow us to admit what we have done. Our inability to eat humble pie means that we can spend half a lifetime suffering from spiritual starvation. What is even worse than the pride that comes before a fall, is the pride that follows the fall, because it stops us from getting up, sometimes permanently.

Every different sport or athletic event has its own techniques that have to be learnt, and Franz was an expert in both track and field events. With his technical advice and his secret training method I saw comparatively ordinary athletes become candidates for the next Olympics. When I went to see my brother compete in the Schools' Challenge Cup for athletics, held at the White City stadium in London, he came eleventh in the Pole Vault. The following year he won the event with a vault of eleven foot six. That was in the era before we went metric, and just one year before fibre glass poles were introduced into the country. He was also trying for some time to break the county record at the triple jump, then known as the hop, step and jump. When, in despair, he turned to Franz, the help he received was immediate and effective. Franz only needed to watch him once before he saw the problem. He had been so enthusiastic, so intent on breaking the record, that he put too much energy into the hop, leaving little energy for the step, and almost none for the final jump. Once Franz corrected him and taught him how to put equal space between the hop, step and jump, his performance changed dramatically and he was able to break the record with ease. "You see." said Franz, "it is all a matter of balance. Until you get the balance right you will go nowhere." Then he added. "It is the same in life too, is it not? Get the balance wrong and everything is wrong." I do not know about life in general, but it is certainly true of the spiritual life. If first enthusiasm encourages you to do too much too soon at the expense of everything else, then it is only a matter of time before you capitulate and give up, as my brother was about to do until Franz taught him the importance of balance. In other words, if you are encouraged to spend too much time in solitude trying to pray without proper direction, then failure will only be a matter of time. Prayer must be part of a balanced spiritual life in which there is also sufficient time for work and for recreation.

Who could be more dedicated to prayer than the Desert Fathers, but every day they also had to give themselves to the traditional seven hours of manual labour. When in later years they were in danger of forgetting this, they had to be reminded in reforms, like the Cistercian reform that was inspired by St Bernard of Clairvaux. In time their prayer life so inspired their work that eventually their work became their prayer, but it takes very many years for this to happen. Cardinal Basil Hume put it this way: "To say your work is your prayer or your life is your prayer is not only meaningless, but quite misleading. It is undoubtedly the ideal, but such an ideal will never be realised, without giving daily time to personal prayer". In the meantime, balance, balance, balance in all things, as Franz used to say.

Let me say a few words about what he called his secret method. It was called weight-training or pumping iron. It was a new method of training, imported from the United States in the early nineteen-fifties, where it had transformed their athletes. It is simply taken for granted today - the principle behind it is very simple. By repeatedly raising the weights above your head you are not just developing the muscles in your arms and legs, but virtually every other muscle in your body as well. The whole person is not only made stronger and more powerful, but is given powers of endurance beyond those who do not use this method. Even those who are naturally gifted, or who have a high degree of technical training, soon realise they will end up the losers without weight-training. A new powerful super athlete can be fashioned by one single action, repeated over and over again.

The priest who taught me how to meditate listened to Franz as well. The next time I went to the meditation group he told us that what Franz had said not only applied to sport, but to the spiritual life too, particularly to prayer. What is prayer but the raising of the heart and mind to God? It is just like weight-training. Whatever form of prayer you are engaged in, whether it is saying your Morning Prayers, trying to meditate or even contemplating you will always experience distractions, so you will always have to keep raising your heart and mind to God time and time again. As a person is doing this then the muscles of the heart and mind are continually being exercised, gradually transforming the whole spiritual metabolism.

However, there is a dimension to spiritual weight-lifting that Franz knew nothing about and which I only came to understand by accident. I was bemoaning the fact that my handicap prevented me from training and taking part in sport like the others when suddenly he interrupted me. "Peter," he said, "beneath everything that I am teaching to gain sporting success there is a medical aspect that is crucial, and which I do not need to explain, except to you. Physical exercise is vital for the good and well-being of the whole person. If you are unable to do the exercises that I am teaching to athletes, then it is essential that you do something to exercise your body or you will suffer medically." After giving some thought to what he said I retrieved my old tricycle out of the bike shed and decided to use it to cycle to school instead of using the bus. Unfortunately, after several years of inactivity both the chain and the cogs had rusted, so that I could not even move the pedals, no matter how hard I tried. I was just about to give up when my father, who had been watching me, came to the rescue. As I tried to turn the pedals once more he began to pour oil onto the chain and then onto the cogs. Gradually with my endeavour and with the facilitating power of the oil, my tricycle was returned to full working order and I was able to use it as I had planned. It didn't strike me at the time, but later I realised that I learnt an important lesson. Human endeavour alone may get you everywhere in the sporting life, but it will not get you anywhere in the spiritual life without the facilitating power of the Holy Spirit. That is why the presence and the action of the Holy Spirit is symbolised by oil in many of the sacraments. It was a lesson I needed to learn.

As we are engaged in spiritual weightlifting in prayer, our endeavour is facilitated and eventually brought to perfection by the Holy Spirit. However, experience taught me something further. I learnt that if we continually act as if everything depended on us in the spiritual life, in general and in prayer in particular, then we will get nowhere, all will be lost. "Cut off from me you can do nothing," Jesus insisted (John 15:5). I have a new definition of prayer then, that takes into account our trying, but which modifies the word trying with another word - gently. 'Trying gently' breathes into our endeavour the realisation that we alone will never succeed without God's endeavour. God's endeavour is the Holy Spirit. The new definition therefore is that prayer is 'gently trying to raise the heart and mind to God'. If you find yourself getting angry because you seem to be getting nowhere, this is a sign that you think everything depends on you, and you have fallen into pride. If on the other hand, you think that everything depends on God and you do nothing, this is a sign that you have fallen into presumption. Genuine Christian prayer involves gently trying to raise the heart and mind to God. Once again, as Franz insisted, it is all a matter of balance, the balanced endeavour of the human and the divine. You cannot have one without the other if prayer is to be successful.

I want to let you into a secret about the spiritual life that for some reason many people fail to see. They think they would progress in leaps and bounds if only they did not have so many distractions in prayer. The truth of the matter is you could not possibly progress in prayer without distractions. My brothers and I used to laugh at an old Victorian painting that our aunt used to hang on her kitchen wall. It depicted a brook flowing down from the mountains. The left hand side of the brook was in all but darkness, the right hand side was bathed in light. In the foreground there were stepping stones and under the picture written in bold Gothic script was, "Make all your stumbling blocks into stepping stones." I do not know why we found it so funny. I suppose the combination of the Victorian picture and the Gothic script made it all seem a little too twee, at least to us. But the truth of the matter is that the little epigram was true, and it still is true, especially in prayer where our stumbling blocks are in fact the stepping stones to sanctity.

It is interesting that St Teresa of Avila said that you cannot pray without distractions. If you go to pray and fall asleep you are not praying, nor are you praying if you are swept up into an ecstasy. When you are asleep you are doing nothing and when you are in an ecstasy then God is doing everything. Prayer takes place in between the sleep and the ecstasy. In that place there are always distractions, so you are forever engaged in turning away from them in order to turn back to God, by continually raising your heart and mind to him. So if you have a hundred and one distractions in half an hour, you have chosen to turn back to God a hundred and one times. In other words, you have been doing what St Peter asked his listeners to do on the first Pentecost day. You have been repenting, repeatedly trying to turn back to God, continually raising your heart and mind to him, to give your love to him, so that he can give his love to you. Prayer is the place where in concentrated periods of time you practise what God wants you to do all the time, as you turn to him in all you say and do each day, and as you turn to him in the neighbour in need. That is why all the saints and all the great Christians who are held up to us as examples of how to live the Christian life, are men and women of prayer. They all knew and practised the art of spiritual weight-lifting in prayer. It was this daily spiritual exercise that, not only taught them the art of how to keep turning to God outside of prayer through all they said and did each day, but gave them the power to do it too, as their weak human powers were surcharged by the divine. As they gave, so they received, and in ever greater measure. The speed with which they turned away from distractions and temptations inside of prayer gave them the facility to keep doing the same outside of prayer too.

Practise does make perfect. The English fleet defeated the French fleet at Trafalgar because they practised more. It was not so much the flair of their Admiral, Nelson, as the daily gunnery practised that enabled them to fire twice as quickly as their enemy. It was the same at Agincourt. The English bowmen could fire six arrows whilst the French crossbowmen fired one. English football teams have lost far more than they should to Germany, because, as their manager put it, "They don't like practising penalties." Germans did practise, whether they liked it or not! That is why you will not find any football managers on pillars in Trafalgar Square!

The spiritual weight-lifting that was always part of prayer before, becomes far more difficult and burdensome when a person finds themselves in the deep purification that takes place in the dark night. The reason for this is that the new distractions that I have mentioned are far more burdensome than before, making it ever more difficult to raise the heart and mind to the God who seems to have disappeared behind a cloud of unknowing. These distractions do not only come from the world that you have just left behind, and to which you will soon be returning. They come from the evil that has been harbouring deep down within and which must be drawn up, seen and destroyed by the action of the Holy Spirit. The reason why the vast majority of those who go into this dark night leave before too long, is that apart from the dryness and the aridity that they have never experienced before, the distractions grow as they try to persevere. The person who despite all this, is prepared to soldier on, develops spiritual muscles that are called virtues, more quickly and perfectly than before when spiritual weight- lifting was comparatively easy.

This is the place where patience, hope and endurance is learned by journeying on when all seems hopeless, where faith is learnt when you are prepared to go on believing when all around and in front of you seems dark and forbidding. It is the place where loving, true genuine loving is brought to perfection, as you go on giving, seemingly without receiving, for love is easy when your love always seems rewarded. Your loving is being rewarded far more fully and far more deeply than ever before, but you do not see or experience what is happening, and that is why it is called the hidden, secret or mystical way. When we are being purified in this mystical darkness, all self-seeking and cupboard loving that infected our spiritual journey before is gradually eliminated. Gradually then, we are emptied of all and everything that prevents the pure love of God and his pure love of us, as we enter into what the Greek Fathers called *Kenosis.* It is while waiting patiently at the foot of the Cross, that in God's good time, not ours, we are open to receive what they called the *Pleroma* the fullness of God's love that Jesus received in his darkest hour. What happens then is told by few, because like any lover the intimacy that they experience when love is transposed into union is deeply personal, even though it is ultimately for all.

However, I must say something about the ultimate mystical experience of God on earth, because it helps to put to right the mistaken beliefs of many bogus mystics, or the teaching of some mystics who are only on the way but believe they have arrived at the summit. In her book *Interior Castle* St Teresa of Avila details the psychological experiences of the love of God that a person encounters as they ascend and finally arrive at the summit. When other authentic Christian mystics write about this journey they are always writing about one and the same thing, and one and the same experience. However, the way they express themselves will depend on whether they are men or women, whether they belong to the Greek or Jewish tradition, whether they are from the East or West, or which particular period of history or cultural milieu they come from. The particular emphasis in their writings will be determined, too, by the point at which they themselves have reached on their own spiritual journey, at the time they are writing, or directing someone else. That is why mystics who have arrived at the summit of the mystic way should be preferred to beginners, or to those who have become bogged down at some point along the way, and have deceived themselves into believing they have arrived at the summit.

Writers will inevitably use different language and different means of expression that can be a stumbling block to the reader, leading them to conclude that there are many different ways that human beings experience the love of God in the mystic way.

That would be untrue. When Christians open and keep opening themselves to the Holy Spirit, the same thing always occurs. At first he fills them with joy, as he did with the crowds on the first Pentecost day to inspire them to abandon themselves ever more fully to his action. Then he purifies them to enable them to be united with the One who sent him. Purification can be long and painful, but it is essential if imperfect love is to be united with perfect love. As this process advances, the light of perfect love begins to flash through the darkness, heralding the arrival of pure God-given love. It first enthrals the mind and heart, before gradually possessing the whole person, body and soul. It is called the Mystical Marriage in the West and Deification or *Theosis* in Eastern Christianity. In the Eastern Church in particular, the Transfigured Christ (Matthew 17:1-8, Mark 9:2-8, Luke 9:28-36, 2 Peter 1:16-18), is seen as the perfect example of what will ultimately happen to us, not just to our hearts and minds, but to our bodies too.

The final stage of the mystical journey here on earth for them is totally other than that conceived by Christian intellectuals and mystics influenced by the Pseudo-Areopagite, and the Neoplatonic school from which the Pseudo-Areopagite learnt his practical Greek philosophy. They will be dealt with in the next chapter. That school which developed into something of a powerful religious force amongst some of the intelligentsia in the aftermath of the Resurrection, lured many unsuspecting Christians into its orbit. In convincing them that the salvation which it promised involved shunning all material things that were a stumbling block to perfection, it condemned them to one of the most superficially plausible of all heresies - Gnosticism. The outward manifestation of God's plan was, for them, no more than a mirage. Union with God could only come about by a disembodied and esoteric mystical search that ended in some kind of sublime ecstasy for a chosen few. The body for them was the prison of the divine spark, and it could have no part in whatever form of ultimate salvation they taught.

There were myriad forms of Gnosticism, from Manichaeism that grew up in the East to Neoplatonism that grew up in the West, including a version espoused by those who called themselves Christian, namely Marcionism. However, they all had one thing in common - material things prevented their spiritual journey so they were committed to freeing themselves from their influence. Salvation for them was to free the sparks of the divine within them from the material body that entombed it and to rise to the spiritual flame whence it came. For Greek Gnostics, like the Neoplatonists, the material world that prevented them from returning to God was not evil in itself, for like them it came from God, but it had to be left behind or it would encumber them. For other Gnostics, the material world was evil, the work of a *demiurge* or an evil god.

Bishop Marcion, son of the Bishop of Sinope, a town on the shore of the Black Sea, was seen as the founder of Marcionism, the most popular Christian form of Gnosticism. For him the incarnation could be no more than a divine deception, for all material things were the work of an evil power. His Gospel begins therefore with the words, "In the fifteenth year of the Emperor Tiberius, God descended into Capharnaum and taught on the Sabbath." Jesus' physical human birth was denied for he could not have had a body. It was merely the appearance of a body used by God to communicate with man. This is why the Apostles' Creed, recited by the Catechumens at their baptism and used regularly by all Christians, was so explicit about the reality of the incarnation.

"I believe in Jesus Christ the Son of God, who was born of the Holy Spirit and the Virgin Mary, who was crucified in the days of Pontius Pilate, and died, and rose again from the dead, and ascended into heaven and sat down at the right hand of the Father, who will come to judge the living and the dead and I believe in the Holy Spirit and in the Holy Catholic Church, and in the resurrection of the flesh."

William Temple, the revered Archbishop of Canterbury, was right when he said that, "Christianity is the most materialistic of all religions," for it does not consist in striving to free the human spirit from its entombment in the body, but rather in allowing the Holy Spirit to penetrate and permeate the whole human personality, body and spirit. No wonder the Neoplatonist Dean Inge found little in common with his Archbishop.

What happened to Jesus at his glorification is our destiny too. Despite the evidence to the contrary, of bodily corruption in the grave, we are ultimately destined to experience the resurrection of the flesh. However, the difficulty of imagining such a physical resurrection, with the further unanswered questions of where, when, and how, make many modern Christians Gnostics, at least when it comes to visualising life after death. It seems far preferable to imagine the human spirit rising to be united with God immediately after death, leaving the body to decay in the grave, rather than to imagine some other physical world, in or outside space and time. For them to imagine some other world, where freed from the corrupting power of selfishness, human beings live together with God in peace and in harmony, and in flesh and blood, would seem to ally themselves with the fundamentalists. The Sadducees, who did not believe in the resurrection of the body, tried to make a mockery of it by asking Jesus which wife a man would live with in heaven when he had seven on earth? The answer that Jesus gave was revealing. He did not deny the resurrection of the body, but merely that there would be no such thing as marriage hereafter.

At first the Judaeo-Christian spirituality made deep inroads into Hellenistic culture as vast numbers of its adherents were converted to Christianity. However old habits die hard and, as the vitality of primitive Christianity began to wane, many ideas and practices from the old Hellenistic culture began to assert themselves. Many early Christians were sufficiently influenced by Gnosticism to suspect that contact with all things material would hinder their spiritual life. And so, like the Gnostics themselves, many aspired to an over strict puritan way of life wrongly believing that it accurately reflected the Gospel, which it clearly does not. The insidious influence of Gnosticism gradually came to denigrate and then undermine the mystery of marriage. In the old covenant God's promise to Abraham had made marriage into a sacred institution to bring about his promise to the father of the Jewish people. The sacrament of circumcision consecrated to God the sacred instrument through which God's promise to raise up a great nation from his seed would be fulfilled.

The truth then is totally other than that spread by the Gnostics and their Neoplatonic cousins. The Word was made flesh so that the love that animated and continues to animate Jesus would make his home within the very depth of our physical human personality, beginning here and now on earth. Furthermore, the plan of God, the Mysterion, determined that this sacred place, this home, would be the place where a mystical marriage would take place between the believer and the risen physical body of Jesus, in and through whom they would be reconciled with God. However, entering into Jesus does not just mean entering into his new and glorified life, but also into his action. Since the moment of his glorification he has been receiving and returning the supra-abundant love of God, while simultaneously overflowing with what he receives. Those who freely choose to receive this love are drawn into a mystical vortex of mutual loving to eternity, in short, into the Mysterion.

Deep down in the heart of every human being, no matter how low they may have fallen, though they may, not only have rejected all known religions, and even the very existence of God, there is a primeval prayer. This prayer may not always be apparent - it is not always there as a form of words, but it is always there as a deep desire, a yearning for love, for security, for a home, for a family, a perfect family. A human being is an embodied yearning for the fullness of love. That is why St Augustine penned those immortal words, "Our hearts are restless until they rest in you." For some it may take more than a lifetime to discover who this You is.

Since the Renaissance, down to the present day, many Christian intellectuals have been deeply influenced by their classical education. Without realising it they have subconsciously imbibed Greek philosophical ideas that proved so enticing to the early Christian Gnostics. Without explicitly accepting it as dogma they tended to believe in a Neoplatonic afterlife where their souls or their spirits are united with God the moment those bodies have been placed in their tombs to decay. The evidence of their eyes does not support the idea of the Resurrection of the dead in any literal sense, so they simply cast it from their minds. They dismiss it with other anthropomorphic expressions of the faith that seem too facile, too banal to believe.

Because the details of our afterlife were never detailed by Jesus, and because they have too often been answered in a way that seems trite and trivial, it must not turn us away from the central mystery of our faith, even though it seems unimaginable. If it were fully imaginable, then it would not be true, for the meaning of the Mysterion is ultimately beyond our wildest dreams and imaginings. However, the teaching of Jesus and the earliest Christian tradition, inspired by the Holy Spirit who Jesus promised would make all things plain after his death, is uncompromising. God's plan is to draw all up into the physical, human but glorified body of his son Jesus, together with their human, but purified bodies. Our bodies and his body are to be united in a mystical marriage, infinitely deeper, more profound and more fulfilling than the happiest possible marriage here on earth.

Frankly I do not know any fairy story or any man-made myth, no matter how outrageous, that comes anywhere near this overwhelming truth. Not even arrogant human beings could have imagined it, even in their most outrageous flights of fancy, if it had not come directly from Jesus himself. However, even he did not try to define or explain the mystery of the Holy Trinity. Jesus was not a Greek who was primarily interested in what a thing is in itself, but a Jew, who is always more practical, more existential, more interested in explaining what a thing can do. He was far more concerned with telling us how to enter into the life of the Holy Trinity, than in giving the sort of theoretical explanations that came later. In order to understand what it means to enter into what St Paul called, "the love that surpasses the understanding" (Ephesians 3:19), the Fathers of the Church, up to and including St Bernard, used the human analogy by repeatedly turning to the *Song of Songs*. They repeatedly turned to this, one of the most beautiful love poems ever written, to explain and detail the profound mystical journey into Christ, and through him into the love that created us all, and to which we are returning as our final destiny. It is here and only here, as we are plunged into an unbounded supernatural fire of loving, that we are united with the first giver and the first receiver of infinite loving. Thanks to the loving that has and will always make them one, we too will all be one in them, in the Father and in the Son, because we are transported into them by their mutual loving that has no beginning and no ending. Love, even our weak mortal loving, always yearns for more, and the more we receive the more we desire, until we become one with the one in whom love has its ultimate realisation.

You may remember that in *Wuthering Heights*, Catherine Linton's love for Heathcliff was so great that she said, "I don't love Heathcliff, I am Heathcliff." In other words, she wanted to enter into him more fully and more completely than their human bodies allowed, and to remain there forever. She was not so much saying what had happened, but what she desired to happen more than anything else. She wanted to lose herself in him and wanted him to lose himself in her. You find the same idea in the story of *Tristan and Isolde*. When the two reached the heights of human love, their union was so sublime that at one moment Tristan calls Isolde Tristan, and Isolde calls Tristan Isolde. You find exactly the same thing in the gospels. At one moment Jesus calls himself the Son of God and at another moment, God. Although the love of Tristan and Isolde is as close as any human mind can imagine, not even Wagner, whose music describes their love more perfectly than any words, suggests that they merge to become a new single identity. Genuine love is between two. Just as there are always two separate persons in human love, so there must surely be two separate persons in divine love.

Although Jesus insists that, "The Father and I are one" (John10:30), and that "I am in the Father and the Father is in me" (John 14:11), it is perfectly evident that their individual identity is never lost, no matter how close their union. However, the Gospels go one step further. The love that binds them together is not a blind impersonal force, but a separate personal love in its own right. To return to the human analogy to try and explain what this means; in *Wuthering Heights* Catherine and Heathcliff see that the mutual love that binds them together seems to have something of an identity of its own, that is equal to the love that each has for the other. If anything, it is greater because it appears to have a personality that can unite them, even when they are separated by time and place, and even by death.

The love that can be experienced in this life in some measure, can be found in its most complete form and without measure, in God alone. Jesus does not tell us these profound truths because he wishes to exercise our minds with dry abstract truths about the inner nature of what was later called the Holy Trinity, but because he wants to inspire us with the truth. The truth is that the Father and the Son have chosen to make their home within us, so that the most sublime love affair imaginable takes place within our inmost being. Infinite loving has its centre everywhere and its boundaries nowhere. Despite all that has been said, even infinite love must be received by choice; it can be excluded when human choice refuses to receive it. This creates the worst black hole in the whole of creation that has traditionally been called hell. If heaven can be found within us then so also can hell. But let us concentrate on heaven and the love that can take us there.

The ultimate experience of God on Earth, known only to those who arrive at Divinisation or Mystical Marriage, is Trinitarian. In other words, they become clearly aware that they are caught up in, and experience in some measure, the love without measure that endlessly revolves between the Father and the Son within their own inner being. This realisation is, in fact, the sign that a mystic is a true Christian mystic, and not some Neoplatonic hybrid.

Read, reread, and reflect on all Jesus said and did in St John's account of the Last Supper, and these profound truths will come alive in a way that nothing I can say ever will. Then you will receive far more than mere words, through the Spirit who inspired them, and what you will receive will bring you to your knees in thanksgiving and in adoration.

But all has not been said, for in this profound mystical vortex of loving that revolves between the Father and the Son, in which we are caught up, we are not alone. We are at one too, with all who have chosen to enter into this ecstatic joy, with relatives who have chosen the same path, mothers and fathers, brothers and sisters, friends and lovers, children and grandchildren, and not just our extended family but the whole extended human family, living and dead. They are not just living with us in Jesus, but travelling with us too into eternity. Our own personal joy and satisfaction is enhanced beyond our wildest dreams by re-meeting our own families and in knowing and loving them as never before. Even in the best of families, the pernicious cancer of selfishness prevented us loving each other as we would have wished. But now that the cancer has been spirited away and we have been transfused with pure love, there is nothing to prevent us from becoming the genuine loving families that we never really were on earth. This supernatural homecoming is, however, the prelude to joining together for the last time, in order to set out upon our final and unending journey into eternal life and loving.

Together we will, not just experience the fullness of ecstatic joy, but the ever more fulfilling joy of experiencing what St Gregory of Nyssa called *epecstasy*, the ongoing and ever more fulfilling ecstasy of infinitely going beyond what was once our capacity for love. As this journey unfolds, that capacity never stops expanding as we travel without any further let or hindrance, as infinite love draws us on to the destiny designed for us by God from all eternity. At last the final stage of his plan – The Mysterion – is in its ultimate stage of completion. And we, together with all whom we love and hold dear, are bonded ever closer together as we draw ever nearer to the blissful union with the pure unadulterated and infinite loving and goodness that resides in Our Father who is in heaven.

* * *

This was the longest, the deepest and the densest talk that Peter had given. I thought that he would have lost his audience long before the end. This may well have been true had any other speaker been delivering exactly the same material, but it was different with Peter. I think it was the singer not the song that totally absorbed them. You could have heard a pin drop throughout the hour and a quarter that he spoke. When he finished, no one clapped, there was just a deep and pregnant silence that seemed to envelop the whole church. Nobody left, most people just fell to their knees in prayer. Then gradually people wandered up to speak to Peter and ask him to pray for them. It was quite evident that this was going to go on and on so the parish priest came and invited Ellena and me to come into the presbytery for a cup of tea. I went down to the church at about half past nine to see if Peter was ready to go, so we could catch the ten o'clock train home, but he was still busy talking to people. The same happened when I returned at half past ten. Many people had left, but many more still remained and for the first time I could see he was actually praying over some of those who sought his help. I had never seen this before. When I returned at half past eleven he was still praying over people, but I had to be brutal. The twelve o'clock train was the last one to Brockenhurst, so I had to drag him away and bundle him into a taxi. It was after two o'clock before we climbed into bed – we were all exhausted.

The next day we all had a lie-in and after the eleven o'clock Mass we drove Peter over to Ashurst on the other side of the Forest for Sunday lunch, to which we were invited with his brother and sister-in-law, to celebrate their twenty-fifth wedding anniversary. We returned home late without Peter who stayed over with them so that he could get an early 'plane back to his home in the Western Isles. We were both exhausted and decided to have another long rest in bed the following morning. However, I woke shortly after seven-thirty enveloped in pitch beyond pitch of deep melancholic sadness. I could not stop the tears incessantly rolling down my cheeks. I was not afraid to die after a long and eventful life, but I was devastated that at the very moment when I had at last been given the wisdom to understand and appreciate the faith that I had not understood at the beginning of my life, that life was all but at an end. At least before the end came I would have just enough time to help put together the book that would enable others to begin, with the wisdom given to me just before my departure.

Then suddenly the telephone rang, at about eight o'clock. It was the parish priest from SS Anselm and Cecilia. Apparently, he had been trying to contact us the previous day to tell us about an article in one of the Sunday newspapers. It was headlined 'Miracles at Lincoln's Inn.' It seems some of the people with whom Peter had prayed over were claiming that he had cured them. Although the Parish Priest was sceptical, as were we, far more had come forward after the article appeared to claim that they too had been cured. One had been, allegedly, cured of terminal cancer, another of blindness and many more of other illnesses, and it seemed the numbers were multiplying because the Monday papers were full of it, and the front door of the presbytery was surrounded with reporters and photographers. He was ringing us to warn us that somehow they had found our address and believing that Peter was staying with us, some had set out for Brockenhurst, if they had not already arrived.

I had just enough time to wipe my tears away, and tell Ellena everything I just heard, when the doorbell rang. Thanks to the warning we peeped out to see about half a dozen newspaper men waiting to interview us, or rather to interview Peter. Thank goodness, we had got him away. Although we dressed and had breakfast we did not answer the door bell nor the telephone that kept ringing and ringing. Finally, we had a counsel of war. They knew that we were in, and they also thought that Peter was with us. The only way we could lift the siege was by confronting them with the truth, so I finally opened the front door and gave them a statement. I told them that Peter had indeed been staying with us, but that he left the previous day and was at that moment flying back to his hermitage home in another country. I did not mention that other country was Scotland and his hermitage home was in the Outer Hebrides for fear they might pursue him. I also said that I knew Peter for almost forty years and all talk of miracles was nonsense, and bade them good morning.

"That's the end of that," I said to Ellena who was busy reading the morning's post. "I'm not sure that it is," she said, as she handed me the letter that she was reading. It was from the hospital giving me an appointment with my consultant for the following Wednesday. They were all puzzled by my latest tests that showed that all trace of the cancer that had given me hardly six months to live, had completely disappeared. Of course, we could not believe it - it was obviously all some mistake, but it was not! After many further exhaustive tests, no trace of the cancer could be found. Ellena was standing in front of me with tears falling from her eyes, as her smile grew larger and larger. She reminded me of a rainbow that grew ever more vibrant and ever more vivid to light up the whole countenance of the landscape with hope, despite the rain that was still falling steadily. "It is time to get started," she said, before we were lost in each other's' arms, both weeping in thanksgiving and both ready to start our lives all over again. All week more and more invitations had been coming in for Peter to speak. Peter had said that after what Padre Pio had foretold, he would have to accept them. It seemed it was part of his destiny, but he told us that he would need our help for he could not do it alone. "There goes my fly fishing," Ellena said, "We have work to do." "Thank the Lord for that," I was thinking, "No more trout to eat, morning, noon and night. Oh, for the joys of egg and chips and sausages and mash."

Chapter 13

Dionysius the Pseudo-Areopagite

After his long journey Peter was understandably tired and it was not surprising that he fell asleep on the train after his first talk. But the next morning, after the usual time he spent in prayer, he was full of life and showed no further signs of tiredness until all his talks were over. This meant that we spent hours asking him questions and discussing the implications of his talks on the train, both going to and returning from London. To introduce you to all he said in our discussions would entail writing three or four more books. I have therefore just chosen those things that he spoke about that shed clear light on the talks he gave. The first was in answer to Ellena's questions about the mysticism of Neoplatonism. She had recently attended a talk on Dionysius the Areopagite given by a Catholic academic, and she found his talk was more a eulogy than an objective criticism of his teaching and its influence on the later Christian mystical tradition. That his influence has been immense is undeniable, but whether or not it has been benign is quite another question. That is why she turned to Peter to shed light on the matter. What follows in this and subsequent chapters is based on our discussions with Peter and on what he said, sometimes word for word.

He began by saying that an unhealthy and untraditional emphasis developed with Dionysius that encouraged believers to give subjective mystical experiences an unwarranted importance in the spiritual journey. In the authentic mystic way, as he insisted repeatedly, the whole emphasis was, and still is God-centred. It was primarily directed to giving all honour and glory to God. The joy, the delight which filled believers as they did this was the by-product of giving themselves to, and living for, another.

In all the spiritual writings of the Fathers of the Church, none of them speaks in any detail about their psychological experiences, nor do they enumerate progressive states of psychological awareness which they experienced in their journey into the love of God. Detailing successive psychological states as steps in the journey is something that comes later, much later in the Christian mystical tradition. Whatever merit this has, and it is not without merit, it was most certainly not there at its outset, and it does have inbuilt dangers. True love is primarily interested in the one who is loved, not in seeking pleasurable feelings and experiences, with emphasis on esoteric states such as ecstasy as the climax of the mystic way, as it is for Neoplatonism. The spiritual life is essentially a journey from selfishness to selflessness. Encouraging a person from the beginning to seek out and then to savour esoteric mystical states is simply using God as a spiritual prostitute.

Since referring to him as Denis the Menace in a previous work, Peter said that he wasted all too much time researching him and his influence further, for fear that he had done the man an injustice. This enabled him to conclude that his influence on the Christian mystical tradition has been, and still is, real but deeply regrettable. Dionysius was in fact a pagan convert from Neoplatonism who wrote his four books and various other writings, somewhere between AD 490 –530, four hundred years after his supposed friendship with St Paul. These works are heavily dependent on the writings of the Neoplatonism of his previous pagan teachers. He was writing long after the Church's reaction to Arianism had created a completely different spiritual landscape from that which prevailed in the aftermath of Christ's Resurrection. He was as far away from Apostolic times as we are from Tudor times, but in order to give a false power to his alien ideas he pretends to have lived in those times himself, and to have been on familiar terms with many great Christian personalities whom we rightly revere. To do this, Dionysius assumed the name and the persona of a well-known personality acquainted with St Paul.

It is one thing to write in another person's name; this is not an uncommon convention for a writer, and is usually quite harmless. But to do it in such an emphatic way, in order to deceive readers into believing in the quality and in the orthodoxy of all that is said, is taking the matter too far. This deceit has had the most pernicious consequences for the Christian mystical tradition. The veneration that was given to this man and his writings in the Christian West, where his works were translated into Latin, cannot be exaggerated. For many hundreds of years almost all Western mystical writers looked to him as to one of the Apostolic Fathers, whose works therefore were even more authoritative than the Fathers of the Church and hardly less sacred than the scriptures themselves. He was even referred to as St Denis. He did not just claim to be the Bishop of Athens and friend of St Paul, but a friend too, of St John, Timothy, Titus, Justin, Carpus and Polycarp. He claimed to have known Mary the mother of Jesus and although he did not profess to have been at the Crucifixion, he did claim to have witnessed the solar eclipse mentioned by Matthew (27:45) and Mark (15:33) that took place when Jesus was dying on the cross. There are many more deceits in his writings, and all with one aim, to fool others into accepting his own Neoplatonic presentation of Christian mysticism.

He succeeded too, for it was almost a thousand years before anyone even questioned his identity, and then for four hundred years more, many eminent scholars still defended him, and for that matter still defend him. He was finally exposed by Hugo Koch and Joseph Stiglmayr at the end of the nineteenth century. These two scholars worked independently, and in 1895 came to the same conclusion. They discovered that whole extracts from his works had been lifted from the last of the great Neoplatonic writers, Proclus, his teacher. Further to this they found an astonishing agreement in the sequence of thought, examples and expressions that had also been taken from Proclus. So henceforth, he genuinely earned the title of the Pseudo-Areopagite. But it took well into the twentieth century before the fraud was generally accepted, although many still look to him with reverence and revere his teaching. Many still continue to allow this teaching to distort the true meaning of authentic Christian prayer, leading myriad well-meaning Christians into various forms of bogus mystical practices that will lead them nowhere.

It must be remembered that Dionysius was writing after the Roman Emperor Theodosius the Great had declared Christianity to be the official religion of the Roman Empire (AD 381). If you wanted to progress in any sphere of life, it paid to be a Christian. If you wanted the widest possible distribution for your works, it would only be possible to do this as a member of the new religion. Although his conversion to Christianity was probably genuine there is nevertheless the distinct impression that he does no more than doff his hat to Christian orthodoxy in order to spread his Neoplatonic philosophy as far as possible. He refers to the scriptures to underpin and support this Neoplatonic philosophy, referring to Christian tradition and to the dogmatic teachings of the Church just to keep onside, when what he is saying is at times at variance with both. It is important to remember that whilst Dionysius was still alive, the Emperor Justinian closed the academy in Athens where Dionysius was trained in Neoplatonic philosophy under Proclus, to prevent erroneous Neoplatonic ideas deceiving Christians.

Where does Jesus Christ fit into the mysticism that Dionysius attempts to pass off as Christian? The fact of the matter is, he does not, and the Incarnation that is the hub and centre of everything is simply bypassed. In his rightfully acclaimed *A History of Philosophy,* the famous Jesuit, Frederick Copleston, put it this way:

"The Neoplatonists objected to the Incarnation and although we cannot be justified in asserting that the Pseudo-Dionysius denied the Incarnation, his acceptance of it does not well adapt itself to his philosophic system nor does it play much part in his writings. One may well doubt whether his writings would have exercised the influence that they did on Christian mediaeval thinkers, had the latter not taken the author's pseudonym at its face value."

Christian prayer begins, continues and is completed in, with and through Jesus Christ, who is, "The Way, the Truth and the Life" (John 14:6). Dionysius hardly mentions him, let alone centres his spiritual teaching around him. He might well have been the first person to have referred to what was later accepted as the three ways of the spiritual life, the purgative, the illuminative and the unitive way, but I can find no evidence to suggest that he passed through them himself. Read the life of genuine Christian mystics like St Augustine, St Bernard, St John of the Cross and St Teresa of Avila and you know immediately you are on holy ground. You know that they are the real thing. When they speak they are speaking from experience, and with them to guide you, you are in safe hands.

The sign of genuine Christian mystics is not their ability to hold forth on abstruse mystical states, nor to hint that they have experienced high states of transcendental awareness, but on the quality of their virtues. You know the real thing by their integrity, their truthfulness, their honesty and their goodness; as Christ said, "You will be able to tell them by their fruits" (Matthew 7:20). There is nothing in the Pseudo-Areopagite's works to suggest that they have been written by such a person. They are full of deceit, and for what purpose but to spread his good news that God is utterly unknowable, and the best you can do is nothing but yearn for what you do not know and cannot have. Yet the scriptures tell us that the unknowable has simply done everything humanly possible to make himself known, as a tender, loving Father who wants to share his life with us. We are invited into a profound I-Thou relationship with God, not an I–It relationship that is quite explicitly the subject of the Pseudo-Areopagite's mystical theology. This supra-being, and everything you can possibly say or conceive about God, can only be approached by entering into what he calls the *via negativa*. This entails stripping away anything that you can possibly say, think or conceive about God, because he is inconceivable, and plunging yourself into a mental nothingness that eventually leads to ecstasy. There is no evidence that he had such an experience himself.

Dionysius is the precursor of what was later called the heresy of Quietism, condemned in 1687 as the counterfeit of true Christian mysticism that all but damned true mystical prayer to the present day. There is evidence that previous Neoplatonists, notably Plotinus, did experience ecstatic states. At least his disciple Porphyry said that he did experience ecstasy on four or five occasions over a period of six years, although precisely what he meant by ecstasy he does not say, but there is no evidence that Dionysius did. You get the distinct feeling that he just mentions ecstasy as the consummation of the *via negativa,* because this is what he has been taught, rather than what he has experienced, and he justifies this way by giving it a spiritual climax in conformity with his Neoplatonic mentors.

Read the accounts of the great Christian mystics when they try to describe the ecstasies that they experienced on their mystical journey and compare them with what Dionysius has to say on the subject and you will see you are comparing dross with true gold. In the authentic Christian tradition, ecstasy is never seen as the climax of the mystic way, but part of the rite of passage. The ultimate goal is the Transforming Union or the Mystical Marriage, when the Holy Spirit who filled Christ to overflowing in every part of his human nature, does likewise for the believer. A saint like St Philip Neri, for instance, actually regretted the ecstasies that he experienced, because they prevented him from going out to do what Christ wanted to do through him. There are some useful things that Dionysius has to say from a philosophical approach to God, but he says nothing regarding the mystic way that was not said better immediately before him by the Fathers of the Church, notably St Augustine, St Basil, St Gregory of Nyssa, Clement of Alexandria and Origen. So too the Desert Fathers, Abbot Macarius, Evagrius Ponticus, and the great St Antony himself, as well as St Gregory the Great, St John Climacus and the whole tradition of Philokalia that followed him. For all of them the spiritual way began and always continued in and through Christ.

For the believer who reaches the heights of mystical union, the very experience itself convinces them that they are drawn up into, and are in fact experiencing something of the loving that unites the Father to the Son, in whom their prayer is reaching its consummation. Their prayer is Trinitarian, and this is the indispensable characteristic of authentic Christian contemplation. None of these profound truths is found in the Pseudo-Areopagite. The summit of the mystical life is, for him and his Neoplatonic predecessors, ecstasy. It is a sort of disembodied experience that takes place in the higher part of the head, the *apex mentis.* But the summit of the Christian mystical life is what happened to Jesus at his Glorification. In other words, he tangibly experiences the love of his Father, the Holy Spirit, not just in his head, but flowing into and remaining in every part of his human body, from the top of his head to the tips of his toes.

When you read St Augustine it is quite evident that he has been influenced by Neoplatonism in presenting his profound Christian theology, but when you read Dionysius the converse seems to be true. With Dionysius you get the impression that he has been influenced by Christianity in presenting his Neoplatonic mystical philosophy. It was said of Judas that it would have been better if he had never been born. It is certainly true that it would have been better for the Christian mystical tradition if this man had not been born. The best thing to do, if you want to pray the Christian way, is to forget all about him. Leave him to the few intellectuals who still like to chart his influence on the Christian mystical tradition, as if they are following a golden thread. This thread is made of fool's gold that only deceives dabblers, non-practitioners, naive novices and spiritual bounty hunters into believing that this way is the authentic Christian way.

The true golden thread to follow throughout the centuries, teaches how a Christian first comes to know and love the most loving and loveable human being to have walked on this earth, by reading, reflecting and ruminating on all he said and did, as a prelude to contemplation. Christian mystical contemplation begins when words, images and even the most heart-felt expressions of love, give way to the still and silent gaze upon God, in, with and through Christ, as purification enables the mystic to be united ever more fully with Christ as he is now. This is the prelude to the Mystical Marriage when the mystic is drawn into the love that endlessly passes between the Father and the Son. Here they come to experience the love of Christ, which is beyond all knowledge (Ephesians 3:18), experienced in every part of their mind and heart, and body and soul.

Sadly, the influence of Dionysius and his disembodied Neoplatonic mysticism on very many subsequent mystics in the Christian tradition has prevented their spiritual development. Dionysius has not only been a menace in the past, most particularly when his influence helped destroy the Christian mystical theology after the Reformation, but he still is today. Thanks to him and to the resurgence of his pagan philosophy, modern spiritual writers influenced by him have rekindled an interest in mysticism in a way that is as misleading today as it was in the past.

One of the most damaging features of his writings was to give a new meaning to the word mystical. With Dionysius, the word mystical comes to mean or refer to a tangible psychological experience. Henceforth, and thanks to him, spiritual writers begin to emphasise this aspect of the spiritual journey. Prior to him, the emphasis was always as it should still be, on how to develop an ever-loving relationship with Jesus Christ, and through him with the Father. Just as in human loving, this relationship leads to an ever-deeper joy and delight, but this is not directly sought for its own sake; it is the natural consequence of giving oneself to another. Most genuine believers quite naturally feel reluctant to talk about the intimate details of their personal relationship with Jesus, just as married lovers quite naturally feel reluctant to talk about the intimate details of their loving relationship with each other. St Francis of Assisi would do all in his power to hide from others the utter bliss that would enthral him when he was overwhelmed by the love of God. If he was walking with others when this happened he would insist on his brothers walking ahead of him, or he would rush away to relish what he was receiving in solitude. If this was not possible, he would pull the hood of his habit over his head so that nobody could see the inner joy that captivated him mirrored in his face. And this, one of the gentlest of men, would become very angry if anyone disturbed him in his solitary communion with the one he called Brother Jesus.

The emphasis on degrees of mystical awareness, thanks to the influence of Dionysius, has in the past and present, encouraged the spirit of the bounty hunter into the spiritual journey. It has also encouraged the erroneous belief that it is totally acceptable for a believer to begin their prayer life, not by learning to love, but by learning man-made techniques to acquire states of transcendental awareness. Love means going out of oneself into another, not using them to get pleasurable feelings for oneself. What is true of human loving is also true of mystical loving.

Christian prayer is above all about love, and therefore first and foremost it is about learning to love a person. Just as in human love, the more you love and are loved by another, then the more you forget yourself. The joy that you experience is the result or the by-product of loving and being loved. If you seek it for itself, you will lose it, if you find it in the first place. The moment that love is turned into its counterfeit is the moment when selfishness desecrates the only thing that makes life worth living. Christian prayer begins by getting to know Jesus Christ, as the first disciples came to know him, and love him, and then through his love, entered into him. Dionysius is wrong to make an utterly unknowable God the object of the spiritual journey. It might be philosophically defensible, if you are a follower of the Neoplatonic tradition in which he was originally trained, but it is not if you are a follower of the Christian tradition in whose name he claims to be writing. In the Christian tradition, the spiritual quest begins with the clear revelation that God is knowable. In short, he is our loving Father whom we can come to know through love, the love that he chose to implant within us, as he promised at the Last Supper on the night before he died.

Let me now put to bed once and for all the insidious fallacy that is the very essence of Dionysian mysticism. It has regrettably attracted and still attracts mystical dabblers and dilettantes to its pernicious teaching in the many different guises that it has assumed over the centuries, down to the present day. Like Dionysius, its adherents are only nominal Christians for they are primarily influenced and guided, not by theology, but by philosophy, not therefore by love but by reason, and by reason alone. They consequently and quite logically conclude that by reason alone, God is utterly unknowable. The practical teaching therefore for someone who aspires to come to know God, is to progress by what is called *via negativa.* In short, it is to strip the mind of everything, of every image, of every idea, of every thought, for none of these can aid a person in coming to know the one who is by definition, infinitely beyond them. Having done this, individuals must then place themselves in a state of inner emptiness or 'nothing'. It is only here that one can come to know and in some way experience God in some sort of disembodied ecstasy.

In clear contrast, the Christian way insists that God is love, and therefore it is by love that you can, not only come to know him, but actually enter into him and experience his love, for that is the very reason for which God created us. At the beginning of his spiritual journey St Augustine discovers God's love as it is embodied in his creation, and then as it is supremely embodied in the greatest work of his creation, Jesus Christ, in whom all things are created. It is then, by receiving the love that continually emanates from Jesus, that human loving is transformed. It is transformed by being purified of all the self-centred and distorted love that can prevent it from being united with God's perfect love that is embodied in Jesus Christ. Once sufficiently purified, human loving can enter into his glorified body ever more deeply, finally entering into his very action – into his mystical contemplation of God.

Let me now try to clarify the confusion that has deceived so many for so long. When Dionysius and his later followers speak of stripping oneself of all and everything that is not God by *via negativa,* they are primarily referring to the stripping of the mind. However, when Christian mystics use what seems to be similar language, they are primarily referring, not so much to the mind or the reason, but to the heart, the heart's desire, or the will.

In the Christian mystical tradition, the one thing that is God-given and implanted within every human being from the beginning, is the yearning for God which initially manifests itself as a longing for love. The mystic way is the place where that sullied self-centred love is purified to enable it to lead a person into union with perfect love. That is why everyone knows the famous saying of St. Augustine, "Our hearts are restless until they rest in thee, O Lord". At first, love seeks its fulfilment in the beauty of creation or in the arts that mirror it. Then, like St Augustine it leads us to Christ, thence, in and through Christ, to the maker of all things who made the love for which we yearn, and who is that love in its infinite and eternal realisation. Christian asceticism therefore, does not enjoin a *via negativa* that would strip a person of everything, but only of all unnecessary, unwarranted desires, and lesser loves that prevent the pure and simple desire for God flowering in mystical contemplation.

Let me take a leaf out of John Bunyan's *The Pilgrim's Progress* to explain what I mean by personalising love and reason. There are two prisoners confined within every human being. One is called reason, the other is called love. Only one can escape. Through knowledge the prisoner, reason, can come to know something or someone, by using their minds to distinguish, understand, and to apprehend, but it cannot escape to encounter anything or anyone outside. However, the other prisoner, love, can escape, for its very nature is to reach out to the object of its desires, not just to know them, but to enter into them through their loving, and to relish the union that they yearned for from the start. Pure reason can never escape; it is destined to remain incarcerated within its cell forever, no matter how it might try to escape. It might repeat mantras to all eternity, but they will never help it to get there. Sadly, it will just to go around and around in circles in a mental cul-de-sac, going nowhere.

If you read the works of the great saints who were also mystical writers, you will notice how they subtly change the teaching of Dionysius. They feel they must refer to him and treat him with reverence, because they have been deceived into believing he is a saint who was on familiar terms with the Apostles, but they nevertheless change his teaching. His rigorous inner asceticism is re-directed from the total emptying of the mind, to the total emptying of the heart or the heart's desire. It is emptied of all other loves that prevent the divinely implanted spark flickering into a flame, and rising to the mystical flashpoint where it reaches out to be united with its maker.

When Christian mystics speak of the inner purification that takes place in what St John of the Cross calls the dark night of the soul, they are referring to the stripping of the heart, not primarily the stripping of the mind. All authentic Christian teaching from the beginning has taught that throughout mystical purification, what has been called the 'Prayer of Faith' must be employed to keep the heart fixed on God. The book *The Cloud of Unknowing* is one of the best examples of how this form of prayer should be used to keep the heart's desire fixed on God. Far from doing nothing in Christian mystical prayer, they have never been more active, but in a fuller and more penetrating mystical activity, as they keep turning to God, practising repentance on a higher level than ever before.

Their profound mystical endeavour is completely unknown to those whose attention usually ends in turning inwards to self, rather than outward and upwards to God. It is only as the purification of love is being brought to perfection in the mystic way that the repentance practised there opens the Christian mystic to the outpouring of the Holy Spirit that St Peter proclaimed on the first Pentecost day. The more the Holy Spirit enters in, the more the recipient is drawn up and into the one who sent him, into the glorified Christ, in whom, and with whom they become their true selves, as they begin to do what they were created for from the beginning. It is here that the Christian mystic begins to love God with his or her whole heart, mind, body and soul. And, because they are doing this in Christ the King, they begin to both receive and experience something of the love that he receives continually from his Father. So, far from doing nothing in this profound mystical loving, we are moving ever closer to doing to perfection that for which we were created in the beginning. We have never been more intensively or better employed before. Why? Because we are doing what we have been made for and enjoying it with our whole being, as we go relentlessly out of ourselves through love, into love without measure.

This unseen life and love is called mystical because, as said before, the word mystical is taken from the Greek word that simply means hidden or secret, because it is beyond all human sight, but not beyond all human feeling. However, the primary meaning of the word mystical simply refers to the mystical life of the Holy Spirit that flows to and fro between the Father and the Son, and now simultaneously between all who are in the Son, whether it is felt or not. This is the primary meaning of the word mystical as it is used in this book. It has nothing to do with having obscure or esoteric states of transcendental awareness procured by man-made methods or techniques of one description or another. This meaning of the word came into Christianity much later in its history from Neoplatonism, thanks to Dionysius.

The word mysticism was never used by the Fathers of the Church, nor was mystical experience anything to be sought for its own sake. In the early Church the mystical life that bound them all together may indeed have eventually led to what 'moderns' would call mystical experiences, but these experiences were never sought for their own sake. It was because they sought God for his sake that the experience of his love sometimes became tangible, as it did for St Paul. In short, and once again it was the by-product of the selfless giving of oneself to God. Put in another way, the spirituality of the ancient Christian mystics was theocentric or God-centred, the 'spirituality' of 'pseudo mystics' is anthropocentric or self-centred, not so much sought for God's honour and glory, as for their own.

In his masterpiece, *Western Mysticism,* Abbot Butler has shown that before St Bernard (1090-1153), the inner or hidden awareness of God's love that is experienced as a by-product of loving him, is generally called contemplation or mystical contemplation. This older and more traditional way of referring to the tangible experience of God's love is generally retained by the mainstream of Catholic mystical writers. I use the word Catholic because genuine mystical writers who perpetuate the most ancient Christian mystical tradition are predominantly Catholic. The reason for this is that the first radical Protestant reformers, and those who are still influenced by their doctrines, believe that man is intrinsically evil, thus making the divine indwelling and the consequent mystical life unthinkable. Anglicanism would in general be a good example of an exception to the rule.

The accepted language that describes mystical experiences is usually taken from St Teresa of Avila's spiritual masterpiece, *Interior Castle*, written at the height of her powers. She denotes different states of the awareness of God's loving presence by their psychological intensity, and in ascending order. They are: the Prayer of Recollection, Prayer of Quiet, Prayer of Full Union, Prayer of Ecstasy, and Rapture. The higher the intensity of a state, the shorter is its duration. All these forms of mystical contemplation are experienced in the head, or in the mind, or in the higher mind that Latin writers called the *apex mentis*. However, the journey finds its completion in this life, not just in the *apex mentis*, but in the body too, as the love experienced in the mind begins to overflow into the whole person, resulting in what St Teresa of Avila and St John of the Cross call the Spiritual Marriage. This marriage, which finally becomes permanent, is preceded by temporary experiences of the 'spiritual marriage' that come and go for a time. It is for this reason that they call them the 'spiritual betrothals'. In the spiritual or mystical marriage, the believer begins, even in this life, to experience the transformation of the whole person that is their final destiny. That is why St John of the Cross refers to this state as the Transforming Union. To see the completion of this mystical transformation they must look through the eyes of Peter, James, and John. It is through their eyes, as they gazed on Jesus as he was transformed and transfigured before them on Mount Tabor, that Christians can see Christ as he would soon become after his Ascension. Then, in seeing who he would become, they were able to see who they would become if they were prepared to be baptised with the baptism that Jesus chose for himself. When asked by James and John for preferential treatment when the Kingdom finally came, Jesus made it clear that this would mean accepting a second baptism, the baptism of suffering involved in the daily carrying of a cross (Mark 10:38). It might be a matchwood cross compared with the one that Jesus was to shoulder, but it would be a cross nevertheless. This suffering would involve the daily dying involved in journeying on through the mystic way. It is here alone that our self-centred love, once hidden in the nether regions of our soul, is laid bare, before being gradually purified to be united with the perfect love that is only fully realised in God's kingdom of love in heaven.

In general, the rare moments of experiencing the love of God in the *apex mentis* occupy little more than one percent of the journey in the mystic way. The clear majority of the time is spent in darkness, the dark night of the soul. That is why so many give up this mystical journey unpurified, and therefore unprepared to experience brief moments of joy in mystical contemplation, not to mention the mystical marriage to which they are invited, which eventually becomes a permanent and lasting experience as it did for Jesus while he was on earth. In the whole of our spiritual journey, God only does one thing; he loves us relentlessly with the fire of the Holy Spirit. At first and for a long time, years rather than months, the fire of his love purifies us in preparation for the union that can only take place when there is a sufficient likeness between the giver and the receiver. The fire that at first purifies in the mystic way eventually begins to kindle the love that results in the forms of mystical contemplation so carefully described by St Teresa of Avila. I will not attempt to detail the journey through the mystic way, because that has been done, and in detail, with the relevant practical advice in the book *Wisdom from the Western Isles, The Making of a Mystic.*

In following this way, we are taking up our daily cross and following in the footsteps of Christ himself. When, after first enthusiasm, we find ourselves in dryness and aridity, endlessly trying to dismiss the many distractions that assail us, we are at the beginning of the dark night. It is here that the purification of the selfish, self-centred person that we are, begins. Many will soon run away and give up the daily prayer that they once hoped would give them experience of God. They do not want to waste their time seemingly doing nothing when they could be changing the world by themselves. However, what they would call doing nothing in prayer is called 'doing the one thing necessary' by the mystics. They know from their own experience that it is by continually turning away from distractions and back to God, although he doesn't seem to be there, that the selflessness that makes selfless lovers is gradually learnt. Only then can they love God and others ever more perfectly. So, when we courageously try to journey on in prayer although we seem to get nothing out of it, we are in fact practising the selflessness from which all the virtues are born. We are carrying the cross daily that Jesus asked us to carry, as he carried his cross all the way to Calvary to show his love for us.

Let me end this chapter by stressing something that cannot be stressed enough. God's purifying action does not just bear fruit when he makes his presence felt in the moments of light, as described by St Teresa of Avila, but throughout the darkness too. In fact, the mystics continually describe how, on emerging from periods of darkness, when they believed they were doing nothing, they find they were in fact being filled with profound spiritual wisdom. But this only happens because they have been trying to respond in darkness. That is why, like Saint Paul, you do not hear them boasting about the moments of light they have experienced, but about the suffering through which they have been able to carry their daily cross, and through which they have been inspired by the wisdom of the Holy Spirit. St Thomas Aquinas is one of the best examples of this, for, unknown to the general reader, the profound wisdom that infuses all his works was learnt in the night, as described in the next chapter. This is not just my opinion but the opinion of the great Garrigou-Lagrange OP. That is why St John of the Cross, like so many other great mystics, praises what they call the 'gift of holy darkness'. Without this gift, the Christian renaissance that is needed cannot begin nor can it be sustained.

Chapter 14

From a Mystical to a Moral Spirituality

When I asked Peter how the spirituality that he described in his talks began to return once more, at least in part, after Christendom's Dark Ages when the centrality of Christ's humanity was not emphasised as it was in the beginning, his answer was as usual, to the point and clear.

He said that although St Bernard of Clairvaux (1090-1153) was not seriously influenced by the Pseudo-Areopagite, he was undoubtedly influenced by the new interest in the historical Jesus when the Crusaders re-opened the Holy Land for pilgrims from the West. The influence of this new spiritual phenomenon was reinforced and deepened by St Bernard's study of the scriptures and the early Fathers, thanks to the precious manuscripts carefully collected and preserved in monastic libraries. They suffused him with a burning desire to come to know and experience the love of God with which all his writings were imbued - earning him the title of 'the last of the Fathers'. However, this new spirituality that once more set the incarnation at the centre of Christian spirituality would not have penetrated far beyond the cloisters of his Cistercian monasteries, had it not been for another man. This time it was a layman, born less than thirty years after his death, who did what even St Bernard's genius failed to do.

This other man was St Francis of Assisi (1181-1226), who, in his own words, was no more than a semi-literate draper's son, who was also deeply influenced by the new interest in the historical Jesus that was exciting medieval Europe. Pilgrims were returning home with stories of where Jesus was born, grew up, preached, died and from where he rose from the dead. He even visited the Holy Land himself and when he returned he built a crib at Christmas at a little hamlet called Greccio, high up on the hillside above the Rieti Valley. From that time, onwards the practice of building cribs at Christmas spread all over the world and down the centuries, to remind a world that had once all but forgotten the world-shaking importance of the Incarnation. By his own example and by the example of his followers, he taught ordinary people to do once more what the first Christians had done, and done daily. He taught them to meditate on every moment of Christ's life on earth and most particularly on his death and Resurrection. It was here that the love would be generated that would enable a believer to enter into the person whom he called Brother Jesus. Just before he received the stigmata on Mount La Verna on the 14 September 1224, he heard Christ himself revealing to him that it was only through love and love alone that he, or anyone else for that matter, could enter into union with him and through him with the Father.

As a Protestant, I was particularly sceptical about private revelations, so I approached Peter about my misgivings one evening during a retreat that he was leading in Franciscan Italy. Peter explained that God's love, like all love, can only be received by those who are open to receive it, for love of its very nature cannot be forced on anyone. His love therefore, can only be received by those who have a pure and humble heart. That is why God seems to choose people who we would think are unfit for purpose because of human weaknesses of one sort or another. Yet it is precisely their human weakness that gives them the inner humility of heart that enables the love of God to do in them, and through them, what could not be done in others. He gave the example of Abraham, an impotent man of almost a hundred years, chosen to be the father of his people. He chose Moses, a man who had difficulty expressing himself, to speak on his behalf to the Pharaoh to save his people from slavery. He chose the stripling David to fell the giant Goliath and save his people from the Philistines. In due course Peter, who denied Jesus three times, was chosen to become the head of God's new people. Paul who persecuted them was chosen to become the Apostle to the gentiles. Augustine who was a slave to sexual sins was chosen to become one of the Church's greatest theologians.

The truth is that even sin itself can lead a person to sanctity, if it leads them to know their utter weakness, and enables them to turn to the only one whose love can transform them. The truth is not just that God can work through weakness, but that he can only work through weakness. The most accurate translation of the first beatitude is not, "Blessed are the poor in spirit," but, "Blessed are they who know their need of God." It is only they who will turn to God in their need, to receive the only love that can change them and others whom God wants to change through them. That is why St Francis of Assisi was chosen to receive and understand the most simple but profound truth that is the heart and soul of the Christian message - the absolute and unconditional primacy of love, forgotten by his contemporaries. It was for this reason that he named the Holy Spirit as the General of the order that he founded. For it was the fire of his love that would first purify them before setting them alight with the love they would use to rekindle the world with what had set it ablaze at the beginning. Peter then went on to explain that because God can only enter and reveal his love to the humble of heart; the rich, the powerful, and those in high places are often the last he can work through. That is why time and time again, history shows the Holy Spirit working through the poor, the weak and the lowly to bring renewal to a Church whose leaders are deaf to his message.

It must be said, however, that not everybody has major physical or moral defects that make them aware of their utter need of God. That is where prayer comes in, the prayer that can and does lead anyone who perseveres for long enough, into the mystic way. It is here that the Holy Spirit makes them aware of the moral weaknesses that cannot be overcome without the grace of God. It is here that saints are made out of the sinners who enter there, as their purification opens them to receive the love that generates the wisdom to see the truth, while at the same time giving them the strength to embody the truth, and to do the truth no matter what the cost. That is why this book is trying to encourage the reader to pray and to persevere in prayer, to the place where Christ-like people are formed, for they are the only people who ever did and ever can bring about authentic and lasting Christian renewal. Any alien teachings or practices that discourage or dissuade or obstruct a person from pursuing a spiritual journey through mystical prayer, are preventing the formation of the saints, the mystics and the spiritual leaders we need to guide and direct us. Over a hundred years after the Council of Trent, a most pernicious heresy influenced by Dionysian mysticism, called Quietism, was responsible for doing precisely this.

I will never forget what Peter said to me late one night during that retreat he was leading in Franciscan Italy, nor did Peter forget it for that matter, because only three years ago, he sent me a document produced by the Church's theological commission in 2014 entitled *Sensus fidei fidelis in the life of the Church.* I would recommend it to everyone. It emphasises that, as the Wisdom of the Holy Spirit can only work through the poor and humble of heart, these are the people, seemingly on the periphery, who must always be consulted. If this is not done, then we will continually commit the sin against the Holy Spirit, who can and does speak through them, and so put the need for continual renewal and reform in the Church permanently in jeopardy.

Like all genuine revelations, the revelation of the primacy of love was of course nothing new, for it had been the teaching of Jesus while he was on earth, and of the early Church after his Resurrection. But the all-embracing love of the Risen Christ that had shone so brightly at the dawn of Christianity became lustreless and dim during the Dark Ages. It took the wisdom given to a man of no importance, to see the most important truth of all, moments before he was united, as never before, with Brother Jesus. This revelation would not only dominate all subsequent expressions of Franciscan spirituality, but all other genuine expressions of Christian spirituality, as it had dominated the daily spirituality of the early Church.

Once again, from meditating on Jesus as he once was, the love would be generated to enable a person to enter into him as he is now, and in, with and through him, to enter into and share in his contemplation of the Father. What was once all but lost to view, rose up once more to inspire and regenerate the Church. The mystical prayer that radically opens human love to the divine, and the divine to the human, was once more to become the principal inspiration to animate and regenerate the Church for many centuries to come.

In the years to come thousands upon thousands of believers would once more be drawn up into God's plan, the Mysterion, beginning a journey here on earth that would only be completed hereafter. In the next four or five hundred years, there would emerge hundreds of first rank mystical writers to support the faithful, following the example set by St Francis of Assisi, making the primacy of love paramount in their spiritual endeavour. From St Bernard to St Teresa of Avila and St John of the Cross and beyond, there would be more great mystical writers and spiritual guides than at any other time in the history of Christian spirituality. The one guarantee of their orthodoxy was then, as it still is, their absolute and unequivocal adherence to the importance of the primacy of love. There were many bogus forms of mystical teaching that did prevail for a time, but after four hundred years there was one, deeply influenced by the Pseudo-Areopagite, that had a pernicious and permanent influence on the authentic teaching and practice of true Christian mystical theology. I am referring to the heresy known as Quietism. The practice and then the condemnation of Quietism had a devastating effect on Christian spirituality in general, and mystical theology in particular, and has affected every aspect of the Catholic Church down to the present day.

Sadly, the mystic way that did still prevail amongst some of the faithful within the Church, never became a way for the Protestant reformers because of their belief in the intrinsic sinfulness of human beings. It was this that made it impossible for them to envisage Christ entering into them, or them entering into him. They may be saved by the merits of Christ, but, entering into a mystical union with God in Christ was impossible. Prayer directed towards union with Christ then, was not only pointless, but gave the impression that human endeavour, through prayer or any other good works for that matter, could attain union with God. All we could do was nothing; any attempt to do anything would be seen as tantamount to blasphemy. After all, if human beings are intrinsically evil so also must any thoughts, desires, or motives which arise from such a flawed creature. All that could be attained could only be attained by the grace of God alone.

Understandably, once the Reformation began to spread, the Catholic Church became suspicious of any form of prayer that seemed to suggest that human endeavour was of no or little value. It was acceptable to engage in what came to be called Discursive and Affective prayer, when the mind repeatedly reflects on the truths of the faith, and the heart reacts with heartfelt love. But if beginners began to linger too long in what was called Acquired Contemplation, just gazing upon the God on whom they had been reflecting, or if they were led into true mystical prayer, such as Recollection, Quiet or Full Union, to use the language of St Teresa of Avila, then they immediately became suspect. What seemed to suggest that they were doing nothing, seemed to suggest they were falling into heresy. When Molino the founder of Quietism wrote in his *Spiritual Guide,* "It is by the way of doing nothing that you will reach the goal of losing yourself in God," his condemnation was only a matter of time. Whether he had actually fallen into the errors of the reformers or not was beside the point; he wrote as if he had, and others who would follow him would act as if they had too. He had to be stopped. The mystic way, like every aspect of the Christian way, is a partnership at all times, albeit an unequal partnership, between the human and the divine.

During this period, the most popular and successful method of prayer was to be found in the Exercises of St Ignatius (1491-1556), and forms of prayer based on, or derived from them, because it involved concerted spiritual endeavour in which there could be no hint of heresy. When the Jesuit superior general, Mercurian, found that one of his priests, Balthasar de Alvarez, acting as spiritual director to St Teresa of Avila was supporting her in the mystic way, he was ordered to stop immediately and return to guiding her according to the Exercises of their founder. His action became the norm for other superiors, down to the present day when all forms of mystical prayer became suspect for fear of leading the faithful into Quietism. It was called Quietism, because it seemed to encourage a person to do nothing in prayer, but remain quiet before God. Here, he or she appeared to do nothing but wait on God's action in total silence. Quietism in all its different manifestations, seemed to encourage the reformer's belief that our own efforts are useless and even blasphemous. Everything depends, not on what we do, but only and exclusively on the grace of God alone. It was Quietism that gradually undermined authentic mystical theology and the role of the mystic within the Church. It carried the *via negativa* of Dionysius the Pseudo-Areopagite to the ultimate extreme. The believer was not only encouraged to do absolutely nothing in prayer, but to do nothing about temptations either. It was, as a result of the Church's zeal in crushing this heresy, condemned in 1687, and in promoting the Gospel of good works, for fear that Catholics would fall into Protestantism that mystical prayer simply fell into abeyance. The enormity of this and its consequences down to the present day cannot be exaggerated. It meant that the primacy of love, that dominated Christian spirituality before, was simply taken away almost overnight.

Mystical theology is that branch of theology that teaches how the love of sincere Christian searchers is gradually prepared for union with Christ. It teaches how this union is brought about through a profound inner purification so that we can finally become one with him, not just in being, but in action, in his mystical contemplation of the Father. Take yeast, salt and sugar out of bread and what is left but an unwholesome indigestible lump of dough. Take purification, processing and polishing out of love and what is left but an unwholesome self-centred nobody who is going nowhere. But the love that is purified, refined and brought to perfection in the mystic way, eventually passes through darkness to experience light, as the new heart formed in mystical purification enables the light of God's love to become tangible. At last, what we thought we knew by faith becomes tangible, and that makes all the difference in the world. Knowledge alone is not enough. Knowledge alone will never change anyone permanently. But the experience of being loved will. All this happens in the mystic way where saints are made out of sinners and where the great spiritual leaders are formed to lead us back to the contemplation that dispels darkness and bathes us in the light of God's love. Without the contemplation that was called into question after the condemnation of Quietism, we will be going nowhere. In his monumental *History of the Church* Monsignor Philip Hughes put it this way:

"The most mischievous feature of Quietism was the suspicion that it threw on the contemplative life as a whole. ... At the moment when, more than at any other, the Church needed the strength that only the life of contemplation can give, it was the tragedy of history that this life shrank to very small proportions, and religion, even for holy souls, too often took on the appearance of being no more than a divinely aided effort towards moral perfection."

The mystic way in which the saints, the mystics, the martyrs and great spiritual leaders of the past had been schooled for thousands of years, was not only misunderstood, it was condemned. This has led to an increasingly superficial spirituality from which we have all suffered. It all too often consists of a vast mosaic of myriad pious practices that have led to a 'pick and mix' spirituality. Although they are not bad in themselves, these practices do not naturally reflect or flow out of the liturgy of the Church, nor do they clearly prepare the way for its meaningful celebration. The best of them may well be good, and good enough to lead a person into the mystic way, where in purification they would see the truth, but then it was highly likely that the way would be blocked to them or declared dangerous. This happens when even the most respected authorities misdirect the faithful, because they themselves are the casualties of the anti-mystical witch-hunts, the effects of which have continued since the condemnation of Quietism to the present day. The original passion of the first zealots, who sought to dismantle, demolish and destroy all forms of prayer that had the mere whiff of Quietism about them, may well have gone, but the convictions that drove them have become endemic in the spiritual ethos that we have inherited. They have thrown out the baby with the bath water, and the bath water that has been thrown out is the water of the second baptism, that Jesus called upon his disciples to accept (Mark 10:38), where love is learnt and brought to perfection under the guidance of the Holy Spirit. All spirituality that has been stripped of the mystical theology that teaches where, and details how, love is learnt and brought to perfection, is going nowhere but around and around in circles. The whole point and purpose of Christian spirituality is to teach believers how to be stripped of self-love, preparing the way for God's love to suffuse their love with the only love that leads to union.

Many people have been deceived into believing that the impoverished spirituality that we have all inherited, that is unsympathetic, if not positively antithetical to mystical theology, is what they are proud to call Tridentine Spirituality. But this is not true; authentic Tridentine Spirituality that flowered for over a hundred years after the Council of Trent, safeguarding the primacy of love, was as deeply mystical as that which preceded it for hundreds of years. In his life's work, *Enthusiasm,* Monsignor Ronald Knox makes it quite clear:

"The seventeenth century was a century of mystics. The doctrine of the interior life was far better publicised, developed in far greater detail than it had ever been in late-medieval Germany or late-medieval England. Bremond, in his *Histoire littéraire du sentiment religieux en France,* has traced unforgettably the progress of that movement in France. But Spain too, the country of St Teresa and St John of the Cross, had her mystics, Italy also had her mystics, who flourished under the aegis of the Vatican. Even the exiled Church in England produced in Father Baker's *Sancta Sophia* a classic of the interior life" (Chapter XI).

Quietism, Knox insists, "is the error of a few incautious souls, trying to repeat the lessons that they have learnt from the saints of the counter-Reformation and getting it wrong" (Chapter XI). They get it wrong because they do not have the time, the energy, the inclination or the authentic teaching to lead them into the place where purification takes place. It is only here that true Christ-like love is learnt. As we have seen, this purification does not begin immediately after a person has seriously embarked upon mental prayer, but later, in months rather than years, if they keep to their daily time for mental prayer. Then it is in years rather than months of being purified in dry and arid prayer that a person first begins to experience moments of inner peace. As the demons within are being put to death, their inner soul is being put to rest. St John of the Cross put it this way:

"On a dark night, kindled in love with yearnings - oh, happy chance! - I went forth without being observed, my house being now at rest".

St Teresa calls this God-given state of rest, when a house once at war with itself, is at peace, The Prayer of Quiet. This infused prayer, the first stage of true mystical contemplation, must not be confused with Quietism. Quietism is the name given to the movement that promises The Prayer of Quiet to those who have not been prepared to undergo the inner purification that would enable them to receive it. If a person wants to become a master craftsman, a stone mason, a sculptor or a great artist, then he or she must go through a prolonged apprenticeship to learn to perfect their art under the direction of a master. The same is true of the spiritual life. If you want to perfect the art of loving, to love God and others as Jesus did, then you have first to become an apprentice for many years. This is where loving is learnt and brought to perfection under the guidance and direction of the perfect lover in what appears to be a continual dark night. The Quietists wanted to bypass this spiritual apprenticeship and attain The Prayer of Quiet by their own ill-advised endeavours and as quickly as possible. The result is an unholy spiritual chaos that usually ensues when human beings try to do what only God can do in those who are pure and humble of heart. Inevitably they confuse others as they have confused themselves. They confuse them, not just about prayer, but about the whole gamut of the spiritual life, from self-absorbed scrupulosity to endless disputes about mystical states. I have spoken about Quietism in the past tense but sadly their descendants are still with us, albeit in slightly different attire.

The role of the great mystical master craftsmen and women is of vital importance to the Church and always has been. They are the spiritual leaders, the teachers, the doctors and the consultants on whom the present and future health and well-being of the Church depends. You would not think of going to seek the advice of doctors who have not passed through the equivalent of their long apprenticeship, nor would you trust a surgeon to operate on you without an even longer professional preparation. The serious demise of mystical life in the Church in the aftermath of the condemnation of Quietism has deprived the Church of the indispensable spiritual teaching, inspiration, and guidance needed for continual growth in the spiritual life. It has further deprived us of the best educated and practised mystical doctors and consultants. In short and in biblical language it has left them as sheep without shepherds.

It was only after Quietism had been condemned that, in the words of Knox, "a joyless moralism" prevailed that was influenced by Jansenism that spread far and wide despite its condemnation by the Church. Jansenism was a sort of Catholic Calvinism, born at the beginning of the seventeenth century, in which the writings of the Greek and Latin Fathers were substituted for the Bible, but sadly love was lost in translation. For them most people were heading for hell on the doom and gloom express. Only the few could board the flight for heaven after a life of unremitting mortification and misery. After visiting their headquarters at the Convent of Port Royal near Paris, visitors would come away as Knox put it, "not so much feeling privileged that they had met people on the way to heaven, but feeling that they themselves were most certainly on their way to hell!"

Fortunately, the gloomy ethos generated by this narrow-minded moralism gradually lifted with the introduction of more uplifting and inspiring devotions like the devotion to the Sacred Heart. Sadly however, when this led people to the mystical crèche where saints are made, there was no one to encourage, instruct, or guide them through the purification, where the love that leads to union is learnt. Genuine mystical theology then withered after the condemnation of Quietism and has never bloomed in quite the same way since.

An understandable attachment to the Tridentine Liturgy has deceived many into believing that the spirituality that we have inherited was born at the Council of Trent, like the Mass that they, like so many of us, rightly admire. Not at all. It was born in the immediate aftermath of the condemnation of Quietism, and it is deficient and defective because it lacks the foundation, the inspiration and the destination that mystic theology once gave it. Let me put it in simple language. The spiritual life begins and ends with a marriage, a mystical marriage with Christ. Take love out of any marriage and what are you left with but a drab and dreary daily monotony in which you exist rather than live together. You merely exist with, at best, a mutual tolerance and a set of unwritten rules and regulations tacitly accepted by both parties to keep the peace, rather than to live in the peace that only love can generate. Extract love from any marriage and law of one sort or another takes over. It is the same with the mystical marriage to which we are all called when love is withdrawn, but with one difference. If something goes wrong it is we, not Christ, who has stopped loving. If this marriage breaks down it is because we didn't seriously try to love in the first place, or because we stopped when we were given the privilege of being led to the place where human love is purified for marriage with the divine.

That generation after generation has been born with an inherent desire for union with God is beyond question. However, it is also beyond question that a spirituality that cannot lead a person on though purification to that mystical union is not fit for purpose. That is why there have been so few great mystical guides in the last three hundred years or more compared with the many hundreds of mystics, saints, and mystical writers who spanned the centuries from St Bernard, who was born in 1090, up until the condemnation of Quietism in 1687.

The moralism that Monsignor Hughes said prevailed after the condemnation of Quietism has resulted in a clear distinction between the ascetical life and the mystical life that did not exist before. The point is made quite clearly by the great Dominican theologian, Garrigou-Lagrange, perhaps the greatest spiritual theologian of the twentieth century. In his book *The Three Ages of the Interior Life* that fuses the teaching of St Thomas Aquinas with that of St Teresa of Avila and St John of the Cross, he states quite emphatically:

"Since the seventeenth and eighteenth centuries, authors have deemed it necessary to distinguish absolutely between ascetical and mystical theology. Thereby they have compromised the unity of the spiritual life. The perfection which ascetical theology speaks of, becomes an end and not a means to a more intimate and more elevated union. Mystical theology then was no longer of any importance except to a few privileged souls" (Chapter 52 page 548).

The unity to which he refers can only be attained in the spiritual life when the ascetical life is primarily seen as the means by which a person opens themselves to receive the love of God. It is this love, the Holy Spirit, who can alone draw us up into Christ, beginning now in this life and reaching its consummation in the next. In him we begin to forget ourselves as we live for God and for his honour and glory in all we say and do. However, take this mystical life away and the ascetical life merely becomes a way of life in which we try to make ourselves perfect by our own unaided endeavour and for our own honour and glory. This is what Fr Garrigou-Lagrange means when he says that since the demise of mystical theology the ascetical life has too often been an end in itself, a method of making oneself perfect by achieving moral perfection by one's own endeavour. Inevitably it leads back into the old heresy of SemiPelagianism and into a spirituality that is self-centred not God-centred, anthropocentric not theocentric. Authentic Christian spirituality is, and always has been focused on facilitating the action of the Holy Spirit within, and that is why, what was first called "The Way" came to be called the spiritual life. For in the spiritual journey the Holy Spirit is at all times at work purifying and refining the love that is being prepared for union.

Sometimes his presence is experienced in darkness, sometimes in light, sometimes in presence, sometimes in absence, sometimes in obscure contemplation, sometimes in pure contemplation. It is then that a person becomes more passive as God's action becomes more active. Never does a person cease to act, but now their action takes place in, with and through Christ under the ever more penetrating influence and inspiration of the Holy Spirit. It is only non-practitioners who try to liken mystical contemplation to putting oneself in the state of 'nothing'.

Before the rise of moralism that began to view the ascetical life as an end in itself, St John of the Cross made it clear that his mystical writings were for all, even though he was writing for the sisters of the new Carmelite reform. Writing almost eighty years ago, Garrigou-Lagrange was delighted to say that the distinction between the ascetical and the mystical life was no longer accepted by himself and a small group of similar minded academics. However, at the beginning of the twenty-first century this view still remains the opinion of a few academics and their followers in the rarefied atmosphere of university campuses, but that is all. On ground level nothing much has changed to reverse the massive spiritual imbalance that began after the condemnation of Quietism. What academics discuss in learned papers has not filtered down to the ordinary men and women in the pew. Or if it has, it has not been transposed into the teaching that encourages, inspires, directs and guides them to journey on come what may, into and through the mystic way where they are transformed by the Holy Spirit.

There are of course some exceptions to the rule. There are still people who have tried to journey on in the mystic way despite living in a spiritual climate in which 'devout moralism' still prevails. Sadly, they are considered mavericks or misfits. I have been privileged to meet some of them who, despite the conventional wisdom that discounts the importance of mystical theology, have managed to travel along and through the dark night regardless. But sadly, they have had to do this as eccentrics, oddities quietly journeying on the periphery when they should, not so much be in the mainstream, but be the mainstream. A new and effective Christian renaissance cannot take place, nor can it be sustained without people like these.

It is only because both the old scholastic theology and the new biblical theology have failed to be transposed into simple accessible and practical mystical spirituality for all, that the simple truths that everyone knew and lived by in the early Church have been forgotten. This truth is, as Peter emphasised in his talks, that by our very baptism we are called to a mystical marriage with Christ. No one doubted for a second that this was for all and that it was the beginning in this life of what would only reach its ultimate consummation in the next. Nor did anyone doubt that like other marriages this marriage involved a daily close mutual interpenetration of loving that reaches its most intimate moments in prayer. The sort of abstruse and intellectual arguments that made even some of the most respected and orthodox theologians question whether the mystic way was for all, would have both mystified and horrified our early ancestors in equal proportions. It is just further proof, if such proof is necessary, that the prevailing spirituality that has reigned since the condemnation of Quietism, is not only seriously deficient but aeons away from the profound mystical spirituality bequeathed by Jesus himself to the early Church. It is both profound and mystical because it calls all who would listen to him to a mystical marriage with himself, which was destined to flower, not just in heartfelt love, but in a love that would completely possess and pervade the body too, beginning in this life and reaching its climax in the next.

No one can maintain a decent moral life let alone a heroic one, as Jesus did, without the same inner spirit that animated him. But once you outlaw the mystical theology that guides a person through the purification then true imitation of Christ, never mind marriage to him, becomes impossible. Before you know where you are, you are back in the world of rules and regulations of precepts and moral directives on which to base your life, with a liturgy to celebrate it that becomes moribund with rites, rituals and rubrics that must be punctiliously performed. In short, we are back in the world of the Old Testament that Christ came to supersede. It is a world where without the all-pervading presence and action of the Holy Spirit within us, we are condemned to the continual moral failure that leads to the feelings of guilt which have, for outsiders, become the hallmarks of Roman Catholics. Jesus insisted that without him, and the love with which he wants to rule and guide us from within, we cannot do anything, never mind maintain even a semblance of a decent moral life. And St Paul repeatedly makes the point that the age when we were to find redemption through maintaining the laws of old is now over. We are now in a new age where the new law of love is supreme. This law of love is a person. This person is the Holy Spirit, who can therefore reside within other persons who choose to admit him. From here his loving can infuse all human loving, making possible everything that was quite impossible without him.

The modern malaise, then, is ultimately due to the anti-mystical witch-hunts that were once rampant throughout Christendom that rooted out all forms of prayer that even mentioned such words as inner Recollection, or Prayer of Quiet and any form of prayer that did not seem to involve the continual inner activity of the mind and heart. In short, all forms of prayer that created the inner environment in which the Holy Spirit can work to purify what St Paul called the 'Old Man' and to refashion him into 'the 'New Man'. In this climate, even the works of St Teresa of Avila and St John of the Cross were considered as suspect, because they were misunderstood. Nothing was done, or for that matter has been done to repair the damage, down to the present day.

To the uninitiated, influenced by the pagan mystics, contemplative prayer did not seem to involve the activity of the heart and mind, but nothing could be further from the truth. In true contemplative prayer, believers are continually trying to keep their hearts and minds directed towards God despite the distractions and temptations that try to divert them elsewhere. This is made abundantly clear in a work like *The Cloud of Unknowing* that sums up perfectly the way contemplatives prayed in the early Church. If, for very brief and rare moments of grace, contemplatives experience the love of God lifting them up and out of themselves, it is not they who have chosen to do nothing, but God who chooses to fill them with the tangible experience of his love for brief but transforming moments of bliss. Nor are they doing nothing in these moments, for they are doing what they were created for. At this moment and at every moment to the end of time, Jesus is fully engaged in the sublime contemplation of his Father. A person has never been so completely and whole-heartedly active as when doing what we are all created for. When we are sufficiently purified that we can join him in this supreme act of loving, then we will never have been more active before, because we too are wholly and whole-heartedly engaged in doing what we have been created for – loving at the highest and most supreme level.

In outlawing authentic mystical theology, the anti-mystical witch-hunts also gradually undermined and finally outlawed the spiritual directors who used to lead those who had come to the end of their first fervour and into contemplation. When they found themselves in the mystical crèche where they were to be purified for the journey ahead, there were no experienced spiritual guides to explain their predicament and guide them along the way into an ever-fuller union with Christ. Shorn of profound mystical prayer and those great saints and leaders who were once inspired by it, Catholic spirituality was seriously undermined in the centuries that followed, and nothing has been done to remedy the situation. If the terrible calamities that have shamed the Church in recent years have not made this abundantly clear, then nothing will.

Aware of the all-embracing spiritual malaise, thanks to the wars, anarchy, anti–clericalism, reformation and revolutions in the preceding centuries, Pope Leo XIII tried to give impetus to a new interest in theology through a scholastic revival in 1879. In his encyclical *Aeterni Patris,* students in Catholic colleges and seminarians were instructed to return to the teachings of St Thomas Aquinas that had inspired the Council of Trent. The new emphasis lasted well into the first half of the twentieth century, but it did little to bring back the mystical theology that was still wanting in the Church. Ironically, those who introduced the teaching of St Thomas failed to see this, and therefore failed to introduce simultaneously the mystical teaching that enabled St Thomas himself to write his great works in the first place. Indeed, without the mystical theology that inspired him, they were merely introducing an unmitigated intellectualism that helped to keep it at bay. Shortly after completing his massive *Summa Theologica,* St Thomas experienced profound and prolonged mystical experiences that were so sublime that compared with them, he insisted, all he had hitherto written was but straw. Let me just note in passing that this is the common experience of those who experience the power of the divine love possessing them for the first time. That is why it was understandable that St Thomas should react as he did, but he was nevertheless depreciating the action of the Holy Spirit who had been 'inspiring him'. For despite what he said his great works are unique and invaluable, precisely because they were 'inspired'.

His mystical encounters should make it abundantly clear to any student of mystical theology that his experiences must have been preceded by very many years of travelling in the night. Otherwise he could not have received such sublime states; had he been unpurified, they would not have been open to him. He himself refers to these purifications when commentating on St

John's mystical analogy of the vine at the Last Supper. He writes:

"In order that the just who bear fruit may bear still more, God cuts away in them whatever is superfluous. He purifies them by sending tribulations in the midst of which they show themselves more generous and stronger. No one is so pure in this life that he no longer needs to be more and more purified."

Commentating on this text, Garrigou-Lagrange insists that, "These are the passive purifications of which St John of the Cross spoke at such length." Without this purification, the great *Summa Theologica* could never have been written. That is why when writing the *Summa,* he defined contemplation as "a simple intuitive view of the truth accompanied by awe". This perfectly embodies his own experience, for he knew that he could only write his master-work thanks to God. It was the Holy Spirit who infused into him the divine truth in his daily journey in the dark night that he then transposed into words in his *Magnum Opus*. Had he defined contemplation after he had experienced the love of God raising him to ever greater mystical heights, when he had completed his *Summa,* he would no doubt have re-defined it as, "a simple intuitive view of *love* accompanied by awe". For it was then that the God who inspired him with the truth before, to enable him to complete his great master-work for his Church, inspired him with his love. This inspiration enabled him to experience something of the fullness of God's love here on earth as part of the reward that he would receive more fully in heaven. Notwithstanding all this, henceforth theological students were predominantly, and almost exclusively, fed on what he called straw, because they were not simultaneously introduced to the mystical theology that had purified the Angelic Doctor, earning him the title Angelic. A purely intellectual understanding of his works would therefore only encourage and sustain the intellectual emphasis in the Church that has kept the study and practice of mystical theology at bay.

This state of affairs continued until the beginnings of what came to be called the New Biblical Theology that enabled the Second Vatican Council to take place. This New Biblical Theology certainly touched hearts, as well as minds, and raised hopes but these hopes were finally to be dashed. The New Biblical Theology was in fact the very ancient theology that prevailed at the dawn of Christianity, but reinterpreted and re-presented thanks to the modern biblical, liturgical and historical research that inspired the second Vatican Council. The sadness was, as I have already emphasised, that one vital branch of early Christian theology had been forgotten, and that was mystical theology. Both the old scholastic and the new biblical theology were to suffer from both the ignorance of, and therefore the failure to practise, the mystical theology lived and practised by our ancient Christian forebears. Sadly therefore, although many genuine attempts have been made to renew the Church in the three hundred years or more since the condemnation of Quietism, what the spiritual theologian Lois Cognet describes as 'devout moralism' continues to be the staple diet of Catholic spirituality.

The Christian renaissance that is needed is still on hold. For a successful new birth to take place, love is the necessary ingredient. Not, as St John insists, our love, but God's love infusing our love with his own. The principle of the primacy of love must not just be reasserted in theory, but in practice, by once again guiding people to and guiding them through the place where true selfless loving is learnt and brought to perfection, as the divine and the human become as one. Mystical theology must therefore be encouraged without qualification, and with practical support and assistance from the top, and with wise and prudent help and direction from below. Only this will enable believers to set the world on fire with what animated and inspired their first Christian ancestors.

By the time the twentieth century had fully dawned, a new interest in the Pseudo-Areopagite and Neoplatonism arose. The original Christian meaning of the word mystical had now completely changed, thanks to writers like William James, with his influential book, *The Varieties of Religious Experience,* and other books inspired by his ideas. It now came to be used, almost exclusively, to refer to inner psychological states of transcendental awareness. Added to this, many of the new breed of mystics believed that the experience of mystical states leads to a new religion without dogmas, where all religions meet and become as one. Evelyn Underhill, for instance, speaks of "the mystics' impassioned love of the Absolute, which transcends the dogmatic language in which it is clothed, and becomes applicable to mystics of every race and creed."

More and more people began to look to the Far East for what had been lost to view in their own mystical tradition. It was not surprising that both progressive and conservative theologians looked on mystical prayer with deep suspicion, so those who promoted the Second Vatican Council, and those who opposed it, were both flawed by an absence of the mystical spirituality that abounded in the early Church. Thanks to Quietism and its aftermath, the Catholic mainstream had long since been convinced that the mystic way was an extraordinary way for the few, if it was a way to be encouraged at all amongst the faithful. Once again, authentic Christian Mystical Theology was undermined and blighted by its counterfeit. Psychological experiences were seen as almost ends in themselves, divorced from the hidden journey into the Mysterion that preoccupied the spiritual teaching of the Fathers of the Church, the early monastic communities, and the teaching of the authentic Christian mystics who followed them for more than a thousand years.

The Jesuits have been the most influential religious Order in the Church from the Council of Trent to Vatican II, but their influence on mystical contemplation, apart from a few famous individual exceptions to the rule, has been virtually non-existent. Their main source of spirituality for themselves and for others, is the Exercises of St Ignatius, but once they achieve their objective by leading a person into a faith full of fervour, failure often follows. This is because when fervour suddenly fizzles out, the vast majority of directors trained to guide people through the Exercises are all but totally ignorant of the mystic way, if they are not positively antagonistic to it. This is not a criticism of the Exercises, long may they continue, but what is needed is a new breed of directors who have learnt by their own experience, as well as by study, to lead people onward into mystical contemplation. When people ask for spiritual help, it is not always the answer to reach for a copy of the Exercises that once helped them, but never helped them to develop further. Nor is it correct to assume that there must be something wrong with the person seeking direction, if they do not find the Exercises helpful. They may very well have used them before or similar methods of mental prayer and been led on by them into the place where contemplation begins. If spiritual directors have not been there themselves, they will not only be of no help, but they could permanently damage the spiritual journey of *bona fide* travellers by suggesting that there is something wrong with them, or that they are taking the wrong direction. Although they have never been in the mainstream in Ignatian spirituality, mystical theologians and practitioners have always been evident. Some have made invaluable contributions in the field of mystical theology, but they have never represented the *status quo* nor have they been encouraged. Let me use one great Jesuit, Fr Alexander Rozwadowski SJ, to sum up all that I have been trying to say, in a remarkable article that he wrote in *La Vie Spirituelle* (January 1936).

"We do not affirm that mystical contemplation in this life is necessary for the salvation of the soul, but the question is, is it necessary for sanctity? By sanctity we mean a great love of God and neighbour. The sanctity in question here is the normal prelude to life in heaven, a prelude which is either realised here on earth or in purgatory which presupposes that the soul is fully purified and so capable of receiving the beatific vision immediately. Finally, we say that according to St John of the Cross infused contemplation is necessary for sanctity. And we even add that the perfection of the Christian life will not be possible without it, because it implies the eminent exercise of the theological virtues and of the gifts of the Holy Spirit which accompany them."

It would be untrue to give the impression that the years following the condemnation of Quietism were spiritually dead apart from Ignatian Spirituality. Prayers were said, the office was recited, the liturgy was celebrated, but vocal prayer depends on the prayer of the heart. In other words, vocal prayer depends for its power and efficacy on the love that is generated in prayer within the heart of a believer. It is this love that determines the quality of our relationship with God, before we even open our mouths. St Paul insists that without love, nothing has any value, for as Jesus insisted at the last supper, "Cut off from me you can do nothing" (John 15:5).

Like every other human accomplishment that is worth possessing, love has to be learnt. In the most ancient and hallowed teaching of the great spiritual writers, prayer is the place where loving is learnt, in prolonged and protracted periods set aside for that purpose. But further to this, prayer is the place where the love without measure unleashed in the sacred liturgy is received by those who participate in it. The measure in which this love is received is only limited by the capacity of a human heart to receive it. Jesus came to inaugurate a new world order in which human beings would be transformed into perfect, caring and compassionate human beings, by pure unadulterated love, his love. This is the love that is unleashed daily in the most sublime liturgical action of all. But the Mass is not magic; mere physical presence does nothing for the faithful, unless they are regularly faithful to the prayer that enables them to receive the fathomless spiritual riches that it unleashes. That is why all the Saints who have ever lived, no matter how different they might have been, have always one thing in common. They were men and women of prayer – the daily private and personal prayer that is practised deep down within their own hearts.

"You should have at least half an hour a day for personal prayer," wrote St Francis de Sales to a priest. "Unless of course you are very busy, then you would need at least an hour." This was of course in addition to Mass and the daily recitation of the Divine Office. However, for the patron saint of parish priests, St Jean-Baptiste-Marie Vianney, this was not enough. He spent whole evenings and well into the night in the deep prayer that inspired thousands of people a week to pour into his parish to listen to him speak. His sermons read like an anthology of pious platitudes, but when they were delivered by a man formed in the profound contemplative prayer that he experienced night after night, they were infused with the compassion and love that characterised the man he committed himself to follow.

When the absolute primacy of love was revealed to St Francis, for fear that what had been lost in the Dark Ages would continue to darken the life the Church, he decided something had to be done and done daily. The primacy of love was not, as St John had taught, referring to our love of God, but to God's love of us that makes our love of him possible. That is why, as the first Christians saw so clearly, every moment of every day had to be dedicated to receiving the love of God, so that this love could first inspire, and then infuse their love. It would only be then that the Father's love could draw them up and into the Son. There, in, with and through him, they could come to experience in ever greater measure, the love without measure that united the Father and the Son to eternity. To enable this mystical love to suffuse his own impoverished love, Francis spent days, weeks and months in prayer. To do this he had to flee far from the madding crowd to lonely places for prolonged silence and solitude. To this day, Franciscan Italy is strewn with hermitages that were built around caves, crevices in the rocks, or over the ground where Francis had built simple dwellings of wattle and daub, where he opened his heart to receive the love that made him into the man the medievals' called the Second Christ. His faithful followers followed him into similar places of solitude, as Franciscan hermitages sprang up all over Europe in the centuries that followed. Lest they lost what they received when they returned to their friaries from where they served the people, two hours a day was stipulated as the bare minimum that should be given to personal prayer each day, in addition to the Divine Office and daily Mass.

We are not all called to such a strict regime as characterised the lives of the early friars, but we are all called to follow their example. We are all called to seek whatever time and place we need to enable us to open ourselves to receive the same love that they sought, because that is the calling of all Christians. Without it we are nothing, but with it we can play our part in building the Kingdom of God here on earth, where justice and peace reign, where greed and discord reigned before. It is time to cast aside the sad and sick inheritance of Quietism that has cast a shadow over the life of prayer, or at least over that prayer in which the Holy Spirit makes us into another Christ. The belief that this contemplative prayer is only for monks in monasteries is a typical example of how ignorance about prayer has plagued the Church, thanks to the anti-mystical witch-hunts that followed in the wake of Quietism. Only Christ can bring about the Christian Renaissance that the world needs more than anything else, but the truth is, even he can only act through those of us who are prepared to receive him.

Chapter 15

The Mystical Crèche

Ever since he had arrived, Peter had carried around with him a document case inside of which was a typescript that he would read from time to time. I presumed that it was something that he had written and which he was preparing for publication. But when I asked him about it he told me that it was indeed a typescript, but that it was not his. It was the typescript of his brother's autobiography *Injured Innocence* that he had promised to read for him before he sent it to his publishers. When Ellena heard that it told of his brother's own prayer journey she begged Peter to read some of it to us. Peter was at first reluctant, but realising that it would soon be published for the world to read anyway, he gave way and read several key passages that we both found deeply moving and inspiring. But first he summarised the first few chapters of the book to enable us to understand the context of the passage that he was going to read to us.

It seemed that David couldn't read or write with any proficiency until he was in his early twenties, and that was only because he taught himself slowly and gradually, because in those days, nobody knew anything about dyslexia. He was written off at school as either bone idle or stupid. Nevertheless, he could hide his disability because he was outstanding at all forms of sport. He was therefore made captain of house, captain of school, captain of rugby, captain of athletics and captain of Sale and Manchester Rugby teams. It was this that, in his own words, made him full of himself, arrogant and full of a pride that blinded him and others to his lack of academic achievement. That is until he arrived at the Franciscan novitiate where there was no sport to enable him to show off his athletic skills, only daily and continual humiliation. The long morning office was all in Latin that he could not understand, nor for that matter could he read it aloud without proclaiming his ignorance. It was the same in the morning classes when the rule and constitutions were studied in Latin. When it was his turn to read aloud in the refectory in both English and Latin, he had his fellow novices in fits of laughter, as he stuttered, stammered and stumbled his way through what others could read with so much ease and facility.

If his days were hell on earth at least his evenings, in comparison, were like heaven on earth, as the meditation on the scriptures that he had learnt at school seemed to progress inside of prayer in direct proportion to how his humiliation progressed outside of prayer. That is until after about three months, when he thought he was about to enter everlasting sweetness and light, he suddenly found himself in what seemed to be everlasting darkness. It went on and on throughout the rest of the novitiate and for two more years into his student days without any form of alleviation whatsoever. How he continued, he still does not know. However, despite everything he nevertheless continued to give an hour a day to personal prayer every evening, until something began to happen to change not only his prayer, but the rest of his life. After putting us in the picture, Peter then began to read from the typescript itself.

"Despite getting nowhere at all, I spent an hour or more every evening in the church after Compline, battling with distractions and temptations. The strongest of these temptations was to stop wasting time doing what more and more seemed to be quite purposeless. Would not my time be far better employed in studying to prepare myself for the future like the other students? However, after months of struggling amidst dryness and aridity, I noticed a change in my consciousness that was so subtle that it was probably weeks before I began to reflect on it. It was as if I were being drawn into an experience of presence that was not entirely new to me, but which I had never experienced in prayer before. It was the same sort of experience that I had for the first time when, as a boy, I had spent many happy holidays at the cottage my father used to rent on the Yorkshire moors to keep us safe from the enemy bombs that had already made several of our friends homeless. It first occurred after watching a kestrel hovering on high. It was an experience similar to that experienced by the romantic poets. It was this experience that now began to envelop me every time I went to prayer. Whereas before on the moors, the experience was so fleeting that I could never predict it, for the first time it became predictable. It began to envelop me regularly each evening when I turned to prayer, and the sense of presence remained with me, so that I was reluctant to meet or talk to anyone before I went to sleep. About a month after this new experience had come to characterise my evening prayer, something more dramatic took place that took me by surprise.

"It wasn't that the nature of the experience changed, but a sudden lifting sensation inside my head raised my awareness in such a way, that the experience to which I had become accustomed, became far more intense, engrossing my inner being far more completely than before. This was a new departure that I never expected and it had such a deep effect on me that I began to keep a daily diary to chronicle what was happening to me. Although there was something so personal about these experiences that made me disinclined to share them with anyone else, I nevertheless felt I needed some sort of help, or at least some sort of authoritative confirmation that I was on the right path and wasn't taking leave of my senses. This need became more pressing when an even more dramatic development took place. The lifting sensation in my head suddenly began to spiral upward with such force and at such speed that I thought I was about to lose consciousness, but mercifully it stopped just short of what I feared. There I remained, so absorbed by the power that enthralled me that I could not move from the spot no matter what. Even if the experience had not occurred again, which it did, that first encounter would have been enough to convince me for the rest of my life that there was a God, and that God had made his presence felt in my life although I had no idea why.

"I read voraciously, if slowly, to learn from the great spiritual writers, from the Desert Fathers to the present day, to confirm the authenticity of my experiences and understand what would happen next. They all agreed that what I had experienced was, thankfully, but an infinitesimal 'touch' of God's power, for no human being could expect to experience his full power without capitulation. As it was, when what I experienced increased in intensity, the effect would be temporary oblivion or what some, like St Teresa of Avila, called ecstasy. This would be a sign of the human weakness that could not contain the divine. Eventually what had hitherto taken place in the mind or the head as a predominantly spiritual experience would begin to overflow into the body. All this would take time however, a long time, and it was in fact many years before the 'raptures' that I had experienced in the highest part of my mind began to brim over from the spiritual into the physical, from my mind into my body.

"Without giving details I broached the subject with a fellow student, John Baptist Walker, an English graduate from Cambridge who could easily identify with the natural mystical experiences so beautifully expressed in the poetry of the Romantics whom he adored. But he was both sceptical and wary about mystical experiences in prayer. 'They usually begin in mist and end in schism', he said, giving voice to a stock institutional prejudice that was uncharacteristic of him and deeply disappointing to me. I went to see Fr Gabriel, our theology lecturer who was generally believed to be the most learned man in the province. Although he admitted that he had never had such experiences himself, he insisted that they were genuine, and when I protested that I was totally unworthy of them and morally no better, if no worse than my fellow students, he said that such gifts are not given as a reward for living a virtuous life, but to give you the strength to become more virtuous. They carry with them, therefore, a great responsibility for which one day I would have to give an account, for, "When a man has had a great deal given him on trust, even more will be expected of him" (Luke 12:48).

"Whenever I protested my unworthiness before, I had only been doing what was expected of any good religious; I didn't actually mean it. On this occasion however I did mean it. For the first time I realised that whereas all the humiliations in the world had not made me humble, this brief experience, especially the most recent and the most dramatic, had the desired effect, at least for a time. An experience of supernatural power of such force and magnitude could not but make anyone feel small and puny in comparison, not least because what happened had happened quite out of the blue and without any reference to anything that I did to deserve it.

"Once more I found myself in a position where nobody understood me, but this time it was not because I was a dyslexic, but because, through no fault of my own, I had become a mystic. I had no other choice but to scour the library in search of the knowledge that nobody else seemed able to give me. I finally unearthed two books that answered all my questions with such precision and clarity that I couldn't understand why everybody else seemed ignorant of their contents, especially as they were generally accepted as the two greatest master works in the spiritual canon. When I first read *The Dark Night of the Soul* by St John of the Cross I could not believe how his description of the darkness in what he called the night of the senses was so identical with my own, and the descriptions of mystical presence in St Teresa of Avila's *Interior Castle* likewise, explained with absolute precision exactly what I experienced. I could now be in no doubt that the dyslexia that I had thought was the curse of my life, had without my realising it, enabled me to stumble into the mystic way. For reasons that I had yet to discover, nobody seemed to know anything about it in the religious life to which I had committed myself.

"In the years ahead I found this strange ignorance everywhere I went, and so I continually found myself an outsider, not just because I was a dyslexic but because thanks to my dyslexia I was a mystic too. On the face of it, having exotic and exhilarating mystical experiences might seem highly desirable, and once having tasted them they seemed highly desirable to me too, but be sure about it, they do not lead to endless and unalloyed joy, at least not this side of the eternal hills. For a start, however powerful they may be, however much joy they may bring, feelings of profound presence are always followed by absence. They suddenly come to an end as quickly as they start, to be followed by ever-deepening mystical darkness and sufferings, both inside and outside of prayer. Then they always fill the recipient with insights that they never had before, enabling them to see the truth that they must needs express. In their innocence, they think their listeners will be only too anxious to welcome the truth, but telling the truth is a very serious and dangerous business. Would-be prophets beware. The simple truth is not a dainty dish to set before the most dangerous animal on earth, particularly if he or she has political or religious pretensions. By choice they prefer ambrosia to eat and nectar to drink - they have little stomach for humble pie. Be warned, for if you serve it regularly enough and in large enough portions it can make them cross, very cross, and when they are very cross, they can crucify. However, I was quite ignorant of all this at the time, and so eager to speak the truth, and so trusting that people wanted to hear it, that without my realising it I had set myself on a collision course that would be my final undoing."

About a year after this something quite dramatic took place in the student house that upset David's spiritual journey, at least for a time, but again let him speak for himself.

"Some well-meaning soul from the teaching staff had a bright idea that resulted in an unprecedented insurrection amongst the student body that had hitherto been compliant, if not respectful to those who taught them. If the Inquisition had still been protecting the faith in the renowned and robust manner for which it was celebrated, then our well-meaning friend might well have been handed over to the secular arm in the hope that a little fire in this life might save him from eternal fire in the next. It would be a warning to others too, that no matter how well meaning they may be, there is no worse crime in the Church than doing anything that might lead the young and innocent to even question, never mind criticise the established order of things. And yet when all is said and done, all he did was to suggest an exchange programme to foster fraternal charity amongst students from different Franciscan provinces.

"As it was only a pilot scheme, just two students were chosen for the first year. Had these students been any other than John Baptist Walker and Cyprian Faupel, all the desired expectations might well have been realised. However, as these otherwise commendable students were both Cambridge graduates, they had unfortunately been trained to use their critical faculties and to have an unhealthy interest in questioning what students of traditional Catholic theology were never supposed to question. Had these unfortunate propensities already been noted by the master of students, as they had by several of their theology lecturers, they may never have been sent and the impending disaster might have been averted.

"The good news for those who sent them, was that they came back oozing with brotherly love. The bad news was, however, that they brought something else with them that would cause volcanic eruptions amongst the student body and set tectonic plates moving that would divide them irrevocably from their teachers. It was what later came to be called the New Biblical Theology. Not everybody capitulated immediately, but gradually the weight of their arguments plus the exciting and positive ideas made sense to all who had open minds. I held out for longer than most because it seemed to me that the mystical experiences that I could not doubt, somehow confirmed the Catholicism in which I had been brought up. But eventually I came to see that the New Biblical Theology confirmed and explained my experiences more clearly than ever before.

"In brief, the essence of the new teaching was in fact the old teaching of Jesus in all its pristine purity. It had been brought to view again thanks to critical biblical research and the theology it generated, together with a new and more honest appraisal of Church history and the early liturgical practices. Our new tutors introduced us to the works of the great biblical scholars, theologians and liturgical historians who became our mentors. However, what began to worry me as the day of my ordination drew nearer, was that I had to learn the new theology while mastering the old, otherwise I would fail my exams and all would be lost. I was caught on the horns of a dilemma. If it was thanks to my dyslexia that I had been lifted up to drink of the elixir of life, then it was thanks to my dyslexia that I had been forced to forfeit it. I had been so busy reading about the love of God, as so beautifully presented in the New Theology, that I had no time to experience it. I knew this could not go on or I would soon become a hypocrite, whose very life would give the lie to what I preached to others. Thank God, I received a wake-up call just in time.

"We were only able to listen to the radio on special occasions and never watched television; in fact there wasn't a single set on the premises. One of those special occasions was the BBC Promenade concerts broadcast on the radio. One summer evening a group of us settled down to listen to a symphony by Shostakovich. It was not one of his better-known works and to this day I have never been able to track it down. I remember that it began with the beating of distant drums. That is all I can remember of the music that hit me more powerfully than anything I ever heard before. Even Beethoven in all his glory never had this effect on me. It lasted well over an hour and the moment it ended

I went straight to my room awestruck by what I heard. I lay on my bed for hours to allow the impact of the music to penetrate the very marrow of my being. It was exactly the same experience that I underwent in prayer when I was first drawn out of the dark night several years before. It was as if someone was saying, 'You might have forgotten about me, but I've not forgotten about you. I can reach out to you through music too, and through anything in which the truth, beauty, harmony and goodness that have their source and origin in me, find their embodiment in what I have created'. Heraclitus once said, 'All things are full of the gods', and he was right, they are all full of God's beauty, truth, harmony and goodness, so when we fail to turn to him, he can turn to us through them.

"The random mystical moments that continued to punctuate my life were reminiscent of that famous theme of fate that dramatically bursts into Tchaikovsky's fourth symphony. Awesome and uplifting though these experiences were, they always seemed to me to be a warning that I had strayed and that I must return without delay to the journey in prayer that I had all but forsaken. I knew that it was here and here alone, that what I experienced but briefly and in part elsewhere, could be experienced with ever greater power. It was here and here alone that I could consistently receive the inner strength that I needed for the full human and spiritual growth to which I aspired. I felt sure that it was the *Hound of Heaven* searching me out because I was no longer searching for him. No matter what the reason, it was I who had fled him and not him me.

"I fled him down the nights and down the days
I fled him, down the arches of the years
I fled him, down the labyrinthine ways
Of my own mind; and in the mist of tears
I hid from him, and under running laughter.

But with unhurrying chase,
And unperturbed pace,
Deliberate speed, majestic instancy,
They beat – and a voice beat
More instant than the feet –
'All things betray thee, who betrayest me."

"Francis Thompson's *Hound of Heaven* would return many more times throughout my life to call me back for I was all too often in danger of losing my way. I did a lot of thinking before I finally fell asleep that night. I realised that I could not always depend on random wake-up calls like these, so I resolved to begin again without delay. It was a resolve that I would have to make many times throughout the rest of my life."

We found the experiences of Peter's brother not only deeply moving, but in some minor way coinciding with our own spiritual journey, and they gave me the heart and the determination to start again. But Peter had not yet finished using his own brother as an example, as I will continue to explain in the next Chapter.

Chapter 16

The Fruits of Mystical Death

The law of compensation usually decrees that most people with disabilities, whether physical or psychological, make up for them in other ways. Dyslexics therefore are often verbally fluent, as was my brother David. He was therefore continually in demand as a preacher. It was for this reason that the Bishop appointed him director of his retreat and conference centre in North London. His tenure lasted from 1969–1981. All the courses for priests and religious were aimed at spreading the New Biblical Theology and to this end he was ruthless in only engaging the best speakers in the country. Sadly, he couldn't find anyone to give lectures on prayer, so he had to do it himself, although I helped him when I could because I knew this was of vital importance. When *Sacrosanctum Concilium*, the *Constitution on the Sacred Liturgy*, was approved by the assembled bishops and promulgated by Pope Paul VI on 4 December 1963 during the Second Vatican Council, I was deeply disappointed, when so many of my friends were all but ecstatic. The ancient liturgy had indeed been faithfully reproduced and in such a way that it was made easily understood and intelligible to modern believers, but the awe-inspiring daily mystical spirituality bequeathed to the early Church by Jesus himself was completely missed out. At first I thought it would be followed by another Constitution, specifically dealing with what inspired and animated the early Christian liturgy, but no such Constitution was ever even discussed. It was for this reason that my brother and I decided to do something about it, by stressing the importance of daily personal prayer in all the courses promoting The New Theology.

When my brother told me that in seven years in the Franciscan Order nobody had ever spoken about the importance of personal prayer, I found it hard to believe. But over the first few years of his tenure he found that far from being the exception to the rule, virtually everyone, priests and religious men and women, described a similar experience. After six years asking the same question and receiving the same answers, we came to the unfortunate conclusion that the anti-mystical witch-hunts that followed in the wake of the condemnation of Quietism had had a devastating effect. This conviction was reinforced as my brother began to travel all over the world speaking about prayer. Every year from the late 1970s to the early 1980s, he went to Rome to give a course on mystical theology to religious from all over the world, as part of the extra-mural department of the Dominican University, the Angelicum. David was, yet again, disappointed to discover that formation in prayer was for them no more than rudimentary. Once again, his earlier findings were reinforced time and time again.

If personal prayer was encouraged, it was only up to, but never into the dark night, that nobody knew anything about. One day when we were discussing these findings, it suddenly dawned on us that if the general ignorance about mystical theology was all but universal, it must also have affected the great scholars whose exemplary theological studies made the Second Vatican Council possible. It was this ignorance that affected their objectivity, at least when it came to prayer, and they were totally blind to the daily mystical prayer, as practised by Jesus and his Apostles and as handed on to the first Christian believers. Without it the ancient liturgy would have been lifeless, and not the hub and centre of the early Christian community, which it certainly was. We both knew that the great reforming councils of the past owed their very existence and their success to myriad mystics and saints who were steeped in prayer, as were the new orders that they founded.

That is why one of the most successful of all Councils called to reform the Church, the Fourth Lateran Council (1215) was so successful, and that is why its moral and spiritual ethos successfully spread all over Christendom and beyond, through the new mendicant orders like the Franciscans, Dominicans, Carmelites and the Austin Friars founded by great saints and mystics. These Orders were teeming with saintly men and women who are still household names today, like St Francis of Assisi, St Anthony of Padua, St Bonaventure, St Dominic, St Albert, St Thomas Aquinas, St Clare, St Margaret of Cortona, Bl Angela of Foligno and so many others canonized for their transparent and heroic holiness. The other great reforming Council of the last millennium was The Council of Trent (1545 -1563). This too was preceded by great saints, like Angela Merici, St Teresa of Avila, St Peter of Alcantara, St Ignatius, St Philip Neri and so many others. While older orders were reformed, new orders were raised up to embody and disseminate the spirit and the teaching of the Council. Orders like the Jesuits, Barnabites, Theatines, Capuchins, Discalced Carmelites and Oratorians were theologically and spiritually guided after the Council by such Goliaths as St Robert Bellarmine, St Francis de Sales, and St John of the Cross. It was in the hands of such great leaders as these that for more than a hundred years after that Council, the Church continued to thrive and prosper, surcharged from within by the profound mystical prayer that had animated and inspired the Church since the great St Bernard. After the Second Vatican Council, not only were similar mystics and saints all but absent, but so also were the sort of new and vital religious orders to help spread and disseminate the teachings of the Council, and the existing religious orders diminished in personnel on a scale not experienced since the Black Death in 1348.

David and I decided that we had to do something to help make up for the spiritual poverty that always follows when serious personal prayer is neglected in the history of the Church. There was, however, a ray of hope. Despite the lack of systematic prayer that we discovered, we also found that, despite it, very many individuals had made their own way, as we had done. In making their own way they had passed through first fervour and come to the beginning of mystical prayer. However, finding no one to help them they had come to an *impasse*. Once they came to the beginning of mystical prayer they were unable go back to the fervent forms of meditation that had led them there. As they did not know how to go forward, they ended up in a spiritual cul-de-sac. My brother met so many of these people because they sought his help. However, as he was unable to help them in the time available in the short weekend courses on prayer that he ran, he prepared notes for them to take away.

It was then suggested that these notes should be put into book form to help others who could not come to his courses, hopefully people from all over the world. That is how in 1975, he wrote his first book, *Peter Calvay – Mystic*. Unfortunately, the book was sent to eight publishers and they all turned it down. There was not much money to be made in propagating the joys of the dark night of the soul. In the end he approached Veritas in Dublin, who did, it seems, know what he was trying to say, but they did not think there were sufficient people who wanted to hear it to justify publication. They suggested starting at the beginning of the spiritual journey first. That is how the book, *Peter Calvay - Hermit* came to be written and published in 1977, just in time for our mother to read before she died. It became a best seller and encouraged my bother to write its sequel *Peter Calvay - Prophet* in the late 1980s to precede and lay the foundations for *Peter Calvay - Mystic* at last, in the late 1990s. Sadly by this time large numbers of priests and religious for whom the book had been written had left, and so, unlike the other two books, it did not sell as well as expected. Shortly after the Millennium all three books were re-edited and published in one volume with a slightly different story line to accede to the editor's request to make it a little more ecumenical.

By the end of the 1990s so many of those for whom the book

had been written had left and those who remained behind had to shoulder a superabundance of work just to meet the basic spiritual needs of the faithful. Even if they had time to read the book they did not have the time or the energy to put into practise the mystical teaching of the great Christian saints and mystics that the book detailed. As subsequent years passed by the problem simply exacerbated, as fewer and fewer were left to minister to the needs of the faithful. The quality of preaching the faith diminished and more and more people voted with their feet. Without the inner mystical life, developed in the deep and prolonged prayer that inspired and animated their first Christian forebears, their spiritual life gradually declined, not just to their own spiritual impairment, but to that of others too, those who looked to them for leadership. Without the same inner life and love that animated Jesus, they were unable to generate the sublime virtues and moral standards that shone through everything that he said and did. Nobody can acquire these virtues merely by desiring them, they are the gifts of the Holy Spirit, given during and after deep mystical purification. St Francis of Assisi makes it clear in his own writings that the virtues that are the making of all true Christians, cannot be received by anyone without the spiritual endeavour practised through dying to self in prayer.

> "All holy virtues, God keep you,
> God from whom you all proceed and come.
> In all the world there is not a man
> Who can possess any one of you
> Without first dying to himself."
> The Praises of the Virtues (Saint Francis of Assisi)

Dying to self is the beginning, the first step in the mystic way that leads to the contemplation through which all the virtues are learnt. Julian of Norwich makes this point so clearly when she uses the example of Our Lady gazing upon God in profound mystical contemplation. "The greatness and the nobility of this contemplation of God filled her full of reverent awe and with this she saw herself so humble and small, so simple and so poor in comparison with her Lord God that this reverent awe filled her with humility. And so, founded on this she was filled with grace and with every kind of virtue" (*Long Text* Chapter 7).

What happened to Mary from the very beginning happens to all those who, through dying to self, are eventually led into mystical contemplation. It is here that, through what is called the theological virtue of love, human loving is suffused and surcharged by divine loving that gradually generates all the virtues within them. This divine loving, which is the Holy Spirit, draws us, not just into the life of the risen Christ, but into his action, into his unending loving of his Father. This enables our prayer to be infinitely more effective than it would otherwise have been. However, it not only enables our love to reach 'upward' and into God, but God's love to reach 'downward' and into us, and through us into others. It is only God's love that enables us to generate all the virtues that no one can attain without it. We cannot see the profound mystical prayer that enables God to enter our human being, but what can be seen are the virtues that are generated as God's love enters human acting. That is why Jesus said, "You will be able to tell them by their fruits" (Matthew 7:16), and most especially as Jesus insisted at the Last Supper, "By this love you have for one another" (John 13:35). As the same love that penetrated Jesus penetrates us, we become capable of acting like him in all we say and do, and of doing what would otherwise be quite impossible (Matthew 19:26).

Many years ago, there used to be a panel programme on the radio called the *Brains Trust*. The star of the programme was an agnostic, Cyril Edwin Joad, a professor of moral philosophy. On one occasion, a bishop on the panel began to wax eloquently about the moral teaching of the New Testament "Whether you are a believer or not," he said, "you must accept that Jesus Christ has given the world the most wonderful moral teaching that it has ever received. If only we lived by it the world would be a far better place." Professor Joad's answer was immediate. "Poppy-cock, rubbish," he said. "Jesus Christ has given the world a moral teaching that no one can possibly live by. If anyone tries to live by it, as you suggest, they will not only fail but their repeated failure will lead to utter disillusionment and despair. Go back and re-read the Gospel, and you'll see precisely what I mean."

He then began to quote from the gospel himself. "The gospels say, do they not, that we should be perfect as God is perfect, that we should not only love each other as we love ourselves, but as Jesus, the supposed son of God, loves us: that we should love not only our enemies, but forgive them seventy times seven, as he did. Further to this, we should love those who would persecute and even put us to death. These virtues would inevitably guide anyone so misguided as to take them seriously, to disaster. They would lead to spiritual and psychological suicide, unless the believer threw in the towel, as so many do, and settled for being just a nominal Christian. The trouble with you Christians is, that you fill your schools, colleges, seminaries and your universities with teachers who propound a moral teaching, that they have failed to live by, and which their students will also fail to live by too. Inevitably by teaching such impossible standards, that neither they nor anyone can possibly live by, they teach a way of life that is nothing but a recipe for disaster. That is why so many of them end up as guilt-ridden hypocrites."

Who do you think was right, the bishop or the agnostic? I side with the agnostic and so do the Gospels. The bishop would have seen this if he had only read the Gospels as well as the professor. However, even the professor had not read them thoroughly, or he would have seen that the Gospels say many times over and in many different ways, "For men this is impossible; for God, everything is possible" (Matthew 19:26). In order to live out all the moral teachings and embrace the virtues to be found in the Gospels you would need to embody the whole range, the complete gamut of every conceivable virtue known to man. The standards and the virtues that you find in the Gospels cannot be acquired by human endeavour alone. Only when the same Spirit who filled Jesus begins to fill us, will we be able to do what Jesus did, and even greater things, as he promised at the Last Supper.

Jesus became and still is the repository of all virtues, because he was at all times throughout his life, open to receive the supernatural love that, in concert with his human endeavour, generated all the virtues necessary to become the most perfect embodiment of God's loving goodness on earth. His pure unsullied and mystical loving of his Father formed a spiritual highway that enabled his love to enter into God and God's love to continually enter into him. If we are to become other Christs, it means above all, copying the way in which Jesus opened himself at all times, to the only love that can make us into Christlike people, enabling us to embody the Gospel teaching in all we say and do, as Jesus did before us.

But this love or his Holy Spirit can only be given to us, as we try to receive it, by the daily endeavour we make to observe the first of the new commandments as Jesus did when he said the *Shema* every day of his life. This means in the efforts we make to pray each day offering ourselves to God, and in our attempts to transpose the offering that we make into actions through all we say and do. For, without the inner, hidden or secret life and love from God given in prayer, it is, and always will be impossible to observe the sublime moral teaching of the Gospels. That is why Jesus was the first great Christian mystic and those who try to follow him are called mystics too. It is only to the degree to which they receive the power from God, that they are empowered to live the teachings of Jesus, from his moral instructions given in the Sermon on the Mount, to the sublime mystical instructions given at the Last Supper. Take this away and, as Professor Joad rightly said, Christians quickly degenerate into guilt-ridden hypocrites, a scandal to their own brethren and a scandal to the world. In short, Christianity is primarily a mysticism not a moralism.

Anyone who tries to attain the virtues they so admire in Jesus, or any of the saints for that matter by their own endeavour alone, will only succeed in becoming caricatures of the person whom they are trying to imitate. There is only one way to attain all the Christian virtues and that is, as St Francis insists, to die. This mystical death takes place in the profound purification where humility, perseverance and faith are learnt, in months, no, rather in years of practising the loving that seems to receive nothing in return. Without the recipient realising it, this selfless loving enables God's mystical loving to enter into human loving, bringing about the change that will be perfected in the love that is experienced, as darkness eventually turns to light. It was while praying in the inner room, in the hermitage within, that Francis received the grace to develop the virtues and receive the gifts of the Holy Spirit, as Jesus did before him.

The Christlike care and compassion, the superhuman quality of selflessness and sacrifice and the heroic virtues that are generated by St Francis and the saints who preceded and would follow him, are but the outward expression of the divine life already possessing them from within. The exercise of the human heart in prayer then allows the divine life in, so that it is transposed through human being into human acting. Not only does this love further strengthen the spiritual muscles of the recipient, but it opens their hearts from the inside to receive even more of the love that it has already received. In this way true Christians are fashioned so they are able to return the love received in kind to the One from whom it came in the first place. This profound interchange of love now bears fruit in all they say and do, for the world that God is now able to reach through them.

Saint Francis was in theory a mystic because he saw so clearly, and stated so emphatically, that all true virtue and all genuine goodness is in God and in God alone, and can only enter human beings through a mystical death. However, he was also a practical mystic because he continually sought out the solitude in which to enable the Holy Spirit to bring about this mystical death within him with a shaft of light and life that contains all the virtues and all the gifts that have their spiritual origin in God, and their physical manifestation in man - the Christlike man.

The sure sign for Francis that what appears as true virtue and not its counterfeit, is that it is never alone, for it is born of the love of God from within, into a whole family of virtues that appear simultaneously, if gradually, in the behaviour of the true believer. If you meet a tolerant person who is a glutton, or a generous person who is a tyrant, or a patient person who is a swindler, then the virtue that might seem to redeem them is only of human origin, born of the genes they inherited, or the upbringing that others gave them, or the expediency that social acceptance demands of them. It is only as weak human love is suffused and surcharged by the divine, that we are now able to love God with our whole heart and with our whole mind and with our whole strength and to love our neighbour as ourselves, and so keep all the commandments, that a promise can be kept. The promise was made by Christ at the Last Supper, when he promised that whosoever keeps these commandments would be loved in such a way that the Father, the Son and the Holy Spirit would make a home within them.

As this whole process of transformation, or Divinisation is taking place, the mystic begins to experience the love they are receiving, sometimes to shattering degrees of intensity, and with a regularity that finally becomes permanent, as the Trinity of love which is God, is finally homed within them for good. This is true contemplation, a pure gift of God that cannot be generated by any man-made methods or techniques from the East or from the West. Those who suggest otherwise are simply deceiving you, as they have been deceived themselves. It is a tangible experiential knowledge from which strength is drawn that enables mystics to sever themselves from all and everything that prevents them living the Christ-life to the full, enabling them to live fully for others. In the authentic mystic, you will always find a fully balanced and complete person who is not so lost in a self-indulgent evangelical piety that they forget the physical needs of others, nor so engrossed in a socio-political involvement that they forget their own spiritual needs in prayer.

Two priorities are always embodied simultaneously in the true mystic - love of God and love of man. See how the theological and the sociological are completely harmonised in the life of Jesus Christ, the greatest mystic ever to walk on the face of this earth. He was totally open and available to all men because he was first totally available to God. If he had not received from God in his daily prayer at the synagogue, in the desert, or on the mountain side, in the inner room or in the Garden of Gethsemane, then he would have nothing to give by the lake side, at the cross-roads or in the marketplace, the temple precincts, or the place of execution where he finally gave his all. Jesus knew this, and stated it so clearly that the true disciples who have followed him throughout the ages heard him, and they have followed his example. Francis may well have been a mystic of the highest order, and spent years of his life in solitary prayer, but what other man in the whole of the Middle Ages did more for his fellow men than he did; for the poor with whom he worked; for the lepers he served with his own hands, and for the peace he brought to the strife-stricken world in which he lived?

On the very first Pentecost, St Peter said that the continual outpouring of the Holy Spirit, the only source of all virtue, can only be received and continually received by an ongoing repentance. This ongoing repentance is learnt and practised, as a person endlessly practises the selfless turning back to receive the love of God in prayer. This is especially true when God seems to be giving nothing back in return. Repeatedly turning to him in these moments, turns cupboard lovers into perfect selfless lovers. The place where this happens above all else is in the mystical crèche where this selfless loving is learnt. To believe that it is only for a chosen few is to completely misunderstand, not just mystical theology, but the very meaning of the Christian life, and to reduce it to a pale and purposeless parody of what Christ meant it to be, what it once was, and what it can be again.

No deep or lasting renewal can ever take place in any individual believer, or in the Church, unless the importance of the inner mystical purification is not only understood, but taken out of the shadows and placed centre stage again. Deep and lasting renewal, permanent spiritual change, can only be brought about by the Holy Spirit and the purification that he effects in prayer beyond the beginnings. It is here in the mystical crèche that saints are made from the sinners who choose to enter there, and continually choose to stay there until one day, as St Teresa of Avila once put it, they will arise like butterflies from the chrysalis. The great mystic and mother, Blessed Angela of Foligno said that prayer is the school where the love of God is learnt. Since the emasculation of Christian prayer after the condemnation of Quietism, there have been no shortages of elementary or primary schools, but secondary schools and places of higher education where this love is perfected through purification, have hardly existed, nor therefore have the teachers.

At the very moment when Christian mystical theology was undermined by Quietism, the Enlightenment, or the Age of reason began (circa 1685). What could not be verified by pure reason alone was rejected. The moral teaching of the classical Stoics that was rediscovered at the Renaissance was accepted, and much of the moral teaching of the Gospels that the Bishop praised during the Brains Trust, but that was all. They had no time for a mystical spirituality that could not be seen and therefore verified. But the sublime moral teaching that Jesus taught in the Gospels was lived by him alone, until the outpouring of the Holy Spirit on all who would receive him. Jesus was able, not just to live and teach such a sublime moral teaching, but he was able to embody it. But he was only able to do so because by praying without ceasing he was always open to receive the inner power of God that empowered him to do it. This same supernatural power was given firstly to the Apostles and then to those who responded to their message on the first Pentecost and thereafter. This enabled them to preach, teach and embody the moral teaching that Jesus taught. It was seeing such unprecedented goodness at work in them that took the ancient world by storm, inspiring them to follow their example.

Once, however, you extract the inner spiritual energy and power that animated the early Christians from a person's life, then moral fragility and debility will inevitably ensue. This happened at the Renaissance and again at the Enlightenment to the new Stoics, preventing them from living the moral philosophy that they championed, like the classical Stoics before them, as Seneca the greatest of the Stoics openly admitted. The same thing happened to Christians too, to those who, thanks to the demise of Mystical Theology were deprived of the teaching and the guidance that they needed. By that I mean the spiritual direction that would direct them to the prayer that they needed, in which they are sufficiently purified to enable them to receive the love of God that makes even the impossible possible.

When medieval monarchs married, it was usually for political reasons, to join two nations together, to seal a treaty or to patch up an old one. When God called the people he had chosen into a mystical marriage, it was for love, for their benefit, not for his convenience. When a marriage breaks down, the law steps in to bring order to what was ordered before by love. Myriad rules and regulations are introduced to try to promote the virtues, or at least some sort of order that was generated by love before, to reinstate the exemplary moral behaviour and the mutual respect and decency that comes naturally to those bonded together by love.

The spiritual and moral morass that prevailed in Israel when Jesus first appeared, perfectly exemplifies what happens when love is lost in any marriage, human or divine. Although Jesus proclaimed the virtues, the moral standards and the precepts that should characterise the new and perfect marriage that God wished to introduce, it was not enough. That is why he insisted that the love lost would only be restored on and after the first Pentecost Day for those who would open themselves to receive the Holy Spirit. He is the love that bonds the Father to the Son, sent by the Son to draw all who would receive him into himself, and then in, with and through him into the Father. This is the ultimate marriage for which we all long, a marriage only distantly prefigured here on earth by human marriages that are at best shadows of the reality for which we all yearn.

The very heart and soul of the spirituality taught by the first Apostolic Fathers and the Fathers of the Church who followed them, was to detail all that needs to be done to welcome the Holy Spirit into the lives of their disciples. Then, to explain and encourage them to pass through the second baptism of fire when the Holy Spirit purifies them of all the sin and selfishness that prevents them from the marriage with the Risen Christ who sent him. This is the prelude to fully entering into the ultimate marriage, where they are drawn up and into a sublime supernatural union. This transcendental marriage with the Father is consummated in, with and through the Son. It is brought about by the loving that has bonded the two together from eternity. It is this loving, called the Holy Spirit who, after totally possessing the human nature of the Son, reaches out through him to possess the human natures of all who would receive him. When this happens, and as it is happening, people are empowered to live the perfect moral life that Jesus once lived, and so inspire others to do what he did by their very presence, long before they open their mouth to teach it to others.

What mystical theology teaches is how a person can be so purified of self-love that they can be united to perfect infinite love, which is God. It is not primarily about showing people how they can have exciting or esoteric experiences of God, but how they can undergo and endure the experience of death to self. It is therefore all about daily death and resurrection. When all the dross of inordinate self-love has been purified away, then the true gold that was deep down within can be united with the infinite gold who created us. This is the ultimate mystical marriage for which every being hungers and thirsts, for it was God's plan for us all from the very beginning, his Mysterion. The way to its completion involves carrying a cross, if not a physical cross like Jesus, then a cross nevertheless; a mystical cross through which we die to what St Paul called the 'old man' so that we can be reborn into the 'new man', which is Christ. This intimate union will begin here and now in this life and end in the next, in a marriage that will have no end. But like all marriages, if they are going to be as successful as we would wish, they demand work, the work of selflessly living and giving for the other for a lifetime. In human marriage success demands the total commitment of two, but in the mystical marriage with God it is different. He is pure unblemished infinite loving. He can do no more for he has given and continues to give his all. If this marriage is not growing and deepening daily, the fault does not lie with him, but with us and our failure to follow in the footsteps of the Son he sent to teach the meaning of true loving.

We place crosses on our walls, and in our churches, in our schools and parish halls; we place them in our homes and in our bedrooms, around our necks and at the end of our rosary beads - all to remind us of a truth that we can so easily forget. It is not just that Jesus died on a cross before us, but that we must take up a daily cross if we would follow him and come to experience the height and the depth, the length and the breadth of his Father's love that he experienced at his glorification, and to experience it to eternity. When a Christian community is deprived of the true mystical theology that teaches us to carry and bear the cross involved in the dying to self that is learnt in prayer, it deprives us too of all that God has planned and has prepared for us. In short, it deprives us of becoming true Christians. Instead we have to settle for becoming purely nominal Christians. We may well believe in the moral teaching that is to be found in the Gospels, but we do not have the power to live by it. So, as Professor Joad said, we often end up guilt-ridden hypocrites, because we cannot live up to what we profess, and therefore inevitably become a scandal to the world that Christ wants to reach out to, through us.

This must be remedied without delay, in the inner recesses of our inner being, for we are the Church. In short, we must start again, right at the beginning if necessary, and learn how to pray. Nor must we run away when we are asked to carry the cross when we are called to the purification without which union with God is impossible. We must undergo it anyway, whether we like it or not, for no self-centred human being can be united with the infinitely selfless creator without personal purification. In this life, it is called the mystic way, in the next life it is called purgatory. Those who undergo it in this life should not be seen as the exception to the rule, as they are today. They are the only ones through whom Christ can continue to do what he began to do in Galilee two thousand years ago. What we desperately need is not two billion nominal Christians, but just a few totally committed ones, twelve would do; that seemed to be enough in the beginning!

The old penny catechism states, "God made me to know him, to love him and serve him in this world, and to be happy with him forever in the next." We come to know him by reflecting and ruminating on his goodness as embodied in his Son Jesus, as he lived, loved and died in our world. Remember it was Jesus who said at the Last Supper, "To have seen me is to have seen the

Father, so how can you say, 'let us see the Father'? Do you not believe that I am in the Father and the Father is in me?" (John 14:9). That is why meditating on the scriptures is so important. It is here that we come to know and love, not just the most loveable person who has ever walked on the face of this earth, but our Creator present in him, although like the Apostles we may not realise this to begin with. As promised at the Last Supper, the Holy Spirit would make all things plain to his Apostles as he did after the Resurrection. What they came to see and then communicate to their followers, was a truth of the uttermost profundity. By coming to know and love Jesus as he *once was*, their love took them up and into a sublime supernatural union with him as he *is now*, risen from the dead and glorified. But that is not all, because they were not just united with who he *is now*, but with what he is doing now. And what is he is doing now? He is contemplating his Father in an act of undying and unending love, not just with his divine nature, as before, but with his glorified human nature and with all therefore who have been drawn up into that transfigured human nature through love. It is in this act of loving that the mystical marriage to which we aspire on earth is ultimately consummated in heaven. However, the spiritual journey through which our transformation into the Risen Lord is brought about is not a magical but a mystical journey. By that I mean that it is not brought about instantly, even by faith, but mystically through an ongoing inner or mystical purification where all the self-love that prevents us from being united to perfect loving is spirited away.

The more perfectly this purification is brought about, then the more perfectly we are, in the words of St Paul, "fitted and joined together into Christ" (Ephesians 4:16). This means that we are not only taken up to share in his loving of the Father, but that we can receive the Father's love in return. It is now that we can participate in God's plan, his Mysterion, as never before. For now, in, with and through Jesus, the love that we are receiving can be channelled to others with a power and effectiveness that are quite beyond our own human endeavour. That is why contemplating the Father with Christ empowers us to do with speed and success what we have never been able to do before. As the Jesuit, mystic Louis Lallemant (1588 -1635) put it, "You can do more in a year with contemplation than can be done in a lifetime without it."

After death, this contemplation leads us on and into the continual and unalloyed happiness that repeatedly eludes us in this life, despite fleeting moments when the love of God touches us briefly. It is a happiness that is increased and intensified because it is shared by all whom we once loved on earth, for they too will have been finally purified in such a way that they too live in Jesus. It is in him that we now all reside to eternity, and in him receive and return in kind from the Father, the sublime spiritual love which is the Holy Spirit. In other words, it is in Jesus and in his transformed and transfigured human body that we are drawn up into the infinite vortex of life and love that endlessly reaches out from the Son and into the Father, and from the Father into the Son.

It is into this Trinity of everlasting life and love that Jesus came to invite us. This is the home for which we were created and for which we yearn on earth. It is here that we experience the love that surpasses all understanding, reaching out to embrace us again and again. There is no end to receiving what we have always desired, because God's Love is infinite and he has given us an infinite capacity to receive it. That is why, as I explained, St Gregory of Nyssa coined a new word, *Epecstasy*, to describe the joy generated in endlessly receiving and experiencing infinite love, entering and penetrating every part of our being with ever increasing intensity.

It is here alone that we are totally absorbed in the beatific vision that God has planned for us from the beginning, his Mysterion, brought to completion in a mystical marriage beyond all human conception. No human language, no superlatives, no metaphors no analogies, even if they could be multiplied by infinity, could enable us to dream of what God has prepared for us, not even in our wildest and most outlandish fantasies. One word reoccurs time and time again in the Scriptures and in tradition to describe the indescribable, supernatural splendour of the place where the Three in One mutually embrace each other, and into which we are invited - it is the word *glory*. When we also enter into him after purification, we too will finally be glorified in him, so that in, with and through him we will be able to experience for ever the glory of the Father as it reaches out to encompass us as he relentlessly embraces his son. This is the end of all our journeying, the end of all our searching, the destination for which we have always pined, the consummation for which we have ever yearned. If we have strayed, if we are straying again now, let the journey begin once more and without delay.

"Come, Holy Spirit and kindle within us the fire of your Love."

* * *

What I have written concludes most of what we learnt from Peter in that unforgettable week. It was the most important week in my life. Like Dostoyevsky I too have had to experience both death and resurrection and I still do. In the remaining chapters I would like to leave you with some practical help. When I originally sought Peter's help it was after my first wife died. He was a tremendous help to me, not just because he was able to comfort me in my bereavement, but because he was able to encourage me to pray again. He taught me how to pray in such a way that I not only prayed for her, but made the whole of my daily life a prayer for her too, through all and everything that I said and did each day. This made me feel closer to her than at any other time since she died. But further to this Peter explained that when I prayed in this way I was also praying with her too, to the Father, in the Risen Lord in whom she now lived and moved and has her new being.

In order to help me he gave me what he called a blueprint for daily prayer. It was based on the words *Pater Noster*. Each letter was a reminder of what should be an essential ingredient of my daily vocal prayer. I found it of particular help, because he also gave me prayers that he had composed to sum up the spiritual themes which each letter was intended to evoke. I found it so helpful over the years that I thought it might be of help to you too. I have put together daily prayers for you to use based on the more recent memory jog that Peter used in his talks, namely the "Our Father". I have included these prayers at the end of the book as an addendum. I do hope they will be of help to you.

Chapter 17

The Time that leads to Eternity

In addition to encouraging me to use the prayers that he composed for me, Peter also encouraged me to return to the prayerful reading of the scriptures, when I felt able after my bereavement. But somehow I never came around to it for within a year there was another death in the family. This time it was the death of my mother at our home in New York.

Her death happened so quickly and was so unexpected that I had difficulty coming to terms with it at the time. Everything seemed so unreal. I just didn't feel anything. Jobs had to be done and I had to do them. Someone had died and I had to make all the practical arrangements. My relatives and friends were there but they didn't support me, I organised them. I heard them say all the things you expect them to say, and I said all the things I was expected to say. It was as if I was acting a part, and I was conscious of it. But what else could I do?

When I returned home and to work, I carried on as if nothing had happened. The work-load had built up during my absence and it took me months to catch up. The sudden cancellation of a major conference gave me two weeks off. Although I did not realise it at the time, it gave me the space and time I needed to come to terms with my mother's death. It took me a week to slow down. In the second week I read and re-read a pile of letters that my mother sent me over the preceding years. The past came flooding back - all she had done for me, been to me, all the sacrifices she made for me. Suddenly something that had been hard within me softened and the feelings and emotions that had been securely locked away welled up and overwhelmed me. Tears began to roll down my cheeks. I not only came to terms with her death but I celebrated her life too, and her continuing life and love that I knew would always be with me.

On the following Good Friday when I was dutifully listening to the reading of the Passion, something inside me said, "You have come to terms with your mother's death, but have you come to terms with Christ's death?" In a flash, I saw how cerebral my faith had become. Here I was, reacting to Christ's death as coldly as I had reacted to my mother's death the year before. Once again there was the same feeling off unreality, as if I was play-acting, as if I was detached from something or from Someone with whom I should be deeply involved. Some truths are just too big, too awful, and too awesome for the mind and the emotions to cope with; they just do not react to them. That is one of the reasons why so many people never get beyond first beginnings with their prayer life. They can manage with the prayers they were taught as children, they can even make up their own, especially when they want something from God, but they cannot get any further. They might believe every article in the Creed, but it does not really touch them deeply. God is far away in his heaven and the Gospel two thousand years away.

I recalled what Peter had taught me over the years. Two things are necessary for prayer to grow beyond the stage of set formulas and petitions, to the stage when it becomes a personal encounter with the most loveable man ever to walk on this earth. The first thing is to find some space and time in which to stop being busy about many things so that there can be time to come to terms with Christ›s death, and to celebrate his life and love, and his continuing life and love. The second thing needed is to read and re-read every word that has been written about him in the Gospels and to read everything that he said, because what he said is addressed to us personally, just as every word in my mother›s letters was addressed to me personally. These sacred words are precious, so they should be read slowly and carefully, as you would pore over poetry to penetrate its meaning and experience its impact. Gradually in time and under the influence of the Holy Spirit, the faith that once seemed solely cerebral will deepen, as hearts and minds that were like stone before, soften and become porous to receive and experience the love of Christ ever more deeply.

When this happens, the feelings and the emotions react as the whole personality begins to respond in a perfectly human way to the most perfect human being of all. Prayer begins to grow, to develop and deepen, as in any other loving relationship. It expresses itself in the language of love as it responds to the One who now seems to rise out of the sacred texts, out of history, and to enter into the heart and mind of the person who has persevered in prayer beyond first beginnings. As love grows and deepens into union, words finally fade away as they give way to a profound and pregnant silence. Meditation gives way to contemplation - the still, silent and loving gaze upon the one whose life we now experience within us, because we have finally come to terms not only with his death, but with his Resurrection.

If those who love us remain with us through their enduring love, even after their death, how much more does Christ's love remain with us? He not only lived and died for us but rose from the dead precisely to be with us and enter into us with a love more potent and more powerful than the combined love of all humanity, concentrated into a single act and multiplied by infinity. In this supreme act, human and divine love are as one. Only we can keep resisting this sublime love. For although all other forms of energy can prove irresistible, love, no matter how powerful can always be resisted by a human heart that refuses to receive it. All the ills in Christendom over the centuries have come from this resistance and continue to do so today.

Over the last forty years Peter explained to me what I must do to allow God to love me, to allow him to make his home within me as he promised at the Last Supper. He always insisted that the only response that will enable God's love to penetrate and possess us, as he promised, is to love him with our whole heart and mind and with our whole body and soul. Let me now try to summarise all that Peter said to me personally that has both inspired and enabled me to respond to the only love that can both transform and transfigure us all, beyond all our wildest dreams.

The first thing that we must do then, which is in effect a prayer itself, is to find in our lives some quality space and time in which to use the scriptures to enable us to come to know and love Jesus as he once was. This is the first step in coming to love him as he is now, and to enter, not just into his life, but into his prayer, into his contemplation of our common Father. However, we will get nowhere without introducing a certain amount of asceticism into our lives. Don't let the word frighten you, because asceticism for a beginner is quite simple, as Peter first explained to me. "Do not give up anything you like or enjoy, except when it prevents you from giving quality space and time for prayer each day". If you think it is too easy, then try and stick to it and you will soon find it is not quite as easy as you think. Do not let first enthusiasm fool you into heroics that you will never sustain. When you have persevered for long enough in prayer, you will gradually begin to receive and then experience the love that will enable you to do what is quite impossible without it.

When people fall in love and begin to experience being loved, there is nothing that they would not do, or sacrifice for their lover. In fact, they will positively look for things to do, the harder and the more exacting the better, to enable them to show the real quality of their love. What was impossible for self-centred egotists only a short time before, becomes not only easier, but also their greatest pleasure. It is the same in the spiritual life. The exemplary behaviour, the extraordinary self-discipline and the heroic sacrifices made by a person who begins to experience the love of Jesus, are not the results of an arrogant stoic trying to make themselves perfect, but the actions of someone desperate to express their love in behaviour that could not be maintained for long without the love that sustains them. With love, all things become possible that are quite impossible without it. All the little pleasures and pastimes that were thought indispensable before, suddenly become dispensable, and with the greatest of ease, virtues that were noticeable by their absence, are born of this love that envelops them. In short, first seek God and his Kingdom which is love, and everything else you want or desire will be given to you.

I found the way Peter explained the nature of God's love in his talks particularly helpful when he said that in the Old Testament God was sometimes referred to as a mother as well as a father. The same can be found in the writings of the Fathers of the Church too, who referred to what they called the *anima* and the *animus*, or the masculine and the feminine in God. Like the Greek philosopher, Plato, they believed that the love that is found imperfectly in men and women on earth, is to be found perfectly in God. If God is love, then his love is neither masculine nor feminine but a perfect blend of both. If they are one in God, they must also be one in the perfect embodiment of his love on earth, namely in Jesus Christ. Despite the fact of his male appearance then, the perfect blend of masculine and feminine loving that characterised his relationships with others, also enabled him to outline the most balanced and the most sublime moral teaching that the world has ever known, together with the inner spiritual strength to practise it. So, both men and women can find in him a person who they can come to know and love in a way that is completely satisfying and fulfilling. Who would not want to know and love such a person, and in knowing and loving him receive the love that he promised to return in kind, but in far fuller measure, to make the receiver into a more perfect, balanced and fulfilled human being?

The question is, how in the first instance do we come to know this adorable human being now, over two thousand years after he lived on earth? How do we communicate with him now? There is nothing mysterious about human communication. How does anyone come to know anyone else except by using words? The spaces between people are bridged by words. They enable us to find out more about them, to draw closer to them and, if they are loveable, to love them. This is why Christians have always regarded the scriptures with such reverence from the earliest times, most particularly the Gospels and the other sacred writings that enable us to come to know and love the man who was the perfect human embodiment of God's infinite loving. When we learn to listen to his words, we learn to listen to God. When we learn to love him, we learn to love God.

In vocal prayer, despite the time given to brief moments of silence we have been doing most of the talking. However, for prayer to lead on to generate the quality of love that will alone permanently change us for the better, we must learn to listen. If our spiritual life is to deepen we need to learn to stop talking and listen, to be silent and to be loved. This is why all authentic Christian prayer begins not by flinging oneself into obscure states of transcendental awareness, but by trying to listen to God's words, as embodied in the words of Jesus Christ. This is how the early Christians used to pray in a method of prayer that came to be called *Lectio Divina* or the divine or sacred reading. It was so called, not just because they believed the words they read were inspired, but because they believed that they too would be inspired by the Holy Spirit as they read them. They believed that through these sacred readings they would be led on and into a sort of profound conversation with Jesus that would lead them on and into "the love of Christ, which is beyond all knowledge" where we are filled with "the utter fullness of God" (Ephesians 3:18-19).

This is why we, whatever other methods of prayer we may at times find helpful, must never forget and always turn back to the scriptures as the Christian prayer book *par excellence*. Four Latin words have traditionally been used to describe how *Lectio Divina* can lead serious-minded Christians onward to experience the love that surpasses all understanding. The words are *Lectio*

(Reading), *Meditatio* (Reflecting), *Oratio* (Reacting), and *Contemplatio* (Relishing the love that is experienced).

The early Christians knew no other method of meditation. As Peter explained in his talks, many of them knew whole passages, if not all of the Gospels off by heart. They had no other prayer books to hand, nor did they have need of them. When the first Christians used the scriptures, most particularly the New Testament, they were not interested in how much they read, but in how deeply they penetrated the sacred texts in their search for wisdom. The wisdom for which they searched was not a body of facts, but a body full of loving, who continues to love now, as he did when he was on earth. They would read a few verses at a time going over them for a second and a third time, poring over them, entering more profoundly into their dynamic inner meaning. Then they would pause in moments of deep interior stillness to allow the same Spirit who inspired the scriptures in the first place, to inspire them too, with knowledge and love for the man who had come to redeem them. When they had savoured one particular text, they would reverently move on to another, and then repeat the process, leaving pauses for silence for the impact of the words to seep into the very marrow of their being. As this prayer grew more and more intense, the moments of silence would become more and more prolonged, and as love blossomed, words would give way to periods of profound inner contemplative loving.

Although Christians can be said to be mystics by virtue of their baptism, the term mystic is only used to describe those Christians who begin to take serious steps to set out on the search, through prayer and self-sacrifice, to enter ever more deeply into the mystical marriage with Christ that will take then up and into what has come to be called the Mystical Body of Christ. It is here alone that they come to know and experience the Mysterion or the hidden plan of God, to unite all with him through the Holy Spirit whom he sent out for that purpose.

Chapter 18

Into the Mysterion made Man

For the Fathers of the Church the prayerful reading of the scriptures was a sacrament, a unique sacrament, because anyone could turn to it at any time of the day or night. In the first centuries, when Greek, not Latin was the language of the Church, meditating on the scriptures was seen as one of the other great mysteries after baptism, because it could lead the faithful on through meditation into Jesus Christ, the flesh and blood embodiment of God's plan. One who regularly turned to this mystery with serious and prayerful intent, was for the Fathers of the Church already a mystic, for the personal journey into the Mysterion had begun. In order to enable the Holy Spirit, who inspired the scriptures in the first place to help us to do this, we need to learn how to read the scriptures in a new way, and learn to listen too, as we have never really listened before. We are so bombarded with reading material every day of our lives that we have had to acquire a habit of reading at a breath-taking speed. Every day there are the newspapers to read, mountains of junk mail to sift through, memoranda to be absorbed and letters and bills to be dealt with, and that is not to mention addiction to the joys and woes of the internet. Our only concern is to glean the relevant facts as quickly as we can, and then to move on to begin the rest of our life. If we apply the same techniques to the way we read the scriptures, we will not be able to come to know Jesus more deeply, nor generate the love that will eventually enable us to enter into and share in his mystical contemplation of the Father. They should be read as we would read good poetry, endlessly going over them to savour their content.

Having read and re-read the sacred texts, it is time to reflect. Pore over them again and again, ruminating on them, as St Augustine would say, allowing the inner meaning of every word to seep deep down into the very marrow of your being, so that their dynamic impact can register with effect. In order to facilitate the use of this profound meditation, some people find it helpful to recreate the scene in their imagination. If you have chosen to meditate on the profound words of Jesus at the Last Supper, begin by setting the scene in your imagination. Try to visualise the time and place where the action is about to take place. Picture the Apostles preparing the tables, see Jesus coming into the room, watch the way he moves, look into his face when he speaks, then mull over his every word trying to penetrate their inner meaning.

The same sort of scene setting could be used to build up the atmosphere before meditating on other Gospel texts. The Passion of Christ would lend itself to this method of praying. Do not just think of what Jesus went through in your mind, go back in your imagination and place yourself in the event. You are amongst the soldiers at the scourging, one of the crowd during the carrying of the cross, an onlooker at the actual Crucifixion. You see everything as it happens, you open your ears and hear what is said, and then you open your mouth and begin to pray by entering into a dialogue with Jesus as he is in the act of giving his life for you. Although this approach does not appeal to everybody, we should not be put off because it can lead to an emotional response. We are not dealing with pious fantasy here but with the most momentous historical events in human history. The word was made flesh precisely so that people of flesh and blood could understand and see God's love made tangible. Christ's death was a brutal and painful reality through which the Word who was made flesh, speaks of love in a way that is intelligible to all. To neglect the Passion as a primary source of Christian meditation and prayer is to neglect the most important manifestation of God's love that ever took place. This is a truth that St Bonaventure emphasised over and over again.

The more we penetrate the inner meaning of the sacred texts, the more we feel moved to react prayerfully with our hearts to what we have assimilated. Real prayer begins now, as we start trying to raise our hearts and minds to God, as we respond to the inspired words upon which we have been reflecting. To begin with, the truths of the faith are too enormous, almost too incredible for us to take in effectively. When I first heard that the stars in the most distant galaxy were over 13 billion light years away, I simply could not take it in. The distances were too enormous for my mind to cope with. It is exactly the same with the truths of our faith, at least to begin with. They are too much for us to cope with, too great for us to take in, as if our minds are paralysed by their transcendent immensity. We simply cannot penetrate or comprehend their meaning.

It is the same with our emotions too. They can only respond to a stimulus of a certain degree of intensity. When I first heard of my mother's death I did not react; it was all too much for my emotions to cope with. It is the same with the truths of the faith, at least to begin with. However, with good will and with genuine and continuous effort, come what may, things will gradually begin to change for the better. This state of mental paralysis gradually begins to lift. The slow meditation on the sacred texts suddenly begins to bear fruit, the spiritual understanding begins to stir and the emotions are touched and begin to react. What began as rather dry academic knowledge begins to strike us with an ever-deepening impact. Knowledge begins to turn into love, as the love that God has for us begins to register with effect, as we see it embodied in all Jesus said and did. None of us can remain the same when we realise that another loves us. We respond automatically, the emotions are released and we begin to express our love and thanks in return. This is the beginning of real prayer that will grow with depth and intensity as the truth of God's love, alive and active in Jesus, is brought home time and time again.

To use *Lectio Divina* most effectively it is perhaps best to turn to the Gospels to begin with, most particularly the Gospel of St John. Turn to his famous discourses, especially his profound spiritual discourse at the Last Supper, from chapter thirteen to chapter seventeen from which I have already quoted, then to his Passion narrative. There is enough food for prayer there for a lifetime. Then turn to the other Gospels, the letters of St John and St Paul, the Acts of the Apostles and then to the other New Testament writers. The method used in *Lectio Divina* can be used to explore other religious texts as well. Use them to meditate more systematically and more deeply on your favourite spiritual poems and hymns. There are many profound and beautiful hymns that we only glance at briefly every now and then when we sing them in church, like *Lead, Kindly Light*, or *Come, Holy Spirit*. The Hymnal can be a rich source of material for meditative prayer. Some of the modern folk hymns are ideal too. The music may be of varying quality, but the words are often both scriptural and profound.

Meditate in the same way on some of the liturgical texts like the great Eucharistic prayers. We rarely have time to penetrate their profundity when they are being read for us at Mass. One of the advantages of using these prayers in this way, is that it helps to remind us that our prayer is continually moulding us into Christ's own prayer. There are many other liturgical prayers and hymns that can be used for personal prayer in this way. The Gloria is a perfect example and so are many other ancient poems, hymns and sequences used throughout the liturgical seasons, helping to site our personal prayer into the context of each successive liturgical season. Use the psalms too, especially those that you feel speak to you in a special way for your particular needs. These were one of the main sources of spiritual nourishment for the Desert Fathers. The use of liturgical texts in this way helps to build a bridge between public and personal prayer. Too often they are seen as two entirely different and separable departments of Christian prayer, when they should be seen and experienced as two indispensable ways of entering into the prayer of Christ.

All these different suggestions are made with one end in view, and that is to come to know and experience, ever more fully, the love of Christ that is always readily available to all who sincerely seek it. As the impact of his love begins to explode with maximum effect, the believer finds that even the most extravagant words do not sufficiently voice the depth of feeling that they experience welling up from within. In the end the words of thanks, praise, adoration and love give way to silence, that says far more than the most potent man-made means of expression. The slow meditative penetration of the texts, now opens out and envelops the whole person, as the believer is ever more deeply absorbed into a silent contemplative gaze upon Christ. However, although it is the Holy Spirit who inspires the believer, human endeavour is required to attain the first moments of loving stillness and repose. That is why, when meditation first leads on to the prayer that simply wants to gaze upon the love that begins to envelop them, it is called Acquired Contemplation because it is in many ways similar to true mystical contemplation that is a pure gift of God.

This initial climax in prayer can also be attained by methods of prayer other than the *Lectio Divina* as I have described it. The Franciscan mystic, Francisco de Osuna said, "Not only the scriptures, but anything inspired by them, can inspire us with the prayer that leads to contemplative union." The fact of the matter is that countless numbers of believers were deprived of the scriptures, as we have come to use them today. When Christianity spread along the famous roads built by the Romans, it found itself in rather rude and primitive surroundings compared with the sophisticated empire into which it was born. How could you give the scriptures to people who could not read or write? From the earliest times, it had always been the custom to translate the

Liturgy and the Scriptures into the language of the people. However, how could this be done when the people had no language, or at least no written language sufficiently developed to allow such a translation to take place?

By the time this became possible and more and more people were able to read, it was reformers, unacceptable to the traditional Church, who first gave the people the Word of God in their own language. This is why the Church has for many centuries frowned upon, if not positively discouraged, the reading of the scriptures. During these centuries when ordinary people were starved of the scriptures, it was the prerogative of the great saints and spiritual leaders to present the central mysteries of the faith to the people in a way that could lead them to prayer. Simple devotions grew up for the illiterate, techniques of mental prayer were introduced and methods of prayer came into vogue, culminating in the meditation manuals that we have known almost up to the present day. Many of these aids to prayer have stood the test of time, like the Rosary, the Stations of the Cross, devotions to the Sacred Heart, the Exercises of St Ignatius and others. These various devotional practices were good, because they genuinely represented the authentic teaching and spirit of the Gospels for those who were deprived of the scriptures. In so far as they continue to do this, they can still be used to help guide people to genuine sanctity as they have done so often in the past.

Despite everything that has been said and the various suggestions that have been made, none of them may be of any help. That does not matter, but what does matter is that you use whatever method of prayer that helps you best. Ways, methods or techniques of prayer are only means to an end. They are in fact no more than props to help keep our hearts and minds raised and open to God. They are means to this end and should be used as such. There are no perfect means, just different means for different people at different stages of their spiritual journey.

What helps a person at the outset of their journey may not help them as they get into their stride. What helped them when they were going downhill with the wind at their back, might be of little use when they are struggling uphill with the wind in their face. What helped them in the spring might not help them in the autumn of their life. No matter what is said in this book or elsewhere for that matter, "Pray as you can, not as you can't," as Dom John Chapman used to say. Whatever method of prayer helps you here and now to keep raising your heart and mind to God, whilst at the same time keeping distractions at bay, is an ideal method of prayer for you.

Now be sure that you will never find any man-made method of prayer that will completely destroy the distractions that pester at the best of times. In fact, you cannot really pray without them. If, as Peter insists, you ever find that they have completely disappeared, then you will either have fallen asleep or been transported into an ecstasy. If you have fallen asleep you are not praying because you are doing nothing, and if you are having an ecstasy, you are not really praying either, because God is doing everything. The place where our praying is done is between the sleep and the ecstasy, where we continually practise repenting as we repeatedly try to turn back to God despite the distractions that try to make us turn elsewhere. Prayer is the place where selfless giving that is the heart and soul of all prayer is practised, until, under the influence of the divine, human loving is brought to perfection. Whatever means of prayer helps you to do this is good, even if it does not help anyone else.

Two main viewpoints have dominated the approach to God in prayer throughout the history of Christian spirituality. Before the Renaissance the older religious orders emphasised the action of God, while the newer orders, founded after the rise of humanism, tended to emphasise the action of man. Both are orthodox, but both have inbuilt dangers that have often led people into spiritual cul-de-sacs. Those who put all the emphasis on what

God does, can easily forget what they should be doing to co-operate with him, and they fall into a sort of Quietism. This leads to presumption as they present themselves to God in prayer, like suet puddings waiting to be soaked in syrup. On the other hand, those who stress the importance of what we can do, can forget what God does, and can easily fall into what was called Semi-Pelagianism. They act as if everything depended on them. It can lead to a sort of spiritual pride, to an arrogance of heart and mind that destroys the prayer that they seem to believe depends more on their endeavour than on God's.

In order to avoid the danger of presumption, Cardinal Hume introduced the word 'trying' into the traditional definition of prayer. In order to avoid the danger of falling into pride I would like to introduce the word, 'gently', to stress that our endeavour will get us nowhere without God's endeavour. If we become angry or upset at our failure, it is not because we have failed God, but because we have failed ourselves, and the goal we thought we could attain by our own endeavour. Prayer then, can best be defined as "gently trying to raise the heart and mind to God". Nevertheless, despite having a perfect definition of prayer, most of us will spend much of our lives trying to walk the spiritual tightrope between pride and presumption, continually falling off this side then the other. Then in God's time, not ours, the Holy Spirit will eventually reward those of good will who persevere despite their human failures. Then they will finally receive the perfect balance that enables them to keep their hearts and minds open to God, free of the pride or presumption that can prevent them receiving the only love that can transform them into the image and likeness of the Mysterion, made man.

What is of paramount importance, is that if a person gives quality space and time to prayer each day, and perseveres come hell or high water, they will eventually come to experience the love of God entering into their lives in such a way, that their prayer will reach an emotional climax. This climax is sometimes called the Prayer of Simplicity or the Prayer of Simple Regard, or Acquired Contemplation, because all one wants to do is to gaze at the love of God as it is experienced entering into one's inner being. In this prayer in which the whole person, heart and mind, body and soul, is more united than ever before, a subtle change begins to take place. Initially it was through meditating on God's love, as embodied in the human body of Jesus that led to this Acquired Contemplation. From meditating on Jesus as he once was, a deep desire is actuated to enter into a loving union with him, as he is now. This is the very nature of genuine love - it wants to be united with the one who is loved. It is not possible to be united with Jesus as he once was over two thousand years ago, so the desire for union with him is subtly transferred, in such a way that it is now directed to him as he is now, in his risen glory.

Now through the profound mystical prayer that begins after Acquired Contemplation, a person is prepared for this union for which God has created us from the beginning. This preparation begins when every form of prayer that we have found helpful before suddenly dries up and disappears, and distractions and temptations seem to reign where peace and harmony seemed to reign before. We appear to be left in a spiritual vacuum where we feel totally incapable of doing anything, but trying as best we can to continue in what Cardinal Hume called the Prayer of Incompetence. I can perhaps best explain what happens at this point in the spiritual journey by telling you what happened to me, as I expressed it to Peter in a letter I sent him many years ago:

> Dear Peter,
> Excuse me for not writing to you for such a long time. It must be six months or more since you last heard from me. The truth of the matter is, I simply didn't know how to express myself. Something terrible has happened and I don't know

how to tell you about it. Until last September, everything was going according to plan. I really felt that I was getting somewhere at last in the spiritual life. Prayer had become easy to me after those early difficulties that you helped me through. A few words from my favourite Scripture texts were enough to engage my whole being throughout prayer time, filling me with an exhilarating sense of God's presence and love.

My newfound spiritual energies spilled over into my work and especially into the prayer groups I founded and led. Then, unexpectedly, sometime in September, I seemed to be holed and my spiritual resources drained away. Almost overnight I found myself out in the cold, banished without rhyme or reason from the warm hearth that I was beginning to believe was my spiritual birth right. At first I thought it was merely some temporary setback and I would return once more to the cosy fireside. But as the months passed by, the cold was clothed with an ever-deepening darkness and I was assailed by hordes of marauding distractions that cut and thrust at my mind from within.

In spite of all this, I kept up the daily time that you insisted I should give to prayer, though my heart was not in it. I must admit, quite frankly, that in recent weeks I have been finding excuse after excuse to escape from the prayer that was once my heaven but is now my hell. I still lead the prayer groups, but I, who was once their mainspring and inspiration, feel like an outsider. The other members of the group must have noticed the change. A regular attender asked me only yesterday if I was feeling all right. Rather than admit that I was on the verge of losing my faith, I admitted to being a little out of sorts and promised to go to the doctor as soon as possible. But it is not the doctor I need. I feel sure you are the only one who can help me, Peter, though I don't know how. I feel I have come to the end of my tether and I don't know what to do with myself. Please do excuse the rather dramatic and desperate tone of this letter, but it expresses no more than I feel. I do hope I will hear from you in the very near future.

With every good wish.

Please pray for me!

James Robertson

Peter's reply came by return of post.

Dear James,

Thank you so much for your long-awaited letter. I already guessed the predicament you were in. Take it from me, everything has not ended – indeed, it is only beginning. In short, you have just come through what is usually called 'first fervour'. Everybody must go through this particular phase in their spiritual development if they are going to come to know and experience the fullness of love for which they crave.

There are four main stages in a person's prayer life: Juvenile Prayer, Adolescent Prayer, Adult Prayer, and Perfect Prayer. At the Juvenile stage a person is very insecure and lacks confidence in themselves and in God, so they choose to live in a stable and secure world. It is the world of prescribed prayers learnt by heart, or read from a book. It is the world of set formulas and well-tried devotional exercises. The Adolescent stage follows, if and when a believer decides to make their own the faith that they have imbibed with their mother's milk. The world of the adolescent is less predictable and more exciting. Sensing that God is calling them onwards, they respond by searching for him in an ever-deepening prayer experience. Fervour, spiritual cocksureness and pride characterise the make-up of the adolescent, although they are usually only aware of their fervour. Traditionally, the experience of the adolescent took place behind the closed doors of interior mental prayer. In more recent years, many people have been passing through this stage in the company of others, as members of prayer groups. You have combined both.

The moment of truth comes when first fervour comes to an end and believers find themselves deprived of all feeling in their prayer life. It is sad to say, but the vast majority give up serious personal prayer at this point, because their most recent experience conditioned them to associate faith with feelings, or the tangible awareness of God's presence with his actual presence. If they only knew it, God has just taken a new initiative and drawn them closer to himself than ever before. However, this new, more spiritual presence of God seems like absence to the adolescent whose previous experience of him was almost entirely sensual. The days of adolescence are now over – never to return again. This is the beginning of Adult Prayer.

This new world in which believers find themselves is the environment that enables them to become adults, by daily learning to give without receiving and to love without feeling love being returned. If you think about it, you will realise that this is the only way a person can become a perfect lover. The love that is always returned in kind must remain forever suspect until it receives nothing in return and yet goes on giving. This is the beginning of mystical prayer. The great spiritual writers make it quite clear that the beginner who perseveres will be stripped of all feeling and fervour, and will be given the opportunity to become a perfect and selfless lover. Naturally the 'bounty hunter' who is only looking for exciting and exhilarating experiences will pack up serious personal prayer altogether at this stage. Throughout the ages, Christian tradition has given various names to this painful period in the spiritual journey. For some it is the Desert, the Wilderness; for others, it is the Cloud of Unknowing, the House of Self-Knowledge, the Prayer of Faith, or the Dark Night of the Soul. All these different expressions are used by Christian tradition to convey the meaning and implications of the challenge with which the Gospel confronts a person who wants to become a perfect follower of Christ.

The challenge is this: do you want to be identified with the full human being, the Perfect Adult who emerged from the tomb on the first Easter Day? Do you want to experience the fullness of love that Christ experienced in his Resurrection, and share it with others? If so, then you must be prepared to share in his self-sacrificial life, in his death too, and even in his descent into hell. It means literally that! Anyone can follow Christ when he is working miracles, turning water into wine and handing out free food and drink. It is not difficult to be his disciple when you can see him curing the sick, giving sight to the blind and even raising the dead. But how many can follow him into the desert to suffer hunger, thirst, loneliness and temptation? How many are prepared to carry a cross behind him, to follow him to Calvary, to descend into the very bowels of evil with him? Juveniles cannot. Adolescents cannot. It takes an adult to do that, or rather, an adolescent becomes an adult by doing that.

Well, that will have to do for now. I am quite busy at the moment putting a new roof on my cottage but I will write again soon because I have a lot to say to you. For the moment, keep up the daily quality time for prayer as you did before, and keep your heart's attention fixed upon God as best you can. Now is the time when you must learn to give without counting the cost, to love without receiving in return, so that your love may be strengthened and deepened in such a way that you may come to know and experience the height and the depth, the length and the breadth of God's love, which surpasses all our understanding.

With every good wish,
Peter

As always Peter was so right although I didn't fully understand it at the time. When Peter had finished his roof, he wrote many longer letters advising me how to continue praying in the strange new world in which I found myself. There is no time to quote from all his letters here so let me briefly sum up what he taught me.

The great Evagrius Ponticus (AD 345-399), who synthesised the spiritual teaching of the Desert Fathers, called the aridity in which I found myself *Accidie* and the experience of presence that follows it, *Apatheia*. St John of the Cross details the characteristics of *Accidie* in *The Dark Night of the Soul* whilst St Teresa of Avila does likewise for *Apatheia* in her masterwork *Interior Castle*. Through a sort of spiritual hide and seek, a person is purified by the alternating experiences of absence and presence that convinces them that it is God and not they who are in control of their spiritual destiny. At times, they are cast into the depth of all but despair, at other times they are raised to the heights of ecstatic joy and to almost every state between the two before purification is complete. Then, what the early Fathers called *Theosis* or Divinisation, and their spiritual descendants called The Transforming Union or The Spiritual Marriage takes place, enveloping the whole person, body and spirit, as they are possessed ever more fully by the same Spirit who possessed Christ.

Even in the light of this brief résumé it is immediately possible to distinguish authentic Christian prayer from its counterfeit. Firstly, in the Christian tradition we are taught how to come to know and love God as embodied in Jesus Christ, by prayerfully reflecting on the sacred scriptures or through other traditional methods of meditation, not by using mantras to bypass the mind to generate pleasant or relaxing psychological states. In the Western Christian tradition, meditation primarily means prayerful reflection on the person of Christ, to enter into him through love. In the Far East, meditation primarily means the repetition of mantras. Forgive me for emphasising yet again that if using these mantras leads to a certain inner stillness, peace, or what is sometimes called mindfulness, it may well contribute to a certain self-generated tranquillity or psychological equilibrium; but it must never be confused with the true mystical contemplation of God. This cannot be generated in a matter of minutes, but only in years of selfless giving in dryness and aridity and it is then a pure gift of God. That is why the Vatican document, *Jesus Christ the Bearer of the Water of Life – A Christian reflection on the "New Age"* to which I have already referred insists:

"There is a tendency to confuse psychology and spirituality. Many of the meditation techniques now used are not prayer. They are often a good preparation for prayer, but no more, even if they lead to a more pleasant state of mind or bodily comfort."

The notion that believers can come to experience profound mystical contemplation by their own unaided endeavour is to fall into the old heresy of semi-Pelagianism, the belief that human beings can come to experience the presence of God within by what are in effect self-generated psychological techniques, or if you like, by various forms of mental yoga. To appeal to the writings of John Cassian and to other Desert Fathers as confirmation that the Western Christian tradition teaches the use of mantras in the same way as the Indian tradition, is quite simply nonsense. But it is worse than nonsense because it undermines genuine Christian searchers and sets them on a wrong heretical way of prayer, sometimes for twenty years or more. That should be evident to any open-minded reader who has not been brainwashed by the propagandists of the centering and mantra movements, who sadly have deceived others as they have deceived themselves.

In the same way, *The Cloud of Unknowing* is a favourite of those trying to justify the use of mantras. The author of this mystical work however, is not writing for beginners, but for those who, after successfully meditating on the life of Christ, are languishing in *Accidie* or in the Dark Night when their minds and hearts are being drawn towards God in such a way that they have no desire nor any ability to meditate as before. In the introduction to this invaluable little work, the author insist that his book must not be given to anyone, indeed it must be kept away and hidden from the general reader. It is only for those in the dark night, it is positively not for beginners, as those who promote mantras suggest. The author of *The Cloud* suggests the repetition of a word, not as a mantra, but as a practical device, or a crutch if you like, to help keep the heart and mind fixed "in naked intent" upon God. The chosen word is not meant to help a person generate inner psychological states where the attention is not placed upon God but on oneself. Using medieval symbolism, he encourages the believer to use a word such as, "God" or "Love" for instance, as a spiritual spear and shield. When used as a spear the word helps the heart's desire to penetrate the "Cloud of Unknowing" that seems to separate them from the God who smiled on them before. When used as a shield the word can at the same time help to parry distractions and then place them under what he calls, the "Cloud of Forgetting" so that they can be free to give their whole attention to God.

The Cloud of Unknowing merely presents to medieval readers an ancient form of prayer, first referred to by Abbott Macarius who taught those of his disciples who were afflicted by *Accidie* the use of a short prayer, to do for them what the author of *The Cloud of Unknowing* wished to do for his readers. He taught them to cry out to God "To the rescue," or call out the name "Jesus" so that he would come to the rescue. This is the origin of what later came to be called the Jesus Prayer. The Prayer of Faith was the collective title later given to various short prayers used most especially by those who languished in *Accidie* or in The Dark Night of the Soul.

Let me end this chapter by telling you how I made use of the teaching of *The Cloud of Unknowing* that Peter recommended to me, by tailoring it to my own needs in the hope it might be of help to you. Instead of choosing a single word, I started by choosing a single sentence, one that I felt somehow summed up how I felt at the time when God seemed to have taken his leave of me. I chose the prayer Jesus made upon the Cross, most especially when everything seemed too much: "My God, my God, why have you forsaken me?" Or the prayer he made in Gethsemane, particularly when temptations came thick and fast: "Father, may this chalice be taken away from me". When I felt really in the pits I turned to the *De Profundis*: "Out of the depths I cried to thee, O Lord; Lord, hear my prayer", or to the prayer from Cardinal Newman's famous hymn, "Lead, kindly light, amidst the encircling gloom". The Jesus Prayer, designed especially for this particular moment of the mystic way, is perhaps the best known of all: "Jesus, Son of God, have mercy on me, a sinner".

When you pray in this dark night choose phrases you feel appeal to you, but use them in the way I suggest, to help you to keep repenting. What you will find, is that in time the full sentence will be too long, and you will feel the need to reduce it to, "My God, my God", or "Out of the depths", or "Lead, kindly light", or "Have mercy on me, a sinner". Then the time will come when you will be back to where we started with *The Cloud of Unknowing*, when a single word will be all you need, like God, or Jesus, or mercy. It is like changing gears in a car; once you get used to using them, you know automatically when to change down. Some count the words or the phrases on beads to keep gently fixing their gaze on God. These suggestions are not prayer but aids to prayer, the prayer of the heart where repentance is learnt. This repentance of heart that is practised in the darkness is worth ten times that practised in the light. It is easy to pray when the well is full and brimming over, but it is far more difficult to pray when the well runs dry.

It is of paramount importance to give exactly the same time to prayer that you gave when prayer was full of feeling and fervour, so that you can show by the very consistency of your daily presence that you are prepared to go on giving even when you seem to receive nothing in return. Only a mature adult can continue to give in pure selfless love when his or her love seems to be received with indifference, if it seems to be received at all. Now you can see the real meaning of the strange spiritual desert in which you find yourself. It is the place where you offer yourself to God through a process of daily repentance as you endeavour to raise your mind and heart to him through selfless loving. It is a loving that will always be returned in kind, whether it is the kind of love that purifies in turmoil and strife, or in peace and tranquility. God will do his part if we do ours. Our part is to keep on gently turning to him again and again, to keep on raising our hearts whether they feel empty or full.

If you persevere, the time will come when the action of God's love will begin to draw you into an ever-deepening Recollection or Quiet or even the prayer of Full Union. Then you will find less and less need for any of the forms of prayer that supported you along the way. All you will want to do is to remain still and gaze in awe-filled silence upon the One whom you feel drawing you onward into the peace that surpasses the understanding.

At rare moments when I felt touched by the presence of God who seemed absent for so long, I turned to short prayers of praise and thanksgiving to express how I felt. The important thing is to choose something that genuinely embodies how you feel at the time. It is no good pretending with God. What is important is that these short prayers are only used to help you to turn back to God from the distractions that would otherwise turn you away from him. Herein lies the profound meaning and value of bravely journeying on despite the dryness and aridity, the darkness and the demons that you must face. It is here that perseverance is learnt, and the patience that St Catherine of Siena says is not so much a virtue, as the sign of all the virtues, that are learnt in the mystical purification. Vices are bad habits, virtues are good habits. All habits are learnt by practising them and virtues are learnt in this prayer of naked faith. As perseverance and patience are practised, they become the channels that allow the love of God in, to suffuse our human loving with the divine. It is this mutual mingling of love that enables a mere mortal to begin to generate some of the virtues first seen to perfection in Jesus Christ. The darkness in which they are born guarantees the humility of the recipients who are only conscious of their helplessness.

Most of the time this contemplation will be in the dark without a spark of light to alleviate the gloom. Quite out of the blue, brief moments of light may shine through if a person perseveres for long enough and with sufficient patience without wishing to be rewarded. We will be rewarded, but in God's time not ours. In this journey we will come to know and experience the agony and the ecstasy as both are part of the purification. The word agony comes from the Greek word to struggle, and the word ecstasy come from the Greek word to be transported out of oneself. The struggle is with one's lower self, pulling down the higher self whose only desire is to contemplate the divine. This struggle embodies, in concentrated periods of time, the practice of repentance that is at the heart of the Gospel. The transportation out of oneself to experience the divine is the work of the divine love itself that has penetrated our weak attempts at loving as we try daily to practise repentance in prayer. This divine love suffuses our human love, surcharging it with supernatural powers opening it to receive and experience God's loving to various degrees of intensity.

In Peter's last talk, he likened a person at prayer to an athlete in training, repeatedly lifting weights to develop all the muscles of the body through one single action. It is a telling analogy because each time we try to raise our heart and mind to God in prayer, we are in effect developing all the muscles of our heart and mind simultaneously. The more an athlete adds weights to the bar, the harder the work, but the quicker and the more surely will muscles grow. That is why the harder and the more difficult prayer becomes in the night, the quicker and the more surely will the muscles of the heart and mind grow, if regular daily practice is sustained. The whole person then becomes ever more ready and open to receive the love that generates the goodness within them from which all the virtues and all the gifts of the Holy Spirit are born. If successful, an athlete might earn many gold medals, but who wants gold medals when eternal life is on offer here and now in this life, as but a foretaste of what is to come in heaven.

That so much of this journey takes place in darkness is a blessing, as St John of the Cross explains. I remember once speaking to an extremely holy hermit who said that if he could choose between having regular visits from Our Lady or Our Lord himself, and journeying on each day in the dark night, he would choose the latter. He said he would find the responsibility of experiencing the former too much for him. How much better to travel by faith in this life, because the rewards are so much greater in the next. People often wish they could have been alive to see Christ when he was on earth, but my friend the hermit did not. Having seen and heard so much, he argued, how much more would be expected of him when it was time to give an account of his life. At the end of his Gospel St John wrote, "Happy are those who have not seen and yet believe" (John 20:29). The hermit said these were the words that kept him going, and confirmed that he would rather journey on in the dark night of faith, rather than having to answer for how he had behaved after seeing Christ in person. His words have been a great inspiration to me too, when darkness enfolds me for longer that I would wish!

The suggestions that I have made on how to pray in the dark night by using short phrases or even single words, can be likened to using oars on a boat used to guide it downriver towards the sea. At first you row hard to get the boat moving towards its destination, but when the momentum has been built up you can sit back and rest for a while as it moves silently forward. The moment the boat starts to slow down, drifts towards the bank or gets caught in a cross current, then you must start rowing again to keep it moving in the right direction. And so you keep journeying on, at one moment rowing to keep the boat on course, at another resting, enjoying the surrounding countryside. As you approach the sea you need to row less and less as you experience the pull of the tide drawing you onwards. Once you have left the river, you can put aside the oars and set up the sails. Now you can travel with ease and with speed, with the tide on your side and the wind in your sails; another power takes over to do for you what you could never do for yourself.

To end this chapter I would like to emphasise that vocal prayer, with which a personal relationship with God usually begins, does not become unimportant, left behind, as mental prayer develops through meditation to contemplation. Vocal prayer will always be part of a person's prayer life. Sometimes it will be the mainstay when all other forms of prayer seem impossible. The example I would give you is that of the greatest mystic of all. Although Jesus was caught up in the contemplation of his Father's love at every moment of his life, he always turned to vocal prayer every day of that life. In the morning and evening he would say the appointed psalms with which to begin and end the day. Three times a day he would go to the synagogue to pray the *Shema* and recite the *Berakah* when he gathered with his family or his disciples for meals. Vocal prayer and mental prayer are complementary, despite the truth that without mental prayer, vocal prayer will gradually lose its power and potency. When we can no longer meditate, and there is no one to lead us on into contemplative prayer, vocal prayer becomes our daily bread, our staple spiritual diet. It may not be the ultimate ideal, but it is far better than nothing, nor must it be discontinued, even when with help, the mystic way is open to us. The continual **"cri de coeur"** *cri de coeur* ***"cri de coeur"*** for help that is made in vocal prayer when all other avenues to mental prayer seem closed, will always be answered by the God who said, "Knock, and the door will be opened to you" (Matthew 7:7). All that is needed is the advice given to the importunate friend, to keep on knocking, knowing that eventually patience and perseverance will ensure that the door will be opened, "For the one who asks always receives; the one who searches always finds; the one who knocks will always have the door opened to him" (Luke 11:10), but in God's time, not ours. However, this patient perseverance must not be in fits and starts, but regular and daily, whether we are in the mood or not, whether we feel like it or not, and with the resolve to begin again and again, as often as failure threatens to make us lose heart and give up. This not only applies to daily vocal prayer, but to all prayer, if we are serious about abandoning our lives to God, as the only possible response for all that he has done and is doing for us now and always. If we do our part God will always do his, even though there seems to be no one else on earth who can help us.

I know that Peter practises the Morning Prayer that he spoke of in his talks every day. In this way, he told me, he is reminded that the whole of the forthcoming day is the place where he offers all he says and does to God, in, with and through Jesus. This is how the prayer that he makes for others is embodied in all he says and does. In this way, his whole day gives honour and glory to God, but is also a prayer for others, that God's glory may be embodied in them too.

When I had all but completed this book, which is not my work, but a compendium of all Peter's teaching given during his talks, and to me personally over the years, I wrote to him to ask how I should complete it. I wanted him to sum up and simplify his practical teaching in a way that everybody could understand and therefore apply to their daily lives. I cannot do better than to end by quoting from his reply in what is the last brief Chapter of this book.

Chapter 19

A letter from Peter Calvay

"It has been the constant teaching of the great Christian mystics that a serious searcher must travel on in prayer beyond first fervour to be purified, in preparation to receive perfect love. Without this love, the whole outward edifice of the Church's liturgical ceremonial will be no more than "gongs booming and cymbals clashing" (1 Corinthians 13:1), for the quality of the liturgy depends on the love which inspires it, and the love that it then generates. The Church's liturgy always tends to degenerate, to the degree that personal prayer loses its central place as the heart and soul of authentic Christian Spirituality. Many years ago I attended a retreat given by Fr Michael Hollings, who was in those days in great demand as a fearless and outspoken preacher. The retreat was for religious from many different orders. After joining the community for the communal recitation of the divine office, Fr Hollings began his first lecture with a tirade that reminded me of the hellfire sermons that I attended as a boy. He blasted the priests for the mindless way they rushed through the office, "like starving cattle hungry to get to their morning feed." Everybody was, not only chastened, but somewhat mystified; after all, they were only doing what they did every day of their lives in their respective religious communities!

"The following year I spent a month on retreat at the Franciscan hermitage of Fonte Colombo high up on the hillside above the town of Rieti in Italy. The hermitage as it stands today was built by St Bernardine of Siena, the great Franciscan reformer. The very essence of his wisdom can still be seen written in words of gold around the sanctuary. It is here that the friars say their daily office, attend their daily Mass and all the other great liturgical ceremonies throughout the year. To remind them continually of the inner spiritual energy on which their liturgy depends, the words he had written were these: "Si cor non orat, in vanum lingua laborat – If the heart does not pray, then the tongue labours in vain". The liturgy is the communal expression in words, psalms, canticles and prayers of the love with which, united in Christ, we give all honour and glory to God. It depends for its power and effectiveness on the quality of love previously generated by each member of the community in what the Franciscan mystic, Angela of Foligno called the *Schola Divini Amoris – The School of Divine Love,* which is prayer.

"A school is a place where you go to learn. The school of divine love is the place where you go to learn how to practise raising your heart and mind to God, inspired and supported by the Holy Spirit, sent by Jesus for this purpose. It is here that the spiritual muscles of the heart are developed day by day, year by year. When everyone who participates in the liturgy goes to this school regularly, as regularly as the early Christians did, then its communal celebration will be alive, vibrant and full of life. It will become the most sublime experience possible on earth because the Christian community will experience together, the joy, the peace and the spiritual intoxication of experiencing all the fruits of giving and receiving love, in and through Jesus, the Risen Lord.

"But as the liturgy is the expression of the communal love of the community, it will, as it always has done, depend on the quality of the love generated in personal prayer long before we even enter the place where the liturgy is to be celebrated. It was this profound mystical dynamic that not only enabled the early Christians to be filled with the love of God, but to be filled with his goodness too. It was the fruits of that goodness, the other-worldly and transcendental virtues that they embodied, that so mesmerised the ancient pagan world that they literally converted and captivated that world. What happened then to that pagan world can happen again to our pagan world if we only learn from our early forebears, if we only follow the example set by them.

"Is the degradation and the depravity of the modern world any better or any worse than that of the ancient world? If you listen to the local, the national and the international news on any day you choose, you will hear of frightful horrors and myriad stories of what the depravity of human beings can do to other human beings. And if you listen to the frustrations of those to whom we have failed to teach the truth, you will hear their relentless cry, "Why does God allow such things to happen? Why does God not do something about it?" In the true answer to this *cri de coeur* lies the essence of all that I have been trying to say. For the human catastrophes that we hear about day after day in the media to be ended, and for peace and justice to reign where hatred and inhumanity reigned before, something that seems all but impossible must be done. All the vices and viciousness that rule in a fallen humanity must be replaced by all the virtues that Jesus preached in the Sermon on the Mount.

"But, all these virtues can only come to humanity sheathed within the supernatural love unleashed by Jesus on the first Pentecost Day. That this love is still being given on every day, is the essence of what is called the Good News that Christians are called upon to preach and teach to others. However, whenever you hear good news, news that seems too good to be true, there always seems to be a 'but'. Here is the 'but'. Love cannot be forced on anyone. Forced love is a contradiction in terms. It is physically impossible, as everyone who has loved or been loved knows by their own experience.

"What is true of human love is true of divine love. That the great plan of God, the Mysterion be brought about, this love must be made available continually to every human being. In order to bring this about God sent Jesus, so that his infinite love could be transformed in him into human loving, so it could reach out through him into other human beings. But we have to choose freely to receive this love, by turning to receive it, as St Peter explained to his audience at the birth of Christianity on the first Pentecost Day. Then, by continually turning to allow the source of all the virtues to be reborn in us, God can indeed do something to change the world, but only through us. The love of God in which all the virtues we need to bring about heaven on earth, is contained within a single shaft of God's love, but love is not magic. It cannot bring about instant change. I believe in instant coffee, instant tea, even instant physical healing and instant physical miracles, but the instant inner spiritual healing that leads to sanctity is quite another matter. As the pure and perfect love of God penetrates our inner being, it must first purify away and do to death all that prevents the indwelling of love. It is this indwelling of love that gives birth to the virtues that the world needs to restore it to wholeness. That is why St Francis of Assisi insisted that we cannot possess any of the virtues unless we first die. That is why death and resurrection is the central mystery of our faith. I do not just mean the death and Resurrection of Jesus two thousand years ago, but our daily death and resurrection as we try to follow him now. This is a lifelong journey. It leads directly to encountering and experiencing the fullness of love imperfectly here on earth, and perfectly in heaven, whilst at the same time, sharing the fruits of that love with others, here on earth so that they may share our joy, the joy that can alone bring peace to the world.

"Ever since the Book of Revelation promised a new heaven and a new earth, social, and political reformers have been preaching their versions of liberty, fraternity and equality to bring it about. After destroying all and everyone who stood in their way, they never realised the dreams they used to inspire others. All victims tend to identify with their oppressors, and revolutionaries are no exception to the rule. Time and time again you find that once they come to power they become little more than the monsters who once oppressed them. The initial idealism they believed could transpose their dreams into reality has long since been crushed out of them by jealousy, greed, bitterness and hate. This is why the revolution that Jesus preached is the only one that can work, because it brings heaven down to earth, not by destroying the past, but by bringing its deepest desires and yearnings to perfection. It does this by re-energising people from the inside, with a love capable of generating all the goodness and fruits of goodness that can bring about a kingdom of peace and joy, of justice and equality here on earth, as the springboard for our infinite fulfilment in heaven."

Maranatha Joshua ben Yahweh

Chapter 20

Author's Epilogue

The return to a spirituality centred on the humanity of Jesus, in the wake of the reconquest of the Holy Land in the twelfth century, came to be called the Franciscan Spring. It was so called because it owed more to the man whom medieval Christians called the second Christ, than to anyone else. It was thanks to St Francis of Assisi that a new way of prayer was restored, not just for monks in monasteries or nuns in their enclosed convents, but for all. Meditation on the love of God as embodied in the most perfect and the most adorable man ever to have walked on the face of the earth, was an entirely new way of prayer for most of his contemporaries, as it was for the first Christians. It enabled ordinary workaday people to come to know and love God, not just by entering into Jesus through love, as he once was, but as he is now. In this way they were able to enter into his mystical contemplation of the Father, just as the first Christians were able to do before them. What was, nevertheless, open to the few during the dark ages when the humanity of Jesus had ceased to be the driving force in Christian spirituality, was now restored for all. The deeply personal and moving devotion to the one St Francis called Brother Jesus, was imparted to all his brothers, and through them to the new Christ-centred spiritualities that would predominate in subsequent centuries.

Although there were spiritual ups and downs as the history of Christian spirituality unfolded, renewals always emphasised the return to prayer and to the personal love of Jesus generated in meditation that led to mystical contemplation. Although it should go without saying, it must nevertheless be said yet again, that the spread of any fake or fallacious forms of meditation amongst genuine Christian believers can be disastrous.

Reducing true Christian meditation to the saying of mantras for instance, can not only hinder genuine spiritual growth, but permanently inhibit it as well, as renewal always comes through authentic mystics and saints who are formed in the mystic way.

The unprecedented numbers of first rank mystical writers who inspired the next five hundred years or so after the Franciscan Spring, would always keep the barque of Peter on a steady course, despite the periodic storms that at times prevailed. The Council of Trent was not primarily called because the Church was in desperate need of spiritual reform, at least at ground level, despite the propaganda of reformers eager to justify themselves by arguing otherwise. This distortion of the truth has thankfully been put to bed by Eamon Duffy in his brilliant book, *The Stripping of the Altars*. The Council was called to defeat intellectually the false theological positions of the reformers that were at variance with the Church that Jesus founded, and with the faith which flourished under his inspiration and under the Spirit of Truth whom he sent to guide it.

As the task in hand was predominantly intellectual, it was a great intellectual whom the council of Trent chose to be their theologian in residence, although of course he was long since dead! His name was St Thomas Aquinas. His theology would be used to restate and defend orthodoxy, not just for the Council Fathers, but also as the means through which the teachings of the council would be communicated to future generations. This would be the preferred theology that would henceforth be taught in Catholic universities, seminaries and houses of further education for religious, and even for the laity, for the catechism was but a simple and concise summary of the theology of the Angelic Doctor.

The intellectual emphasis that was needed at the time was successful, not least because it was counterbalanced and supported by a strong and deeply entrenched spirituality that emphasised the heart. It was this that continued to inspire the dominant mystical theology that prevailed as an enduring foundation for the vibrant spirituality that was current at the time. A massive upsurge in Christ-centred spirituality throughout the fifteenth century, initially led by great Franciscan reformers, spilled over into the sixteenth century. It inspired two new Franciscan reforms, the Observants and Capuchins whose re-emphasis on the humanity of Jesus inspired, not only older orders like the Benedictines, but new orders too. The Society of Jesus particularly, through the exercises composed by St Ignatius, would keep systematic meditation on Christ at the forefront of Christian spirituality. But perhaps most important of all for the preservation and explanation of mystical theology, this new upsurge in spiritual renewal influenced the foundation of the Discalced Carmelites. Their two great spiritual geniuses, St Teresa of Avila and St John of the Cross, would become Doctors of the Church for their unprecedented and precise description of the mystic way.

William of St Thierry, a devoted follower of St Bernard, once said that, "You will never love someone unless you know them, but you will never really know them unless you love them." Before, during and after the Council of Trent this balance was safeguarded. The balance in orthodox Christian spirituality between the mind and the heart, the intellect and the will must always prevail. The balance between the intellectual understanding of God's plan, the Mysterion, and the heart-led journey into that plan-made-man in Jesus Christ, must always be maintained or serious setbacks, if not disasters will follow. Sadly, unforeseen consequences of the teachings of the first Protestant reformers were to unhinge this balance, and setbacks were to follow.

When at the Last Supper Jesus detailed the mystical metaphor of the vine, he insisted that unless we, the branches, remain part of him, the vine, we would have no power to do anything. You do not need to be a theologian to realise that Jesus was teaching that both the action of the main stem and the branches are essential, working together, if the vine is to bear fruit. In believing that God does everything in prayer and we do nothing, the Quietists were clearly falling into a teaching alien to the Gospels and to traditional theology. The Church therefore had to act.

It had to try to stamp out what might appear to be primitive Protestant ideas within its own ranks. This meant that any form of prayer that seemed to suggest that we do nothing but wait in total inactivity for the grace of God to do everything, had to be condemned and rooted out. But zealous spiritual ignoramuses went too far. They persecuted those who taught and practised authentic mystical theology, and encouraged the anti-mystical witch-hunts that followed in the wake of the condemnation of Quietism. The result of this has been that in the last three hundred years, Catholic spirituality has been systematically stripped of the profound mystical theology that was once its indispensable foundation and inspiration.

All this was completely unknown to me until, like so many others, I was led into the dark night. Whilst vast numbers, finding no help packed up the journey, I was blessed. What was happening to me in Obscure Contemplation was understood by a theologian to whom I turned for help. Although he had the humility to admit that his knowledge came from learning rather than from practice, he insisted that my experiences were authentic and that I must persevere, and he recommended books that were of great help to me. During my tenure as the director of a Retreat and Conference centre in London, I came across many others who found themselves in a predicament similar to mine. Finding no one else, I had to take on the responsibility of running courses on prayer and writing books to try and redress the imbalance in Catholic spirituality, caused, not only by the demise of, but the antagonism towards authentic mystical theology. Just as the Black Death has filled almost all of us with an inbuilt and systemic aversion to rats, so the condemnation of Quietism seems to have filled Catholics with an inbuilt and systemic aversion to mystical theology. During the twelve years running the retreat centre, I discovered that countless priests and religious had no teaching whatsoever in mystical theology. Even more shocking, very few had any systemic training in personal prayer at all; it was simply assumed. They were, of course all taught how to sing, recite, chant or say the divine office, and warned of their obligation to complete it each day. However, virtually nothing had been taught of how the heart should be taught to pray in deep personal prayer, to suffuse and surcharge the Divine Office and the liturgy with the love that can alone animate it and make it the perfect expression of the deep inner life that should inspire the whole Church.

I made it my prime objective from the beginning to recruit only the best and most qualified lecturers in the country to promote the teaching of the Second Vatican Council from, people whom I too could learn with everyone else. One particular theologian was outstanding in his mastery of what we then called the New Biblical Theology, although he was initially trained in Thomistic Theology. I therefore approached him with my misgivings about the demise of mystical theology. His answer shocked me to the core. The conversation that I was eager to initiate, ended abruptly when he simply said, "I am afraid I know nothing whatsoever about mystical theology," and then walked away. His mastery of the teaching of the great scholars whom I had read and respected, whose teaching was responsible for the initial success of the Second Vatican Council, was second to none. How, therefore, could he say that he knew nothing about mystical theology? It took me some time to realise that what he said could have been said by any one of them too, because on reflection, despite years of personal study, it had finally dawned on me that I had found no deep understanding of mystical theology in any of their writings.

It was evident that they too had been influenced, like the rest of us, by the anti-mystical ethos that had pervaded Catholic spirituality over the last three hundred years or more. Suddenly I began to see why the great document on the liturgy that meant so much to me in the beginning failed to have the dramatic influence on renewal that we all hoped and prayed it would have. It was a masterly reconstruction of the ancient liturgy as practised by the first Christians, adapted for the modern world. However, the liturgy is the outward communal expression of the faith of the community from which it draws its power and strength. Nothing was done in any of the conciliar documents to complement the document on the liturgy by uncovering and explaining the vibrant and all-consuming faith of the first Christian communities, and adapting and recommending it to modern Catholics.

It took me a long time to get over my encounter with the theologian, who had taught me, and whom I had been proud to engage as the most respected speaker on the many courses that I organised. But gradually the penny dropped and I began to realise for the first time how the condemnation of Quietism has not just affected the troops in the trenches, but the generals too on whom they depended to lead and guide them. Theologians became highly specialised highbreds, academics, who mainly lived in ivory towers on university campuses, in seminaries, and in houses of study, who held forth on obtuse aspects of theology that meant nothing or little to the punters in the pews. Yet originally the object of their study was the God whom St John told us is love, who had called his people to a marriage with himself. That is why the great mystical writers like St Teresa of Avila had described the culmination of the journey into God as a spiritual or mystical marriage that would begin in this life and have its consummation in the next. Above and before everything else therefore, theologians were first seen as both experts and practitioners in the art of arts, the art of love. It was their profession to teach people how, when and where the love is generated that can enable them to enter into a mystical marriage with God, a marriage to which we are all called. That is why the great theologian Evagrius Ponticus who summed up and synthesised the teaching of the Desert Fathers, said that a theologian was a person of prayer. How else would they be able to teach others? For, as I have said many times over, prayer is the place where love is learnt, where it is refined and purified to enable us to enter into and to enjoy to eternity the marriage for which we have been created. Theologians must be reminded of their primary calling for they are all too prone to become specialists, gaining doctorates in abstruse, obscure or arcane areas of theology that blind them to what the first Christians called 'The Way', which is the way of love, in, with and through The Way, The Truth, and the Life.

Towards the end of the 1970s a visiting professor of theology from the Dominican University in Rome, known as the Angelicum, attended my talks on prayer. I was dumbstruck when he asked me to lecture on mystical theology for a course that he had set up for religious from all over the world in Rome. The reason why I was dumbstruck was that he admitted that he could not find anyone else to do it, despite the massive choice available in a city bristling with Catholic universities. Even a friend of his, the senior spirituality lecturer at the Angelicum declined, on the grounds that he only dealt with the subject from an academic and historical perspective, not from a pastoral perspective. The course that ran for several years resulted in invitations to speak from all over the world, and confirmed the frightening conclusions that I had to draw from the audits that I had made in my own centre where I had taught for twelve years.

The reader may be excused for viewing my conclusions with dismay, if not scepticism, but reflect for a moment as I have reflected for years. How could tens, if not hundreds of thousands of priests and religious have left the Church, if not their faith, if they had been men and women of profound prayer? How could they have left in droves if they had been men and women who had been transformed in the mystical crèche where saints are made from sinners? How could so many who remained have shamed themselves and the Church by performing acts of the most despicable indecency, destroying the lives of so many thousands of innocent children, if prayer of any sort had been any part of their lives?

These were some of the experiences that led me to realise that there can be no deep or lasting reform or renewal in the Church without returning to the profound prayer tradition, culminating in mystical contemplation that was once the inner energy and vitality that gave life to the Church. It was to rediscover this sublime mystical spirituality that prevailed in the early Church that I have tried to follow in the footsteps of Blessed John Henry Newman and go back to the early sources. This was not to rediscover what has already been discovered, but to discover the profound priestly and mystical spirituality that set the early Christian communities alight with a unique quality of pure unadulterated goodness. They proclaimed the glory of God, not just to each other, but to the world that God's love was able to reach out to them and through them.

This book contains a summary of my findings that has forced me to draw a few but necessary conclusions that can enable the modern Church, from the highest to the lowest, to learn from the ancient Church. In short, we must return without delay to that awe-inspiring and all-consuming daily mystical spirituality that was lived by the first Christian disciples, learnt firstly from living it with Jesus himself. The essence of this spirituality was recaptured in the twelfth century thanks to St Francis and the re-understanding and the re-instatement of the primacy of love. It was this above all that was at the heart and soul of the return to mystical theology that inspired the spiritual leadership in the Church until the regrettable effects of Quietism.

Before these unfortunate effects did long lasting damage to Christian spirituality, there was a balance between the mind and the heart, the intellect and the will. It was this spiritual balance that enabled the Council of Trent and those who promoted it, to act effectively to achieve their objective. Once mystical theology had been undermined, however, the spirituality of the heart was denied its natural flowering in the mystic way. For whenever the Holy Spirit led individuals into the crèche where saints are made, ignorant anti-mystical zealots did all in their power to undermine them, and to question the mystical teaching that could help them. Even St Teresa of Avila and St John of the Cross who were later to be made doctors of the Church for their detailed explanations of the purpose and the final destiny of the mystic way, were suspect. In the last three hundred years or more, it has been the re-education of the intellect that has been the prime object of ecclesiastical action in any renewal. This has been instanced by several Thomist revivals.

The most recent Thomist revival was introduced by Pope Leo XIII on 4 August 1879 when he promulgated the encyclical *Aeterni Patris*. From this time forward and well into the twentieth century Thomism became compulsory, not only in seminaries but in all Catholic Universities and houses of further education. Ignorance of the personal spiritual journey of St Thomas himself, however, and of the mystical insights that inspired him at the end of his life, resulted in an unbalanced theological education. It introduced an intense and unmitigated intellectual program for the study of philosophy and theology that had no place in it for the profound mystical theology that had, according to Garrigou-Lagrange, OP such an influence on the Angelic Doctor and on his writings. Many would-be Catholic mystical leaders felt that they would be crushed by the heavy-handed imposition of this intellectual straightjacket together with the carte blanche condemnation of all currents of thought outside the Catholic Church under the catch-all heresy known as 'Modernism'. It prevented a great writer like the Anglican mystic Evelyn Underhill, for instance, from becoming a Catholic and turned Martin Heidegger away from the church, into which he had been born, because it outlawed the traditional Catholic mystical teaching. It was this that had originally inspired him and it was to this that he later returned, but sadly outside the bosom of the Church. The teaching of St Thomas will always be the most complete and comprehensive presentation of the Catholic faith, but when it has been shorn of the profound mystical theology that inspired him, it will inevitably be unbalanced and therefore mislead. It is sadly a mistake that has been made in the past. How very many leaders have been affected by this omission in the ensuing years will never be known. However, what would become known would be the effect of neglecting the spirituality of the heart and the necessary mystical teaching needed to perfect it. A spirituality that does not teach people how to love creates loveless leaders who for want of genuine spiritual love seek its counterfeit. This can not only destroy them, but also the myriad innocents whose lives have been, and continue to be devastated. Thankfully this is only the fate of the minority, but that is bad enough. The majority may not have indulged in such shameful scandals, but sadly they have only been fed on half or less than half rations, because the fullness of love that is open to them daily cannot be fully received. The profound mystical theology that can alone teach them how, has been, if not derided, denied them.

When the New Biblical Theology suddenly took the Church by storm, before, during and after the Second Vatican Council, it excited a whole new generation of students, including me. However, beneath the surface it too was primarily a renewal that appealed to the intellect. Despite an initial response that did indeed appeal to the heart, the initial emotional response soon withered without the mystical purification in which the heart was purified. The balance between the mind and the heart that is always the hallmark of an authentic Christian spirituality, like that originally inaugurated by Jesus himself, was once more lost to view. Casualties were inevitable.

St Augustine said, "The New Testament lies hidden in the Old and the Old is unveiled in the New." I, with countless fellow students, was excited to read the works of a new breed of theologians who, each in their different way, clothed and detailed this insight of St Augustine. This new theology was so alive, so engaging, so enthralling after the purely intellectual reasoning of St Thomas Aquinas, minus the mystical theology that had inspired him. After he had completed his *Summa Theologica* even he later described his own works as 'straw' compared to the experience of God's love that then enraptured him. We did not want straw, we wanted the new exhilarating theology that so excited us. What we had failed to realise, together with the mentors who taught us, was that despite its pristine newness that excited our feelings and emotions, it was still predominantly intellectual. It was good as far as it went, but it did not go deep enough. Furthermore, it was still predominantly concerned with the outside of the cup. It failed to lead us on to embrace the profound mystical spirituality that underpinned it, the spirituality as lived by Jesus and his disciples both before and after the Resurrection.

Sadly, it was the antipathy, if not the open hostility of the new biblical scholars to mystical theology in general that prevented them appreciating the early Christian mystical theology in particular. I have tried to make up for this deficiency in this book, in the hope that others will follow so that a new balance will return to Catholic spirituality, heralding a new dawn. Whether a new Council is needed to promote this is for others to decide, but it would need to inspire our best scholars, theologians and liturgists to follow in the footsteps of Blessed John Henry Newman and go back to the first Christian centuries as they did before. No need to seek out the shape and form of the Liturgy - that has already been done - but this time to seek out and detail the profound mystical spirituality that Jesus practised each day with his disciples. Then see how it was continued and brought to perfection after his glorification, to transform the lives of all Christians by teaching them the daily prayer that leads to the prayer without ceasing. Let them not only show how Christ became tangibly present in those who gave their lives for him in red martyrdom, but how the same happened in those who gave their lives for him in what came to be called white martyrdom - in those who tried to convert every moment into the daily liturgy of selfless living and giving, that enabled them to carry their daily cross for Christ. Let them explain for us the new means of Christian prayer called meditation that taught how, from meditating on Christ as he once was, we can come to contemplate him as he is now, and through him to contemplate the Father. Let their scholarship and spiritual guidance help us to focus more attention on the weekly domestic and workplace liturgy that was so important to our early forebears. Once this is done, the same Sunday liturgy that we celebrate now will be transformed into what they called the Heavenly Liturgy, because that is what it will become, as our giving enables God to give to us in ever greater abundance, making something that we can so easily take for granted into a foretaste of heaven on earth.

Laws, precepts, rules and regulations not only failed to renew the faith of the Jews before the coming of Christ, but they contributed to its demise. They did this because they so highlighted hundreds of daily rules and regulations that the real law of love was forgotten, as Jesus continually pointed out. This first law of love that was so emphasised by Jesus himself and by the great apostle Paul who followed him, was to become the daily bread that nourished the first Christian communities. This law of love and the journey those who aspire to practise it must undertake, should now once again become the essence of the Christian life. To do this the teachers must be taught. For too long, aspiring priests and religious have been given an education that is primarily directed towards developing their intellectual knowledge. This education was understandable when they had to be equipped to combat the errors of the reformers. However, even then there was a balance, because mystical theology was both taught and practised, at least in the beginning.

The effects of Quietism, however, have led to the imbalance

that must be corrected. It must be corrected, not just to effect a balanced equilibrium in the education of future priests and religious, but for the preservation of their humanity. If young men and women are asked to make a vow of chastity, without at the same time being taught how to come to know and experience the love of God through deep prayer, then disasters will follow, as we have all witnessed. Disaster will follow, because no one can live fully without love. If a person has had to forego the experience of God's love reaching out to them through another human being in the sacrament of love, then it is an obligation on those who insist on this sacrifice, to teach them how to come to know and experience God's love in prayer. By prayer I do not just mean saying prayers, or performing prayers of obligation, but by practising the deep prayer that leads onward beyond first beginnings into the mystic way. It is only here they will come to know and experience the love that surpasses the understanding. This is the only love that can compensate them for the love they have given up. It is the only love that can make them fully human, as they are being prepared, like Jesus before them, to use their human nature as the God-given instrument that will enable them to communicate what they have received to others. Mystical theology, as the foundation and completion of spiritual theology, must be taught by practitioners to all young men and women in seminaries and houses of further education. This is their right that must be granted to them by those who have placed on them the obligation to forfeit their natural desire to seek God's love in and through the sacrament of marriage.

All laws, all precepts and all decrees of the Church must be directed to enabling every member of the Church to come to know and experience the love of God by learning how to love him, with their mind and heart, with all their soul, and with their whole being. However, when those who have been asked to take vows of perpetual chastity are asked to do this, then they must at the same time and from the outset, be taught how to generate this love in personal prayer. This will enable them to be prepared and purified to come to know and experience the only love that can bring them to the human and spiritual maturity for which they yearn. There is also a secondary reason why all young priests and religious must be taught mystical theology. Even if they do not make full use of this knowledge for their own spiritual advancement, they will be able to help others who are in need of help in their prayer life. This is why St Teresa of Avila detailed the psychological experiences that a person may experience in prayer beyond first beginnings. It was not to encourage bounty hunters to seek mystical experience for their own personal satisfaction, but to reassure and encourage fellow travellers who might be disconcerted or even frightened by their experiences when God's love begins to make its presence felt within them. She also wanted to reassure them when others, ignorant of mystical theology, tried to suggest that their experiences were spurious or even demonic. If, at a crucial moment in my own life I had not met a priest who understood what was happening to me, and who was able to encourage me to continue on my way, then I would never have written this or any other of my books.

Sadly, because of the prevailing climate in Christian spirituality, for the reasons that I have given, there are very few knowledgeable spiritual directors capable of encouraging and helping a person through mystical purification. So, while we are hopefully waiting for a new generation of priests, religious and laypeople schooled in mystical theology, let me make a few suggestions. Follow the example of the first Christians who learned from Jesus himself how to pray, morning and evening and throughout the day, as they sought the prayer without ceasing. Then set aside some quality space and time to reflect on the life of Jesus, meditating on everything he said and did. When it becomes apparent that this meditation that generates a fervent spiritual love suddenly burns out, don't give up prayer as many do, but look for help and instruction. It is in fact one of the signs that the purification that must precede the mystical union to which we are all called, is beginning. This spiritual burnout to which I am referring may well have happened to readers very many years ago when their first enthusiasm ended abruptly, in the middle of what I have previously called Acquired Contemplation. If this is the case they will have found that they have not been able to go back to their first fervour, however much they wanted to. Instead, if they had not given up prayer altogether, they will have reverted to vocal prayers of one sort or another to sustain them, remaining ignorant of the true way forward into mystical contemplation through purification. Only genuine and adequate teaching, preferably by a practitioner, can help them to progress and to journey onward in the mystic way. There is no going back. That is quite impossible. There can only be a going forward.

This going forward means passing through a profound personal purification. At the end of it they will eventually discover that the brief experience of the love of God that they encountered during Acquired Contemplation will resume, but with ever greater intensity than before. Acquired Contemplation is in fact a brief mystical premonition of the beginnings of what St Teresa of Avila calls the *Spiritual Marriage*. It only ends abruptly because it cannot develop into the full-bodied union with God that the searcher desires. That is until all the obstacles that prevent this union, the sin and selfishness that will always stand in the way of love, are destroyed. We cannot be united with God until the selfishness that contaminates us is purified away. This is the second baptism of fire to which St John the Baptist referred (Matthew 3:11). How God brings this about by the fire of the Holy Spirit in the mystic way is the prime object of Christian mystical theology. Only when this is done here on earth before death, or in purgatory after death, can God's plan, his Mysterion be brought to completion - the ecstatic union and eternal bliss of all, purged of the spiritual dross that has no place in God.

Religious publishers have been producing books for years that are written to galvanise their readers and to inspire them to rise from a nominal faith to an active life of prayer and personal devotion, as the Ignatian Exercises have done for centuries. Many of them are excellent and achieve their objective, but none of them prepares their readers for the time when first fervour fizzles out, and they must be purified in the dark night. Thanks to the mystical drought that has followed in the wake of Quietism and the anti-mystical witch-hunts, the teaching that they need has not been available as it was before.

This teaching is to be found in the Christian spiritual tradition from the very beginning. By studying the whole tradition, up to and including the teaching of St Teresa of Avila and St John of the Cross, I have tried to put that teaching into simple modern English, with contemporary metaphors and examples. To understand what is happening and why, in more detail, when the dark night seems to envelop you, turn to the book, *Wisdom from the Western Isles – The Making of a Mystic (Part III)* which I wrote to help people journey on in prayer when the well runs dry. Finally, and to further what is my life's work, lectures originally given in the late seventies and the early eighties in Rome on mystical theology can be found on my website. This time, however, they have been recorded in a more modern context and given to a group of lay people in England. http://www.davidtorkington.com

T S Eliot once said that he spent his whole life trying to say the same thing in as many ways as possible. Readers will have noticed that I have been doing the same in all that I have written in this book and over the preceding years. I do not apologise, unless, discovering my ploy, readers have become bored rather than inspired by what is after all the teaching of the Good News. It is not my Good News, but the Good News so easily forgotten of the man who rose from the dead on the first Easter Day. To him be the glory and to the Father whom we glorify in, with, and through him, for all that we have received and all we hope to receive. This is our prayer as we journey on into eternity, to experience the ever-increasing joy and delight of receiving love without measure, together with all whom we have ever loved and held dear.

Non nobis, Domine, non nobis, sed nomine tuo da gloriam.

Addendum

A Blueprint for Daily Prayer

Begin with Psalm sixty-nine with which St Benedict instructed his monks to start the divine office. Then it can be followed by the Glory Be, immediately followed by Psalm sixty-two.

O God, come to my aid
O Lord, make haste to help me (Psalm 69).
Glory be to the Father and to the son and to the Holy Spirit.
Amen.

O God, you are my God, for you I long;
For you my soul is thirsting.
My body pines for you
Like dry weary land without water (Psalm 62).

Morning Prayer

Say the Our Father and then using the Our Father as a memory jog, say the following prayers:

Our - Offering – the Morning Offering
God, our Father, I wish to consecrate all that I say and all that I do to you in this forthcoming day, just as Jesus did every day of his life on earth. Please accept what I do so imperfectly and unite it with the perfect offering that Jesus continues to make to you in heaven. I offer to you my joys and my sorrows, my successes as well as my failures, because these especially show how much I have need of you. I make my prayer in, with and through Jesus in whom we all live and move and have our being. Amen.

Our - Union
Father, I know that the more your Holy Spirit draws me into your son Jesus, the more I am united to all who are within him. I therefore ask Mary and Joseph, Peter and Paul and all the saints, especially those to whom I have a special devotion, to be with me now as I pray so that my prayers may be fortified by theirs. I also want to pray for all my family and friends, and all who have asked me to pray for them. May they benefit from the day ahead that I wish to make a perfect prayer, as I offer all I say and do to you, through Jesus Christ Our Lord. Amen.

Our - Resolutions
Jesus, help me to review the day ahead to anticipate all that I should do, so that I can love God as you did, through everything that I do and love my neighbour too, as you love all of us. Help me to forgive my enemies as you forgave, as well as my friends. And give me the grace to seek forgiveness from those I have offended; and never to cease trying to be like you and to behave like you in all that I say and do. Amen (Short pause to make resolutions for the day ahead.)

Daily Prayer

Father - Faith
Father, I know and believe that you are all loving, that your love has been permanently transformed into human loving through the human nature of your son Jesus. I know and believe that his love is perpetually poised to possess me at this moment and at every moment. Penetrate and possess me now, permeate my whole being as I try to turn and remain open to receive you. Melt my heart of stone, re-make it and re-mould it, so that it can at all times be open to receive you. "For I, unless you enthral me, never shall be free, nor ever chaste except you ravish me" (John Donne). Amen.

Father - Abandonment

Father, you have freely chosen to share your own inner life and love with me now through Jesus, as a foretaste of the ecstatic joy that you have planned for me and for all who love you in heaven. As there is no limit to the way you have poured out your loving goodness and mercy on me, I can only totally abandon myself to you in return. I therefore solemnly consecrate every moment of every day to you and to your honour and glory, in and together with your son, Jesus Christ. Amen.

Father - Thanksgiving

Father, although you are infinitely distant you are infinitely near too, for you inhabit the inner marrow of my being. I thank you for being with me, and for all you have given me today, for life itself and all and everyone that has made it worth living. Give me the grace to praise, honour and thank you, as much as I am able and more than I am able, not just in words but in a life that I freely dedicate to you. Amen.

Father - Holy Communion

Jesus, at the Last Supper you promised to make your home in all who would obey your new commandments. Help me to obey them now and at every moment of my life. For when I love the Father and love my neighbour, as you did, there is nothing to stop you making your home in me and me making mine in you. Let the joy and the peace that comes from abiding in you suffuse all I say and do, so that others may be drawn into the Holy Communion that begins in this life and comes to its completion in the next. Amen.

(Now is the time to remain still and silent for a few moments of contemplation to relish what, or rather whom we receive in this Holy Communion. A short prayer could be repeated gently whenever distractions threaten to draw the attention elsewhere.

A prayer such as *Come, Lord* or *Come, Lord Jesus* would be ideal or another short prayer of your choice.)

Father - Examination of Conscience
Lord, that I may see, so that all that prevents you making your home in me may be spirited way. Strengthen me to live the new commandments as you lived them, so that the same Holy Spirit who filled you, guided you and raised you from the dead may do the same for me. Show me the sins that keep you out and give me the power to overcome them, for without you I have no power to do anything. Amen.

Father - Repentance
Father, I ask your forgiveness for the sins that have prevented you from possessing me as you would wish this day. (A short pause to review our behaviour in the past day.) I am deeply sorry for failing you yet again, and with your grace I will never let my pride cause me to delay from turning back to you the moment I fall. Until I can love everyone as I should, help me to do them no harm and give me the sympathy and compassion of the person in whose footsteps I want to walk. Amen.

Conclude with an Our Father, a Hail Mary and a Glory Be.

Night prayer

A suggestion taken from an ancient tradition traced back to the Desert Fathers.

When you are in bed say a short prayer and repeat it slowly and prayerfully. It may simply be the word *Jesus*, or the full Jesus prayer, *Jesus, Son of God, have mercy on me, a sinner.*

This prayer and others like it came to be used most particularly in the Eastern Christian Church, with slow rhythmical breathing. It was not just a device for relaxation, but for reminding the believer of the all-pervading action of the Holy Spirit. The ancient Jews believed that the breath of believers was their life-principle, their spirit, so naturally they believed that God's breath was his life-principle, his Spirit. As a mark of respect, God's breath or his Spirit came to be called the Holy Spirit. So, deep rhythmical breathing that often accompanied short prayers of the heart, helped remind Eastern Christians of the incoming Spirit who dwelt within them with ever increasing power the more they prayed. It can be a reminder to us too, particularly when preparing for sleep.

The prayer *Come, Holy Spirit* can accompany the slow intake of breath followed by the prayer *Conceive Christ in me* as we breathe out. With the next breath pray again *Come, Holy Spirit* followed by *fill every part of me,* and again with the next breath *Come, Holy Spirit,* followed by *bring Christ to birth in me.* Then the three prayers could be repeated again and again. Other short prayers could be used like *Come, Lord,* or *Come, Lord Jesus,* or whatever short prayer you feel helps you best. When this practice becomes a habit it can be far more effective than sleeping pills, and there are no side effects either. Whenever you have finished trying to pray, be at peace. You have done the best you can, now leave the rest to God, remembering the words of St Padre Pio: *"Pray, hope and don't worry."*

Circle Books

CHRISTIAN FAITH

Circle Books explores a wide range of disciplines within the field of Christian faith and practice. It also draws on personal testimony and new ways of finding and expressing God's presence in the world today.

If you have enjoyed this book, why not tell other readers by posting a review on your preferred book site.

Recent bestsellers from Circle Books are:

I Am With You (Paperback)
John Woolley
These words of divine encouragement were given to John Woolley in his work as a hospital chaplain, and have since inspired and uplifted tens of thousands, even changed their lives.
Paperback: 978-1-90381-699-8 ebook: 978-1-78099-485-7

God Calling
A. J. Russell
365 messages of encouragement channelled from Christ to two anonymous "Listeners".
Hardcover: 978-1-905047-42-0 ebook: 978-1-78099-486-4

The Long Road to Heaven
A Lent Course Based on the Film
Tim Heaton
This second Lent resource from the author of *The Naturalist and the Christ* explores Christian understandings of "salvation" in a five-part study based on the film *The Way*.
Paperback: 978-1-78279-274-1 ebook: 978-1-78279-273-4

Abide In My Love
More Divine Help for Today's Needs
John Woolley
The companion to *I Am With You, Abide In My Love* offers words of divine encouragement.
Paperback: 978-1-84694-276-1

From the Bottom of the Pond

The Forgotten Art of Experiencing God in the Depths of the Present Moment

Simon Small

From the Bottom of the Pond takes us into the depths of the present moment, to the only place where God can be found.

Paperback: 978-1-84694-066-8 ebook: 978-1-78099-207-5

God Is A Symbol Of Something True

Why You Don't Have to Choose Either a Literal Creator God or a Blind, Indifferent Universe

Jack Call

In this examination of modern spiritual dilemmas, Call offers the explanation that some of the most important elements of life are beyond our control: everything is fundamentally alright.

Paperback: 978-1-84694-244-0

The Scarlet Cord

Conversations With God's Chosen Women

Lindsay Hardin Freeman, Karen N. Canton

Voiceless wax figures no longer, twelve biblical women, outspoken, independent, faithful, selfless risk-takers, come to life in *The Scarlet Cord*.

Paperback: 978-1-84694-375-1

Will You Join in Our Crusade?

The Invitation of the Gospels Unlocked by the Inspiration of Les Miserables

Steve Mann

Les Miserables' narrative is entwined with Bible study in this book of 42 daily readings from the Gospels, perfect for Lent or anytime.

Paperback: 978-1-78279-384-7 ebook: 978-1-78279-383-0

A Quiet Mind

Uniting Body, Mind and Emotions in Christian Spirituality

Eva McIntyre

A practical guide to finding peace in the present moment that will change your life, heal your wounds and bring you a quiet mind.

Paperback: 978-1-84694-507-6 ebook: 978-1-78099-005-7

Readers of ebooks can buy or view any of these bestsellers by clicking on the live link in the title. Most titles are published in paperback and as an ebook. Paperbacks are available in traditional bookshops. Both print and ebook formats are available online.

Find more titles and sign up to our readers' newsletter at http://www.johnhuntpublishing.com/christianity. Follow us on Facebook at https://www.facebook.com/ChristianAlternative.